7.-95

WEST HAM UNITE

WEST HAM UNITED

The Making of a Football Club

Charles Korr

Duckworth

Second impression November 1986
First published in October 1986 by
Gerald Duckworth & Co. Ltd.
The Old Piano Factory
43 Gloucester Crescent, London NW1

ISBN 0 7156 2126 2 (paper)
ISBN 0 7156 2143 2 (cased)

The author and publisher wish to thank the following for
supplying and giving permission to reproduce illustra-
tions: BBC Hulton Picture Library (p. 81); Jack Helliar
(pp. 5, 14, 37, 39, 48, 59, 66, 92, 105, 113, 118-19, 126, 128,
145, 149, 150, 162, 163, 164, 192, 212, 220, 223, 224, 227);
Local Studies Library, London Borough of Newham (pp.
3, 8, 10, 11, 29, 83, 197, 216); Sport & General Press
Agency (pp. 82, 106, 158, 159, 161, 169); Mrs Betty
Thomas (p. 32); Jack Turner (pp. 103, 137, 151, 152).

British Library Cataloguing in Publication Data

Korr, Charles
    West Ham United : the making of a football
    club.
    1. West Ham United—History
    I. Title
    796.334'63'0942176   GV943.6.W4/
    ISBN 0-7156-2126-2
    ISBN 0-7156-2143-2 Pbk

Photoset in North Wales by
Derek Doyle & Associates, Mold, Clwyd
Printed in Great Britain by
Redwood Burn Limited, Trowbridge, Wiltshire

Contents

To the 3rd of August duo
Anne and Eddie

Foreword

by John Lyall
Manager of West Ham United

It is perhaps fitting that this book should have been written by an American professor, as it is another great example of the interest, even intrigue, that West Ham United creates among its followers and others. I believe the club and its history to have a natural appeal to anyone with an enquiring mind; this is certainly true from a personal viewpoint within the club. I am often asked, 'Why do you stay?' My reply is always the same: 'West Ham is a way of life.'

It was my good fortune to arrive at the club as a young man. My aim was to achieve status in my career as a footballer; little did I realise that the club would 'mould' my life. The fact that I had relative talent as a sportsman was important, but West Ham's greatest influence on me was the way it taught me to set standards for the club and for myself both on and off the field. There was no one accepted formula, it was simply done and agreed by all involved. During my injury-troubled career the character of the club and its people became clearly apparent to me. Before I underwent an operation in 1958 Ted Fenton told me, 'If you had been fit you would have made your debut in the first team.' He had other problems to worry him but he still had time to help. Upon my final injury Ron Greenwood came into the dressing-room and offered me the chance to rest for a year and begin again in an effort to maintain my career. Having briefly met Charlie Paynter in my early days at the club, I was acutely aware of the understanding offered by the management and staff in difficult times, and yet equally full of respect for their forthrightness in criticism and praise. Perhaps it is best put by saying that they did their work very well, but offered the individual a little more.

During my career with the club there have obviously been many great players, ranging from Dick Walker to Alvin Martin; not only have there been great Internationals but many others who have been, and are now, my great friends. We all have many marvellous memories, and are grateful to 'our club'. As my career has progressed I have had to relate to the business and administrative side of football and, as one would expect, I have always been aware of the importance of a good working relationship with my chairman and directors, and also with chief executive Eddie Chapman.

The early days were not easy, but gradually I was 'educated' by my employers to manage the club according to the tradition built up by previous managers and directors. On reflection, it has been the same process as I was aware of as a player – one of growing respect for the club and our profession. I recall my great mentor Ron Greenwood being told that his job as manager of West Ham was the best in the game; he immediately replied that it was possibly both the best and the hardest, because of the tremendous help and loyalty of its people, and in particular its supporters. That statement could not have been better conceived, as I firmly believe we are prepared to give our all in support of something that is very special to all of us.

As in every club, there have been troubled and difficult times and these have been overcome with the determination and aggression that the situation has demanded. The difference at West Ham is that problems have been resolved not by destroying traditions with wholesale change or adopting completely new strategies. Change has always been important to us all, but only if for the good of the club and its supporters. Progress in this modern age is vital, and last season's best-ever league position is fitting testimony to the ambition of everyone concerned to add to the memories and successes of the past.

In this brief personal look at the club, I have attempted to give an insight into the feeling of comradeship which I have lived with during my career at West Ham. Overall, I believe it has been good for us all – although we are all aware of our troubled times, we have 'united' in our efforts to maintain the accepted standards and traditions of West Ham United.

Finally, my thanks to Professor Chuck Korr for allowing me the opportunity to write the Foreword for this most interesting and intriguing insight into the club and its history.

Preface

Football has not been a sideshow of this century. What happens on the
football field matters, not in the way that food matters, but as poetry does
to some people and alcohol does to others; it engages the personality.

Arthur Hopcraft *The Football Man*

This is a book about a football club – West Ham United. It is not a simple
litany of the great matches, triumphs, heartbreaks, players and officials
that have been the history of the club, but a detailed look at how the club
has been run and what it has tried to accomplish. At the same time I do
not ignore the game, for without it West Ham United would have been no
different from many other local businesses and civic enterprises. West
Ham United has become an integral part of the daily life of its
surrounding community. The club has been and continues to be the focal
point for the emotional loyalties of thousands. The activities of the club
have produced a special sense of community in a part of London that has
always seemed mysterious and out of the way to other inhabitants of the
metropolis. West Ham United has been shaped by the area in which it
developed: by the attitudes of its working-class residents and the sense of
proper conduct that permeated the local business class. In this book, I
have looked at football and West Ham from the inside out: my analysis is
based largely on evidence from the club's own archives, and from
directors, managers, club officials and players, whose accounts do not
necessarily coincide with the views of writers, supporters and other
interested parties. This approach enables us to judge the club's decisions
and actions in their proper context. The freedom West Ham gave me to
study their financial records and the minute books of board meetings has
been invaluable in understanding the operation of the club. Whatever
sympathy we might develop for the men who ran the club should not
blind us to the fact that they took on their duties freely and were
responsible for the consequences of their actions. For better or worse,
West Ham has never allowed itself to lose the personal attributes that
make it a club, rather than just a business. It has come close to living up
to what it likes to think of itself as being, 'a family club'.

My involvement in the study of sport and West Ham United was greeted by many of my colleagues and acquaintances with the academic equivalent of that stock phrase of music-hall performers and concerned grandparents: 'What's a nice boy like you doing in a place like this?' What was I, a historian with a solid scholarly training in seventeenth-century politics doing wasting my time studying something as trivial and unintellectual as sport in the twentieth century? The supposed triviality of sport raised important issues about the purpose of historical scholarship. Anyone who has grown up in post-1945 America should understand the important role that sport has played in American life. The entry of Jackie Robinson as the first black major-league baseball player in 1947 not only made a positive statement, it forced many Americans to face the realities of racial discrimination. Patrons of the *status quo* pointed with pride to Robinson's place on the field, others saw that he was only one black and had to face taunts, obstruction and legally enforced segregation. The massive influx of television money into sport showed the power of technology and a consumer culture. The politics of the 1960s often polarized around sport, which supposedly embodied a unique set of moral and social standards. It was no accident that an athlete, Muhammad Ali, came to personify the issues dividing the nation. Reality invaded the self-proclaimed pristine, non-political realm of sport: the state of mind and influence that the American journalist Robert Lipsyte called 'SportsWorld'.

My periodic residence in England made it clear that America's involvement with sport was matched in England – it was impossible for me not to become interested in football and cricket, since they dominated the sports pages. Even in England, the habits of a lifetime died hard. I read the sports section of the newspaper first, even when I did not know one team from another. Talking about sport was the easiest entrée into conversations with English acquaintances. As an American visitor, I was forgiven when I forgot that, like most things in England, sport has class connotations. I have no idea how many times I talked to people about 'football' without realizing that they thought I must mean rugby and doubted my intellectual credentials when they found out I was actually interested in the game 'played by ruffians'.

When I started my research into the role of football in London, I looked for general histories of the sport and the various clubs. I quickly discovered that the latter were virtually non-existent except for those dealing with on-the-field exploits. That was when I decided to focus on one club; the question was, which one? I narrowed the field to three: Charlton Athletic, Millwall and West Ham United, all of which had a recognizable community in which they had developed and from which they continued to draw their support. By the mid-1970s West Ham seemed to be the most interesting of the three. After a few brief discussions, the club helped to arrange interviews and allowed me to microfilm its financial records, internal memoranda and minute books. To my knowledge, no other football club has given a scholar such open access. At no time did the club place any restrictions on what I asked, who I spoke to, or to what use I put the material. There were never any suggestions made about the approach I should take, the questions I should ask or the conclusions I should draw. The club is made up of individuals, some of whom could have put a stop to my research at any time, had they so wished. I will thank many of them below, but I must say here that Eddie Chapman, the then secretary, and the late Reg Pratt, the then chairman, were the catalysts behind the creation of this book. Their involvement made it possible, and I hope that the book lives up to their expectations.

In 1977, someone in an electronics shop in London was fixing a broken audiotape for me that contained an interview I had recorded. When I picked up the tape, the mechanic asked, 'What's a Yank like you doing talking to "Big Mal"?' This book not only answers that question, but shows why more academics should be 'in a place like West Ham'.

I wish to thank a great many people for their help and encouragement. I must begin with some members of the West Ham 'family': Len Cearns, who was very forthcoming in his remarks about his father, his own role and the family tradition at the club, and Betty Thomas, who gave me a different view of the Cearns family as well as presenting me with a unique reminder at the 1980 Cup Final that attracts attention each winter in St Louis. Ernie Gregory, Albert Walker, Pauline Moss, Edna Sheridan, Wally St Pier and Eddie Baily helped in a variety of ways and all made me feel welcome. They answered my questions with unfailing goodwill.

Ron Greenwood and John Lyall were very special: Ron enabled me to understand some of his interests and concerns that had little or nothing to do with the tactics of football. John and I spent a great deal of time talking about how he had grown up playing street football, a background very similar to my early years with schoolyard basketball. He also talked about his early years at West Ham. He was informative, and he was a constant reminder of how West Ham would like to see itself. Most of all, I could not have done anything without the enthusiastic support and friendship of Reg Pratt. I am very sorry that he did not live to see the publication of this book.

Players like Jimmy Ruffell, Dick Walker, Ted Fenton, Ken Brown, Noel Cantwell, Malcolm Allison, Frank O'Farrell and John Cartwright gave a dimension to the club that no one else could have provided. Whether our talks took place in homes, roadside cafes, rooftoop restaurants, offices, or dressing-rooms, the constant feature was their eagerness to discuss West Ham and to analyse their own relationship with the club. They were responsive to questions and talked about the club and personal issues with great frankness. No former player or official refused to talk to me, though arrangements to see some of them fell through.

Jack Helliar, Alec McGuire and Jack Turner brought unique experiences to this book: McGuire explained some of football's financial curiosities; Turner gave a view of West Ham that varied from almost everyone else's. He was provocative and always raised as many questions as he answered. His style and his insights were as different as had been his role with the club. Helliar's heritage with West Ham has few parallels. He has maintained an irrepressible interest in the club, even when events might have dampened it. Any conversation with him was always filled with surprises and stories that are as quotable as they are delightful.

Many people who were not directly connected with the club helped me to understand West Ham. They included Bernard Joy, Terry Venables, Basil Amps, Harry Welsh, Colin Green, Dick Barnard, Ken Astin, councillor Tom Jenkinson, Johnny Speight, and Dame Anna Neagle. The settings of our meetings included the offices of the FA, a primary school and the dressing-room of a West End theatre: some indication of the appeal of football. Trevor Smith and Peter Lorenzo, first-class journalists who grew up with West Ham, went out of their way to be helpful. They shared their knowledge and instincts and led me to other people who they knew could contribute to the book. I benefited greatly from the work and advice of writers such as Arthur Hopcraft, John Moynihan, Lionel Francis, Eric Dunning, Alan Ingham and Ian Taylor.

Academic friends like Eugene Weber, Jim Walvin, Christopher Hill and Robert Latham provided the encouragement that I needed to make the shift into the history of sport. My friends and colleagues Jim Roark and Jerry Cooper were very supportive. After I started writing, other friends kept prodding to make sure the book got finished: Bill Baker with his comments that it was about time to stop living off one article; Maryanne Ellison Simmons, who reminded me that a perfect job of cleaning grouting was far less important than writing an imperfect paragraph; Ted Rowlands, who demanded to talk about the book even before we discussed our political leaders; Joe Losos, who used his considerable powers of argument to deny me the luxury of ignoring what was important; and Storer, who knows how much I prize loyalty to friends.

Wray Vamplew, James Jones, Tony Mason, Iain Hampshire-Monk and Willie Lamont went beyond the call of friendship when they read the manuscript and made pointed and important suggestions for revisions. Tony may have finally forgiven me for not writing about a non-London club, and Wray brought a whole new meaning to the phrase 'wandering scholars'. I want to make a special note of two friends who meant a great deal to me and influenced what I hoped to do in this book – S. T. Bindoff and Bob Wheeler. They died three years apart, on the same day, and I miss them very much.

Tom Jordan and Art MacKinney used some of their very limited budgets to support my research on West Ham. Mary Hines turned my draft and its collection of strange corrections into a readable text. Ed Fedder's first reaction to my idea was, 'You don't really mean "football"?', but after that no one could have been more helpful. He is what a friend, colleague and academic administrator rolled into one should be. Bill Fishman played a unique role. His knowledge of the history of the East End and his passion for the subject is exceeded only by his generosity of spirit and his willingness to help others.

Paddy and Mandy were part of many of the adventures that made London important to me: football, theatre, long talks, 'the rat run' and friendship. I have mentioned often that the community in which West Ham is located gives it a distinctive flavour. I never would have experienced it without Arthur Clarke, Peter Scriven and Alex MacMillan. Arthur is the personification of what East London generosity and decency can be. There is no way properly to acknowledge his kindnesses, except to ask him to keep the packages coming.

One point should be clear by this time. What started as just another scholarly research project became an activity that encompassed much more. It was impossible not to become involved with the fortunes of the present-day Hammers. I developed close friendships with some of the people I met during my work, which will be important to me long after the impact of the book has faded. I hope that did not unduly influence the judgments I reached in the book.

I had the excitement and pleasure of sharing much with Kath and Gavin – insights, people, arguments, Ellington and Philly Jo Jones, light-bulb stories, Pruitt-Igoe and St Andrews among them. They did something I thought was impossible – made me feel as though I had a second home.

From the first moment I arrived at West Ham United, one person was the key to everything that would follow. I developed great admiration for his integrity and ability. I am proud to know that Eddie Chapman is a friend. I hope he and Edith know how much they contributed to this book and my life. The only person to whom that applies more is Anne, and I am sure she is aware of it.

St. Louis, Missouri   C.P.K.
13 January 1986

CHAPTER 1

It started with the 'Irons'

It may be necessary to introduce a little ferment of professional experience to leaven the heavy lump.

Arnold F. Hills, owner of the Thames Ironworks, 1899.

The West Ham Football Club Ltd was registered as a company on 5 July 1900. According to its Memorandum and Articles of Association, the first objective of the company was to 'acquire and take over, or succeed to the concern and undertakings of the unregistered Association or Club known as the Thames Ironworks Football Club'.[1] The Thames Ironworks in Canning Town, West Ham, was London's last surviving major shipbuilding firm. In 1860 the Ironworks had employed 6,000 men, but by 1900 that figure had dropped to 3,100:[2] the yard was fighting a losing battle against competitors on the Clyde and in the north of England. The docks were an important source of work in the area of Essex that was part of the extended East End of London and included the borough of West Ham. Dock work was casual labour, and it was essential for dockers to live close by. The Victoria and Albert Docks were the biggest single source of employment for men in West Ham, and a great deal of cheap housing was built in the Canning Town Tidal Basin and Custom House areas of West Ham near them. However, although more than 7,000 men worked on the docks in 1904, factory work provided employment for three times as many people in West Ham. A few industrial concerns, like the Thames Ironworks, were associated with the docks, but the majority of the West Ham working population was not composed primarily of either casual labourers or dockers: the largest employers of skilled labour were the repair shops of the Great Eastern Railway. By 1904 there were more than 11,000 men working in the metal and machine trades in West Ham.[3]

In governmental terms, West Ham was not in London, it was an Essex suburb – a manufacturing centre, containing factories that had moved from London. Many of these were offensive industries producing dirt, fumes and chemical residues.[4] West Ham was the only local government area in the region in which the majority of the workforce lived within the borough. The increasing population of West Ham in the last two decades of the nineteenth century created a serious problem of overcrowding:

1

there was an average 6.46 people per house in West Ham, while the average for England and Wales was 5.21. But there were tremendous differences within the borough. Overcrowding was severe in Canning Town, Custom House and Silverton – areas containing the highest percentage of casual labourers. In Upton Park and Forest Gate, comfortable housing was occupied by professional and business families. The northern part of West Ham was described as a dormitory for London, and this increased as one went into the surrounding areas of East Ham, Barking and Ilford.[5]

The inner area of West Ham lacked open space and public recreation grounds. Most children and men who played football did so on the spaces between factories and industrial areas. Howarth and Wilson's detailed survey of the social problems in West Ham in 1907 compared its lack of open space with 'planned towns' like Bournville where it was thought necessary to have undeveloped areas within a five-minute walk of homes. It was impossible to achieve this in West Ham, but the report made the point that a lack of open space 'is conducive neither to health nor to morals', and concluded that it 'was not surprising to have bands of young hooligans whose energies are expended in petty larcenies in the streets.'[6] This belief in the value of sport as character-building was a significant feature of the Victorian gospel of hard work and hard play – the 'muscular Christianity' – that developed at the public schools and universities, and found new expression in the settlement houses and parishes in the poor areas of cities. The 'vicars to the poor' took the gospel of sport to their flocks with the same fervour with which their fellow missionaries brought the light of Christ to Africa and Asia. Sport was part of the moral code of young men who filled senior positions in the civil service and sat in the boardrooms of industrial enterprises. It is difficult to imagine a more complete product of inherited money, position and the ideals of Victorian upper-class education than Arnold F. Hills, owner of the Thames Ironworks and creator of the Thames Ironworks Football Club.

The club represented a blend of Hills's two major non-business interests, sport and social welfare. He had inherited the business from his father and joined the board of directors after his education at Harrow and Oxford. He had been the English mile champion and had played top quality football. As a young man of 23 he showed his interest in conditions around the Ironworks in a rather dramatic fashion: he moved into a small house in Canning Town, a short walk from the Ironworks, and lived there for five years. He often remarked later that the lack of recreational facilities was one of the worst deprivations in the lives of West Ham residents.

In 1895, Hills vigorously supported a plan to bring the borough of West Ham into the county of London. West Ham had most of the problems of the metropolis such as overcrowding and filth, but its rates were so low

Arnold F. Hills, President of the Thames Ironworks

that it could not afford good sanitation and open play areas. In Hills's words, 'the perpetual difficulty of West Ham is its poverty, it is rich only in its population'.[7]

Hills was a militant temperance advocate, a vegetarian and a believer in crusading for 'good causes'. He started a number of leisure pursuits at the Ironworks, including a string band, football club, temperance society and drama club, primarily because he believed that such activities were both good business and socially responsible. He began to publish a company magazine, the *Thames Ironworks Gazette*, in 1895 as a 'fresh link of interest and fellowship between all sorts and conditions of workers in our great industrial community'.[8] The *Gazette* appeared for the next twenty years, until Hills was paralysed by arthritis. It was a combination of technical journal, company newsletter, popular history magazine and general local newspaper. The lead article almost always consisted of Hills's discussion of an issue that had attracted his interest. Another feature of the *Gazette* was a summary of the activities of the various clubs.

The football club was formed in the summer of 1895. The *Gazette* contained a short notice asking interested workers to contact the secretary, a senior clerk at the Ironworks.[9] The formation of the club was part of the policy that Hills had enunciated in the *Gazette* under the headline 'The importance of co-operation between workers and management'. He was anxious to wipe away the bitterness left by a recent strike and to gain support for changes he had initiated: 'But thank God this midsummer madness is passed and gone; inequities and anomalies have been done away with and now, under the Good Fellowship system and the Profit Sharing Scheme, every worker knows that his individual and social rights are absolutely secured.'[10]

Hills set up a central council to co-ordinate the efforts of the many new clubs, and insisted that the council encourage the development of the clubs as separate entities. He saw these clubs as much more than a diversion for the participants: they could provide moral lessons while raising the morale of his workers and the reputation of his firm. He wanted the clubs to be good at whatever they were doing. Every club should 'rally loyally around the Central Council...and thus united...the social movement which has already done so much will go from success to success...It will set the seal upon the business prosperity of the firm and crown the labours of the Works with the laurels of the road, the river, the racing track, the field, and the public hall.'[11] The team planned to use a nearby football ground for practice and matches. The club was financed by members' subscriptions and a contribution from the Ironworks. More than 50 men had joined, which necessitated finding enough matches for two teams.

The football club had a hectic and successful first season. Its committee (all of whom were clerks, foremen or supervisors at the Ironworks) set up fixtures and entered the club in cup tournaments. In the committee's own words, it had been 'somewhat presumptuous' in entering the premier competition in England, the English Cup; it had no thought of winning, but the competition would test the team's ability and publicize the new club. If they were 'lucky enough' be drawn against a good professional club, this would add considerably to their funds.[12] During the season there was a move initiated by the players to have the governing committee composed of non-players. 'A number of gentlemen' were asked to fulfil this important function, which proved most beneficial to the club.[13] The schedule of the club was much closer to that of many professional teams than it was to the local amateur or industrial clubs. It had matches against one first division League team and two clubs from the Southern League. During its first season the club showed it was more than an ordinary local side. It performed well in the English Cup, won the West Ham Charity Cup, and did not lose a match to any

Cycle racing was a regular event at the Memorial Ground, the first home of West Ham United

local club. Before the season was over, the committee showed its ambition by having the club elected to the newly-formed London League.

The secretary painted an optimistic picture for the start of the second season. The club had increased its membership and would field three teams. There were 30 first-team matches scheduled and six cup competitions. The team had added some new players, including four first-team men from St Luke's and the Castle Swifts, the latter a company club sponsored by the Castle Shipping Line. After only two years, the Thames Ironworks Football Club had become the ranking team in an area that was described as 'football mad'.[14] At the end of its second season, the club took a step that distanced it from its local competitors. In March 1897, Hills announced that he had finally found a suitable piece of land in the neighbourhood, and that on the sixtieth anniversary of the Queen's accession he would open a stadium with 'a cycle track equal to any in London' and complete facilities for football, cricket and tennis.[15]

The club's third season opened at its new home, the Memorial Ground. The team had smart new outfits, a complete schedule of matches and a ground 'good enough to hold the English Cup Final'. The committee insured the players against loss of wages that might result from injuries sustained while playing football. There were six new players in the first team, five of whom were from the Greater London area. None of these men were Ironworks' employees.¹⁶ The secretary's article in the *Gazette* clearly showed the new focus of the club. He reminded the workers that any football players in the Ironworks could join the club for 2s 6d, which 'entitles them to take part in practice matches and training on Tuesday and Thursday evenings'.¹⁷ Nothing was said about any possibility of playing for the team or being included in the full training programme of the senior players. There was no pretence that the new members would participate in the prime function of the club: winning matches against first-class competition.

Although the club was the most powerful in East London and on its way to winning the London League championship, the secretary was disappointed: 'the support we have received has not been so large as we should wish for, the gates not totalling near the number we might expect and certainly not so many as the quality of the play of our men should warrant.' He could not understand why so many people went to matches at grounds that 'are much less pleasing and where the football is nowhere near as good... Things will have to improve when people realize how splendid the ground is and good is the club.' This appeal must have been directed at men at the Ironworks, since it was published in the *Gazette*. The secretary's remarks imply what the club had become and account, however unwittingly, for its lack of support. The Thames Ironworks Football Club had incorporated leading local clubs and was winning, but it had no particular constituency to whom it could appeal. It was not representative of any single area of West Ham, and it had only nominal ties with the Ironworks. It had no trouble defeating its local rivals on the field and '*was undefeated by any amateur team*',¹⁸ but this did not ensure success at the gate. In late-twentieth-century terms, the club was faced with an image and marketing problem. The governing committee decided it must produce high-quality football to get support. This meant becoming an unabashedly professional organization.

In 1898, the club joined the second division of the Southern League, determined to gain promotion as quickly as possible. This was clear from the composition of the club that started the season. It had 30 players, only three of whom had been with the club the previous year. It no longer represented the Ironworks, and very few of the new players had any roots in the East End.¹⁹ There are no records of the wages payed to the players in 1898, but it would be naive to think that they were attracted from professional clubs as far away as Middlesbrough, Aberystwyth and Inverness just to enjoy the sights, sounds and smells of Canning Town.

The newly constructed club won the second division title, but the secretary still had a dismal report to make in the *Gazette* at the end of the season.

> The only thing needed to make this a success is more support from the men inside the Works. Up to the present we have received very little indeed and can only regret that so many followers of the game prefer to patronize other

clubs to the disadvantage of their own. I hope, however, that next season will see a different state of things.[20]

The secretary's complaint might elicit more sympathy if there had been any strong reason why the men at the Ironworks should have thought of the club as 'their own'.

By 1899 the club had reached the top of the local London football ladder, the first division of the Southern League, where it joined such established clubs as Tottenham, Millwall and Southampton. There was a further turnover, with new players coming from professional clubs throughout Great Britain. The club engaged in an aggressive ticket-selling campaign, using the *Gazette* and local newspapers. The price of season tickets rose from 5s to 10s in two years, but the club offered a variety of admission plans. Also, for the first time 'ladies and boys are specially catered for' with a special reduced price of 5s 6d for ladies ('tickets issued to the grandstand only') and 5s 6d and 3s 6d for boys.[21]

The efforts of the committee to put together a first-class club did not have an immediate effect on attendance, but they did draw a sharp reaction from Hills. In the *Gazette* of June 1899 his article 'Our clubs' spoke of his former hope that successful teams might attract better workers and good publicity to the business. He feared that the club had lost sight of its priorities.

> But in the development of our Clubs, I find another tendency at work which seems to be exceedingly dangerous. The Committees of several of our Clubs, eager for immediate success, are inclined to reinforce their ranks with mercenaries. In our bands and in our football clubs, I find an increasing number of professionals who do not belong to our community, but are paid to represent us in their several capacities.[22]

The committee running the football club would probably have taken what Hills said as a compliment. They were trying to build a competitive football club in order to attract supporters. Hills suggested that the club represented the community of the Ironworks and should find its players and supporters there – but if he believed that, why had he provided a ground that could hold as many as 120,000 people and said nothing when the club started to recruit players and participate at a level that made professionalism inevitable?

By 1899 Hills realized that a club with a broad enthusiastic following might not be compatible with amateurism, and he drew back from the logical consequences of the club he had founded:

> Like the ancient Romans, in their period of decadence, we seem to be willing to be artists and sportsmen by proxy; we hire a team of gladiators and bid them fight our football battles...Now this is a very simple and effective method of producing popular triumphs. It is only a matter of how

Laying the keel of the dreadnought HMS Thunderer at the Thames Ironworks. The company lost substantial sums on the ship

> much we are willing to pay and the weight of our purses can be made the measure of our glory. I have, however, not the smallest intention of entering upon a competition of this kind: I desire that our Clubs should be spontaneous and cultivated expressions of our own internal activity; we ought to produce artists and athletes as abundantly and certainly as a carefully tended fruit tree produces fruit.[23]

The committee thought it was producing fine 'fruit' – the combined labours of the best footballers whose services could be retained.[24] The club could not prosper in the twilight zone of semi-professionalism: it had to choose between becoming a recreational facility for the Ironworks or appealing to the football fans in the local community.

Hills's dilemma was a familiar one at the turn of the century – the middle-class missionary repelled by the success or perversion of his good works. In 1905 Gibson and Pickford, two of the most important men in football journalism, pointed out that 'none but a good class team could fill the Memorial Ground'.[25] Hills's solution was a backward-looking compromise:

> The clubs of ours have to grow, but let them always represent our own people. It may be necessary, at the beginning, to introduce a little ferment of professional experience to leven the heavy lump; but even then let these professional experts come into the yards to work as well as to play.[26]

Hills's proposal was made up of equal parts of naivety and what a contemporary football writer called, in another context, 'shamateurism'.[27]

In 1900 the Thames Ironworks bought out another engineering company and, in order to raise new capital, became a public company. For the first time, Hills was responsible to shareholders. The football club was a money-losing operation that was only justifiable if it created better conditions at the Ironworks. Hills no longer believed that its primary purpose was recreation for his workers or company morale. What should he do with the club – abolish it, or transform it? The club had not developed according to his plans, but it was the product of his urging and generosity: if it went under that would be an admission of failure. There was also the problem of the Memorial Ground. Like the club its most salient characteristic was that it was there. If the Memorial Ground was not used it would stand as mute testimony to the failure of Hills's dreams to provide a football team for the community.

Hills kept the team in existence but severed its formal connections with the Ironworks. He proposed a limited company, but he did not use the situation to cut his personal losses and run. On the contrary, he became a major shareholder, encouraged business associates and his workmen to invest in the club and provided use of the Memorial Ground on very favourable terms. West Ham United's Articles of Incorporation stated that the purpose of the company was 'to conduct the business of a football and athletic club in all branches' and to promote a whole series of other sports including cricket, tennis, bowls and lacrosse. The company was 'to carry on any business which the company thinks fits in with the above and is calculated to enhance the value of the company or to bring a profit to it'. At the foot of the Articles is the provision that the company is 'to employ and pay professional football players...and other athletes'.[28] All seven subscribers to the Articles were elected to the first board of directors. They were joined by three others: an engineer at the Thames Ironworks and two local businessmen. Seven of the ten were residents of the inner parts of Essex, Canning Town, West Ham or the areas bordering directly on it. The other three were residents of the slightly more expensive outer areas of Essex; one was a secretary at the Ironworks who had been a member of the committee of the Ironworks Football Club. The board included two clerks, two engineers (both of whom were connected with the Thames Ironworks), a brassfounder, a timber contractor, a house agent and a resident of Poplar who was described as having private means (see pp. 245-6).[29]

The capital of West Ham United was £2,000, 4,000 shares carrying a face value of 10s each. There was no rush to buy shares. The new club was financially stable only because Hills promised to buy one share for every one sold to the public. Despite this arrangement, by 1902 only 1,777 shares had been sold,[30] and 92 people held shares. Besides Hills, 21 men

West Ham United in 1900, the first team to bear the name, from the *Thames Ironworks Gazette*

owned more than ten shares. Ten of these men served as directors – ownership of ten shares was a qualification for board membership. Twenty of the 21 major shareholders lived in the vicinity of the club and all were self-employed or semi-professional men. The pattern of shareholding suggests that many of the first subscribers bought shares from a friend connected with the old club or purchased a share to maintain some connection with the former Ironworks Club.

The directors were responsible for the club. Each year, a third of the board had to resign, but any resigning director could stand for re-election. Directors were specifically empowered to make nominations to the board. It was probably assumed that the board would bring like-minded men into its ranks. The annual general meeting (AGM) of stockholders was the setting for a report from the chairman and the election of the board. The Articles provided for periodic directors' meetings when they could exercise all the powers of the company including the purchase of property, the issue of stock, the appointment, suspension and removal of managers and secretaries, the investment of funds and entry into contracts. All football directors were prohibited from receiving compensation for service on the board to avoid the taint of professsionalism that had affected the players. Public esteem, service and personal satisfaction were reward enough.

Green Street in 1905, the year after West Ham United moved to the Boleyn Ground. It was a street of small shops and houses, very different from the dockland surroundings of the Memorial Ground

In 1901-2 the team did well on the field, finishing a strong fourth in the league and showing a small profit. The sale of season tickets doubled for the next year (to 110) and 500 additional shares of stock were sold. However, the next season saw a loss of £151. The directors were shaken by this reversal and tried to explain it by the 'bad state of trade in the area and the bad start of the team', which had kept attendance below expectations.[31] But the big change on the balance sheet was not a fall in the gate receipts – the wages bill had gone up by 50 per cent. The following year saw a huge operating loss of £793 although expenses had remained constant. This time the culprit was a big drop in season ticket sales.

On the eve of the 1904 season the directors had reason to worry about the club's future. It had lost £900 in the past two seasons; it had an overdraft of £770 and assets of less than £200.[32] The local bank that extended the credit did so solely on the reputation and word of the directors, for the club had neither the resources nor the property to secure the overdraft. In the midst of these troubles, however, the chairman was optimistic about the coming season. In the spring of 1904 the directors took the most significant decision since the incorporation of the club: they took West Ham United away from the Memorial Ground to a new site, the Boleyn Ground on Green Street in East Ham.

West Ham's new home was everything the Memorial Ground had not been. It was easily accessible for large numbers of spectators, as it was within walking distance of the industrial suburb of West Ham and the residential areas of East Ham and Barking, and in easy reach of Canning

Town and the working-class areas surrounding the docks, the poorer areas of East London and the suburbs of Ilford and Stratford, because the ground was close to a railway station and the tram stopped less than a five-minute walk away. And the Boleyn Ground had more than convenience to recommend it: the setting was radically different from the docklands location of the Memorial Ground. Boleyn Castle was the site of a Catholic school in a neighbourhood surrounded by small shops and residential streets. It was very different from the squalid conditions that outsiders usually assumed to be typical of East London, and was much closer to the support upon which the future of the club would be based. The new ground symbolized a visible break with the Ironworks. Supporters would remember the 'Irons' roots, but the new club was trying to establish itself as part of a much wider community.

West Ham United's move to the Boleyn Ground laid the foundation for its success as a professional club. Ironically the move was forced on it by Hills, who found the concept of professional sport morally repugnant. Between 1900 and 1904, a series of small episodes occurred that showed the growing estrangement between Hills and West Ham United. Among them were the rejection of some of his nominees as prospective directors and disputes over the rent for the Memorial Ground and the services provided with it. At the end of the 1904 season, Hills informed West Ham rather sharply that he trusted that they could make new playing arrangements for the coming year. He also wanted them to vacate the office space they had been using in buildings owned by the Ironworks. Hills stated that his refusal to rent the Memorial Ground to the club after 30 April was because it was needed 'for the *Amateur* [my italics] Thames Ironworks Team'.[33] Hills may have done West Ham a great favour by forcing the club to move, but the way in which he handled it left bitter feelings. In late April the directors heard a rumour that the Clapton Orient football team (a leading amateur club in East London) might use the Memorial Ground. The West Ham board voted to 'publish a copy of Mr Hills' letter to us in full in the press' if any team besides Thames Ironworks used the Memorial Ground.[34]

The directors had looked at the Boleyn Ground even before they knew they would have to vacate the Memorial Ground, but they were not prepared for Hills's sudden action or the new rent. As soon as the lease was signed, the board passed formal resolutions to start a 'million penny' collection scheme to aid the new ground and to 'communicate with advertisement contractors re boardings on our new ground and also ask the brewers for their personal assistance'. The result of Hills's ultimatum was thus a firm slap at two of his cherished causes: amateur sport and temperance.[35] The final move to the Boleyn Ground was made in May 1904. The rental provisions included the amalgamation of West Ham United with the Boleyn Castle Football Club, 'taking their best players into our reserve team', and giving an opportunity to four Boleyn Castle directors to purchase stock in West Ham, with the understanding that one or more of them would be recommended by the West Ham directors to be elected to their board.[36] The consolidation had all the appearance of a small business being amalgamated with a larger competitor. Nothing in the arrangements gave any hint that football was a sport or different from any other type of business activity.

During the first season at the Boleyn Ground, West Ham turned the previous season's £800 loss into a £400 profit. There was a small decrease in wages, but this was more than outweighed by the 100 per cent increase in expenses for the ground (from £331 to £662). The important difference was in the gate money, which rose from £2,900 to £4,300. This was accomplished even though the club did not improve its record on the field.[37]

Before the 1904 season, the chairman's report had been a combination of gloom (the past season's problems) and optimism, 'with a new ground and new surroundings and with an almost new team, the success that we have long hoped for will at last be ours'.[38] The directors had done much more than hope. They had raised more than £3,000 in loans and had obtained a new site. The only creditors named in the club's balance sheets were Hills (£107) and the Thames Ironworks Club (£85). Both these debts were liquidated in 1905. The new loans came from the chairman, the three retiring directors who stood for re-election and the new directors.[39]

The loss of the Memorial Ground had given the directors a chance to plan for a new future. From 1905 the tone of West Ham United was set. It would be a team competing at the highest level, one that depended on quality football to attract supporters. It established itself in the heart of an area where playing football was the usual recreation. The inclusion, for the first time, of local politicians as vice-presidents, was another sign of the attempt to consolidate community ties; the club was guided firmly by members of the local business and professional class who were willing to invest money and time. The directors could no longer be seen as extensions of Hills or the Ironworks: they were civic personalities in their own right. Virtually every retiring director stood for re-election and they were consistently re-elected. This ensured continuity and excluded outsiders from the club.

West Ham United, with roots firmly set in the Boleyn Ground and with new investments in the club, was committed to appealing for support to the broadest possible audience in the area. In 1906 Syd King, the secretary, wrote a short history of the club in which he commented on its early problems: 'The charge that the club was out of sympathy with the local public was not repeated...A lot of prejudice had been lived down...and I don't suppose that any club has had to fight harder for its existence than West Ham United.'[40] King's comments were echoed by Pickford and Gibson who described West Ham as a club that had had dark days despite the local talent that was available: 'Indeed there is

WEST HAM UNITED FOOTBALL CLUB—THE PLAYERS, SEASON 1905-6.

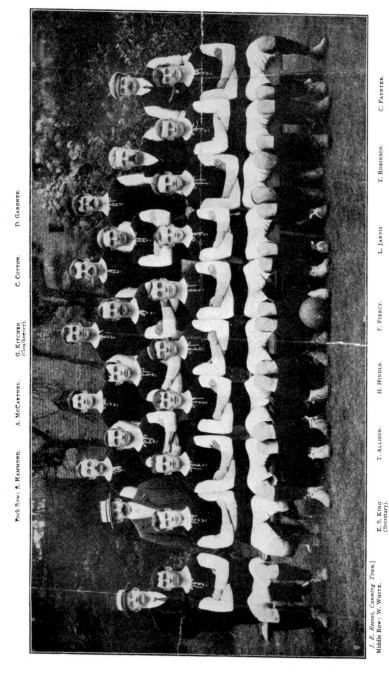

Back Row: S. HAMMOND.   A. McCARTNEY.   G. KITCHEN.   C. COTTON.   D. GARDNER.
(Goalkeeper).

J. E. Reeves, Canning Town.]
Middle Row: W. WHITE.   E. S. KING   T. ALLISON.   H. HINDLE.   F. PIERCY.   L. JARVIS.   T. ROBINSON.   C. PAYNTER.
(Secretary).

Front Row: W. FORD   H. WINTERHALDER.   S. McALLISTER.   C. MACKIE.   G. HILSDON.   W. BRIDGEMAN.   H. WILKINSON.   L. WATSON.   F. BLACKBURN.   A. WINTERHALDER.

probably no club in the metropolis which has experienced the slings and arrows of outrageous fortune more than they...It was a club that did well on the field, badly at the gate...and at the close of the 1903-4 season it was not at all certain that the club would continue.'[41]

West Ham continued to show an operating profit in every season between 1905 and 1914. In 1911 the assets exceeded the liabilities for the first time. In that year, the directors made their first major investment of almost £1,000 to improve the ground. Two years later, the huge sum of £4,000 was authorized to build a new stand and improve the enclosures.[42] The directors demonstrated their belief that the way to build support for the club meant more than having a winning team. They were prepared to spend heavily to make the ground a more comfortable place for spectators, a far cry from the picture often painted of the football supporter willing to put up with (and even to revel in) the hardships connected with attending a match.

We cannot overestimate the link between spectator support and a winning team. In 1892 Charles Edwardes summarized the importance of the result: 'the British public controls itself under trying circumstances when five favourites in succession lose at Epsom or Newmarket. This is not the case in football between league sides. One group must lose when the other wins.'[43] East London newspapers discussed changes in the West Ham team and made it a point to stress the higher quality of the new players. The signing of a local player might bring out some sense of pride, but the acquisition of a player from another club (especially a League or Scottish club) drew much more attention. Journalists usually pointed to the latter signing as evidence that the directors were willing to pay the extra money that was necessary to improve the performance of the club.

The wages offered to players joining West Ham showed that the directors recognized the need to spend money to boost the level of the team. Between 1904 and 1907 the club purchased or signed on more than 30 new players, which meant transfer fees, signing-on bonuses and higher wages. By 1907 all of the first-team players earned between £3 and £4 per week during the season. The wage distinction between players was often what they were paid during the close season: in the summer of 1907 three players were paid £4 per week while three others were given £3 per week.[44]

In 1906 the average wage for the whole team (a pool of 30 players) was £2 10s per week over the whole year. At least 12 were paid between £4 and £4 10s during the season and a minimum of £2 10s during the summer.[45] New players who were signed on from other clubs almost always received higher wages than returning players. Veterans who had been with the club since 1900 filled the reserve and third teams, and their wages ranged from £2 during the season to as little as 15s per match. The directors insisted that all players earning more than £2 10s during the season should not take another job; they were full-time professional footballers and were being paid as such.[46] By comparison, in 1906 casual dockers earned between 5s 6d and £1 2s 7d for a 44-hour week. Tram drivers made £2 3s for a 60-hour week and men employed in the building trades averaged £2 8s for a 44-hour week.[47] At West Ham United between 1907 and 1914 the maximum wage was £4 in season and £4 in the summer. By 1910 this was offered to every player West Ham transferred from a first division team. They also received a signing fee – normally £10 for a top-quality player.

At its first meeting in May each year, the board made decisions on the salaries to be offered for the next season. Provisions were made to increase the offer if important players baulked at the amount, but the maximum wage was controlled by agreement among all the clubs in the Football Association. The board also offered to meet individual players who were dissatisfied with their prospective salaries, but few players chose to appear.[48] The club had the ultimate sanction against a player who baulked: it could decline to raise its offer and refuse to transfer him. The player might protest, and if he did (as one West Ham player did in 1910) the club could respond by informing the Football Association that he was not eligible to play for any other club.[49]

The board saw itself as an employer of football players. Salary negotiations were handled by the secretary (the paid administrator), but the directors retained close control over him and over the finances of the club. There was also a strong strain of paternalism among the directors: players were fined for missing matches due to a reaction to a smallpox vaccination because the vaccinations had been obtained 'without prior permission from the Directors'.[50] Players who could not perform because of injuries or sickness had to be indoors by 8 pm every evening. 'The penalty for the first offence was a 5s fine, any subsequent offence had to be dealt with by the Directors.'[51] Curfews were enforced on players, wages were held in trust for individuals who had drinking problems and a doctor's certificate was required for any failure to play or train.[52] In many ways, the term 'club' might seem an odd way of describing the business of running a football team – an organization that recognized very different roles for the employer and the worker.

In the case of West Ham United, the 'working classes' did not 'claim the game as their own' if this means any control over the club.[53] West Ham United needed something more than players and love of football to succeed: it needed money and management. The combination of an amateur's generosity, local businessmen's sense of community pride, and a desire to gain recognition laid the foundations of a first-class professional club. In the creation of West Ham United, as in so many other areas of English life, working-class participation was limited to work either as players or as supporters.

CHAPTER 2
Whose club is it?

The club reflected how important it was to have a sense of loyalty to people.

Noel Cantwell, West Ham player, 1952-60.

It is easy to assume that the system by which football has operated in England over the past 100 years is the only way in which a professional league can be run and to forget that there are features unique to it. As a backdrop against which to view English football, it is worth taking a brief look at what happened to the Dodgers baseball club in the USA in 1958. In that year, the first year-book of the Los Angeles Dodgers Baseball Club contained an open letter from its president, Walter F. O'Malley, to 'Los Angeles Dodgers Fans'. The team had recently moved to Los Angeles from Brooklyn and the letter was written before a single game had been played in Los Angeles. Tens of thousands of people were waiting to see the Dodgers play, many of whom would call themselves 'Dodgers Fans'. O'Malley stated that the other teams would be coming to Los Angeles 'to do battle with our Dodgers. We bring to Southern California a team proud of its achievements.' He continued: 'We are extremely grateful for the warm reception the Dodgers have received in Southern California and we look forward to many years of happy association with our new fans.'[1] O'Malley stressed the recently successful history of the Dodgers and said that he had hoped to 'bring back warm memories of Dodger triumphs'. He was talking about *his* Dodgers, not the Brooklyn or Los Angeles Dodgers.

Walter O'Malley was more than the president of the Dodgers: he owned the club and had the power to move it across a continent to set up shop in Los Angeles. His team was already the second most profitable financial enterprise in baseball, but the potential market in Los Angeles was immense. This move was the start of baseball's 'Gold Rush'.

It is too easy to look at the 'instant tradition' created in Los Angeles in 1958 as one more example of the Southern Californian plastic 'with it' society. The pre-1958 Dodgers had been much more than just a winning and profitable team. More than any other team in American professional sport, the Dodgers were the symbol of a unique community. The 'trolley dodgers' (surely no nickname could have been less suited to the

automobile culture of Los Angeles) had grown up in Brooklyn at the end
of the nineteenth century. When players put on the 'Dodger blue'
uniform, they became part of Brooklyn, a borough of New York City that
had been an independent community. The Brooklyn accent was
instantly recognizable, and the wisecracking Brooklyner became a
familiar character on radio and in the cinema. The Dodgers personified
the borough: it was a team of underdogs with fans who revelled in
adversity. The Dodgers were 'us versus them', especially when they
played against the New York Giants or the Yankees, teams from other
areas of the city. The Dodgers had a volunteer band, songs, a collection of
local characters famous for their insults and strong lungs to project them,
and a small, ramshackle old park, Ebbets Field. There was no baseball
setting in which an English football supporter could feel more at home
than in Brooklyn.

The Dodger tradition grew in Brooklyn: the team blossomed in the
atmosphere of the borough and the players felt a special tie to their fans.
'Where else in baseball did they know you well enough to recognize you
on the street just by the way you walked?' wondered one of the star
players years after his retirement.[2] The team became a major force for
social change when it brought Jackie Robinson, the first black major
leaguer in the twentieth century, to the team in 1947. He was followed by
a succession of top-quality black players who formed the basis for teams
that won six National League Championships between 1947 and 1956
and came second twice. The fans' famous cry of 'Wait Till Next Year'
was echoed by a newspaper headline, 'Next Year is Now', when the
Dodgers won their first World Series in 1955. The combination of success
and black players made the Dodgers the top draw throughout the league.
In financial terms, only the Yankees were more successful.

But the team did not belong to Brooklyn; it belonged to Walter
O'Malley. When he looked at Brooklyn he saw an affluent white
population moving into the suburbs, leaving behind the poorer blacks
and Puerto Ricans, rapidly deteriorating housing and a small,
antiquated stadium. O'Malley wanted a new larger ballpark with car
parking space, closer to new paying customers. When New York City
officials did not meet his demands, he looked elsewhere. He realized that
he could make more money on the West Coast and gain the prestige of
being the owner of the first major league club in California. O'Malley was
able to dismiss decades of tradition, the emotional loyalty of thousands,
and the support that had been given to the team over the years. He
redefined most of the words that had previously described the Dodgers.
He took everything that surrounded the team and put it in a new setting.
The thousands of Brooklyn fans who bemoaned what was happening to
their Dodgers were living in an unreal world.

For years Brooklyn fans had cried, 'We wuz robbed', referring to the
decisions made by the umpires. In 1958 the ultimate robbery took place,

but the 'crime' was legal. The perpetrator was the club itself and the victims had no recourse. The Dodgers suddenly 'belonged' to Los Angeles. They were not the first to move: in the previous five years, the Braves had gone from Boston to Milwaukee and the Browns from St Louis to Baltimore. But both the Braves and the Browns had been losing money (the Dodgers were the *only* National League team to show a profit for ten successive years) and both of them were in two-team cities.

What happened in 1958 to the Dodgers has been repeated often in various American sports since then. It is a commentary on American society as well as its sport. A comparison with America's 'national pastime', baseball, may bring the structure of English League football into sharper focus.

An English football supporter might deride the plight of the Dodgers and ascribe it to America's youth and traditions, but the National Baseball League was founded twelve years before the Football League. The Dodgers are older than West Ham United. However, it is impossible to imagine the Hammers outside East London. Clubs like West Ham not only create traditions and a sense of permanency, they are also their captives.

A strong sense of shared loyalty exists between supporters, local residents, and the club. Thousands of supporters have spent their money and emotional energy over the years to keep West Ham going. Even people who know little about football talk about 'our club', 'our lads', or what 'we' did last Saturday. The phrases carry a sense of common interest and an almost proprietory view of the club. When sentiments are expressed that the club doesn't care enough about the supporters, they usually coincide with a bad record or an unpopular transfer, but when the emotional rhetoric is stripped aside, even the most dedicated supporter realizes that 'his' club does not belong to him. If West Ham does not belong to the community or its supporters, who exactly does own it – and what difference does this make?

The answer to the first question is straightforward and has been repeated at every AGM since the club was founded. The shareholders are the legal owners of the company. The lists of shareholders show the roots of the club and the changes that have taken place over the years. In 1900 Arnold Hills was the only shareholder whose address was not in an East London postal zone.[3] He was the only shareholder whose occupation was listed as 'gentleman'. He lived up to his promise to support the fledgling club by purchasing one share for each share that the public bought, a pattern that continued for almost a decade. Even the unpleasantness that accompanied the move to the Boleyn Ground did not cause Hills to sell his shares or try to exercise any control over the company. Between 1900 and 1904 an important change occurred. The number of shares sold increased by almost fifty per cent until slightly more than 2,000 were held. The number of shareholders rose from 121 to 177 and those who owned more than ten shares rose from 23 to 48.[4] In 1910, at the end of the club's first decade, the pattern of shareholding was set for the future. For the first time, Hills owned less than half the shares: 1,100 of 2,810.[5] Thirty-four additional people had bought shares since 1902, and more than a dozen shareholders had increased their holdings. The most significant change was in the shareholders' occupations. The number of shareholders had risen from 121 to 211, but the number of shareholders who were labourers had dropped from 51 to 41 and none of them owned more than ten shares. There was an approximately 50 per cent rise in the number of shareholders who were business or professional men and a similar increase in the number who held clerical jobs. Those who owned a minimum of 20 shares were in skilled trades, proprietors of their own businesses or professional men.

In 1909 the ten directors owned 214 shares between them, though only three owned more than 40. Six others owned over 40 shares but none were board members and only one was ever nominated. Two of the six continued to buy shares.

By 1924, 12 men controlled 781 shares between them, their individual holdings ranging from 40 to 133. Two men, Henry Brickell, a builder, and George Hay, a businessman, each owned more than 100 shares. Neither was a director. Mr Brickell had shown his dedication to the newly promoted club by purchasing an additional 50 shares in 1923, which made him the largest shareholder other than the family of Arnold F. Hills. The directors held a total of 153 shares, fewer than they had in 1909. Only one director, Henry Iggulden, owned more than 22.[6]

After 1924, the number of West Ham shareholders began a slow decline, and by 1939 had dropped from 210 to 186. Those owning more than ten shares declined from 61 to 52.[7] There were many share transfers involving members of the board and their families. A contraction and centralization of power was taking place at the club. The board that led West Ham through the Second World War contained the statutory minimum number of five members, who owned 403 shares between them, the smallest holding being that of Mr J. H. Rooff, who had 45. He had purchased his shares when he joined the board in 1933.[8] From 1945 an increasingly large number of shares was held by an increasingly small number of people. The directors bought shares as they became available, always paying the 10s par value. There was no competition for the shares and no reason to buy them as an investment. As long as the Hills family owned its block of 1,100 no one besides the directors could gather enough shares to gain an important voice.

There were two attempts to purchase Hills's shares. Shortly after his death in 1927, the board resolved 'if the shares come on the market advertised for sale that this Company purchase them up to par value'.[9] This had the obvious appeal for the directors; the £550 would come from revenues of the company, which was showing a steady profit. The shares could then be sold or retained at the board's discretion. Undoubtedly the buyers would have been directors, their families, or close friends. The purchase would ensure that the benign neglect with which Hills had treated the management of West Ham United would not be changed by either his heirs or another purchaser. Hills had told the directors of West Ham United that he would not interfere in their enterprise and had been true to his word. The club was run by men in whom he could place his trust and who shared his ideals about the importance of the club – even if they had not been able to resist turning it into a professional team. After 1905, the failing fortunes of the Ironworks and Hills's involvement in developing a new car engine pushed the football club well into the background. His arthritis made him virtually an invalid, and West Ham United became a relatively unimportant part of his past. Thus, the only person who might be called an owner of the club played no direct part in its operation. But every year, the 'Form E, Summary of Shares Capital and Shares' filed with Companies House listed 1,100 shares next to Hills's name. Those shares ensured that the vast majority of individual shareholders mattered very little in the life of West Ham United. The Hills family declined to sell in 1927, but reassured the board that the traditional arrangement would be maintained. At no time did a representative of the largest single shareholder in the company attend an AGM, ask to address a meeting or present any demands or suggestions to the club.

The directors made a second attempt to buy the Hills family shares in 1949. After an extended correspondence between representatives for Mr A. L. F. Hills and the club, the chairman, W. J. Cearns, took it upon himself to telephone Mr Hills. The only commitment Cearns received was that Hills would consider the matter. The issue was not raised again. This conversation took place a year after there had been significant changes to the board: A. C. 'Bert' Davis, its longest-serving member died, F. A. Enders left, and Len Cearns and Dr O. Thomas joined. W. J. Cearns might have been trying to consolidate control of the club as he saw his old comrades leaving. There is a poignant quality about Cearns's efforts, for he died the following January. Was he trying to ensure that his legacy would pass to his heirs on the board without fear of outsiders gaining control of the club? Another aspect of Cearns's life might explain his actions. One obituary described him as 'Mr W. J. Cearns – Builder of Stadiums'. At the time of Cearns's death, West Ham was planning to build a new stand, the most expensive project in the club's history. The stand remains a monument to Cearns, as a builder and as chairman of the club.[10] Was he trying to insure against all contingencies at a time when the club was embarking upon so grandiose a project?

The last new shares were purchased in 1924; 1,142 shares remained unsold until 1961. The board controlled the shares and the decision to sell them was important enough to be the sole item on the agenda at an

extraordinary general meeting called immediately after the conclusion of
the AGM in March 1961. A resolution authorized the directors 'to
subscribe at cash par for all shares presently unissued'. A month later the
shares were allocated to directors: 200 each to R. H. Pratt and L. Cearns,
and 142 to R. G. Brandon, a recently elected member of the board.[11] This
was more than merely tidying up the loose ends of the shares. The
financial situation looked good; profits were steady and attendance was
up. The working account showed a healthy balance, but this was almost
offset by a marked increase in transfer costs. In addition to buying
quality players, the club was making an effort to purchase houses and to
upgrade the properties that it already owned. This, combined with the
projected expenditures on the ground, meant that West Ham was
involved in financial obligations that dwarfed any previous commitments.

West Ham's commitments were made against a background of
uncertainty over the contractual nature of the sport. The Professional
Footballers' Association, under the direction of Jimmy Hill, had started
the process that would culminate in the successful legal action
undertaken by George Eastham. Hill understood how to use television
and radio to get across the players' message, and consistently
outmanoeuvred League officials. Support from the TUC gave a sense of
credibility to threats of industrial action. Long before Mr Justice
Wilberforce handed down his somewhat ambiguous judgment in favour
of Eastham and freedom of contract, it was clear that some changes were
going to take place in the game. At the same time, another almost
unnoticed change took place within West Ham United: a new member
was co-opted to the board, R. G. Brandon, a businessman of George
Street, London W1. Despite his address, he was not an outsider. Brandon
was a school-friend of Reg Pratt's (chairman of the board from 1950 to
1979) and a life-long supporter of West Ham. In Pratt's phrase, he was 'a
man with a wealth of business experience'. He had contacts that could
bring additional funds to the club and he was willing to use his influence.
He saw the club's future as a question of rising or falling – it could not
remain a middling first division club for an indefinite period and survive.
If the club was to rise in the first division money would have to be spent
on players as well as on facilities. Reg Pratt had already come to the same
conclusion. Brandon's appointment to the board strengthened Pratt's
position and gave the board a much better chance of raising the money
necessary to implement those plans. West Ham United was entering a
new stage, even if the path was not clear. There would be increased
expenditure and greater responsibilities for the board. The directors
wanted a firmer sense of who controlled the club. After March 1961 West
Ham could present itself to potential financial backers with a clear sense
that the men who spoke for the club were in a position to make good their
promises.

The AGM was a necessity imposed on the directors by the Companies Act. It was an annual opportunity for the shareholders as the owners of the club to express their opinions on how their investment was being handled. Before 1914 attendance at the AGM varied slightly around 25. Three times (in 1904, 1907, and 1909) attendance shot up dramatically to between 40 and 50. Each of these meetings dealt with a specific issue that had potentially divisive effects on the club: the move to the Boleyn Ground, the necessity to raise money to acquire players, and bad gates. The rare event of a contested election for the board brought a large attendance to a meeting. In 1914 51 shareholders were present to vote at the AGM. There were six candidates for three open seats on the board, each of them long-time shareholders and prominent figures in the community. The three successful candidates received between 39 and 48 votes, the losers between 12 and 19. The board's dominance was apparent. There were no serious challenges to incumbent directors in the future and attendance at the AGM dropped.[12]

West Ham United was more than a company, it was also a collection of shared traditions and beliefs. It was rooted in its geographic and cultural setting more than other businesses. By 1947, the generation of men who had purchased the original shares had died, grown old or moved. Fewer shareholders could identify personally with the club, as opposed to the team. As a result of the war and new economic developments, residential patterns had changed drastically. Each year larger numbers of shareholders appeared in the register with addresses that were no longer close to the ground. By 1950 more than 40 per cent of the shareholders were listed as 'address unknown', and of these the overwhelming majority were small shareholders: 83 owned a total of less than 220 shares. West Ham United and its shareholders began to resemble a normal company more than the community-based institution of the 1930s.

The chairman's annual statement emphasized financial matters, showing that the board and shareholders were involved in a business enterprise, however unusual the product might be. The decision to build a new stand, issue debentures, or purchase the ground merited special attention from the chairman. The shareholders showed little interest in obtaining such information. The annual report stressed that the directors were careful in their management of the company.

The shareholders knew that they were operating under a dividend limitation imposed on the company by the Football Association. Because the club became financially successful shortly after the its move to the Boleyn Ground, it was able to pay the maximum allowable dividend. This, in turn, led to the feeling that the maximum dividend was normal. There is no evidence that the board ever considered granting a partial dividend. In 1938 Mr A. W. Hone, a long-time shareholder, raised an objection and asked that no dividend be paid that year. He made the rather simple point that since the company had showed no profit, the shareholders should not be rewarded. W. J. Cearns's response placed the whole business philosophy of the company in a clear perspective. 'The adverse appearance was due to the acquisition of assets which it was not the custom of football companies to show, i.e. the transfer of players. Last year we spent over £5,000 more in this direction than in the previous year.'[13] The new accounting procedures gave a more accurate picture of the club's assets: it could sell players if it was facing severe financial problems, but unlike many tangible assets, the value of a player could fall dramatically. Injury, age, emotional problems or bad form could drastically reduce a player's value. The sale price was based on the complex and changing character of a market mechanism that varied with the needs of other clubs and the League standings. Cearns reminded Hone that in previous years the company had shown a substantial profit that would have justified a much larger dividend than had been paid. The limits imposed by the FA distorted financial realities and the board was justified in going against normal business practice to make up for these anomalies. Cearns concluded that, in any case, the amount involved in the dividend was so small that it would make no difference to the financial situation of the company. He was correct. The money involved mattered little to the club or most of the individual shareholders. The dividend was something more: it was symbolic of the stability and good management of the club. The board's attention to the dividend was something that came naturally to those solid businessmen. Concern with the dividend sent another message to the shareholders; attention to the financial realities emphasized the care with which the board protected the resources of the company. It was easier to defend the club's seeming refusal to spend money on players (or at least to spend enough to satisfy supporters and the press) and on other items when it was clear that the directors believed that it was a company first, and a team second.

The dividend was paid so regularly that any break in its continuity is noteworthy. No dividends were paid from 1941 to 1944, even though the club showed a profit in the last three years. The money was used to reduce the substantial overdraft and to redeem most of the outstanding debentures. It also minimized the uncertainty facing the club in a world beset with unsolved questions more important than the financial viability of an East End football club. In 1943 the chairman told the shareholders that they could not receive a dividend because the club needed to carry forward a large credit balance.[14] The FA empowered football clubs to pay a cumulative dividend for the war years, and the chairman hoped that West Ham would take advantage of this opportunity. The 22.5 per cent dividend paid in 1945 made up for all but one of the war years. Business was back to normal, even if the first post-war AGM took place in a setting that had suffered severe damage from flying bombs.[15]

The AGM was the most dramatic reminder that the club was a business *and* a publicly owned company. But, as we have seen, the shareholders were almost superfluous to what was happening at the meeting. Their real purpose was to provide an audience to whom the board and the chairman could direct their comments. The chairman's brief talk summarized the balance sheet and the season and gave the directors a chance to disclose the plans they had for the future of the club. The style of the chairman's presentation reflected the realities of West Ham United: a carefully run conservative business, firmly directed by the board. It made more sense for the board to talk about the retirement of debentures and 'a gentlemen's agreement' by the directors to secure loans than it did for the chairman to describe the players needed for the type of football that the 'Hammers' should play. Reg Pratt, for instance, could speak with authority about the decision to purchase the Boleyn Ground and new amenities, but his views on what had gone wrong on the pitch would carry little weight. The shareholders, as well as the general public, assumed they knew as much about football as any members of the board. 'Bert' Davis's involvement in public controversy (see pp.34-6) showed how dangerous it was for the directors to utter anything other than platitudes about football. This suited the personalities of the men who ran West Ham United. They entrusted football to their managers just as they had been entrusted by the shareholders to ensure that West Ham remained a viable company.

After 1960 the club entered a new phase in the relationship between the shareholders and the board. The responsibilities imposed by ownership of the ground and possible freedom of contract for players were so serious that no dividend was paid in 1958 or 1959. However, a three-year cumulative dividend was awarded in 1960. The ten shareholders who attended the AGM in January 1962 got a revealing look at what the future might hold. Pratt's speech began with a subject 'that was not a happy one for us', the replacement of Ted Fenton (see Chapter 8). West Ham had now obtained a manager/coach in whom the board had great faith. The big question was 'the future'. Gates had fallen dramatically, although a partial recovery was taking place. 'The new deal' for the players presented a worrisome uncertainty. The club was not alone in its problems; the 'dwindling support for football' continued and no one knew when it would stop. This probably meant that clubs, including West Ham, 'would be forced' to raise prices at the gate, and that could result in 'floaters looking around for the best value for their money'. Pratt then announced that West Ham intended to spend a great deal of money on improving the north bank, the lights and anything else that appeared to be necessary. There were no questions and the meeting adjourned, having lasted twenty minutes.[16]

Throughout its history the major decisions taken at West Ham United represented a curious blend of the freedom of action possessed by the board on the one hand, and the serious constraints under which it operated on the other. Directors assumed they knew what was best for the shareholders and their actions were seldom challenged. They attempted to make sound business decisions, based on the same standards as their outside business operations, but there many exceptions to the norms of business. The most obvious was the dividend limitation, which made it difficult for the club to raise large amounts of capital. Investors interested primarily in financial returns had no reason to get involved with a football club, even one that seemed as secure as West Ham United. As long as financial gain played no role in the ownership of professional football the board was secure. It did not have to worry about potential challengers, the corporate raiders who lived in the world of business.

The dividend restriction was part of the paternalistic heritage of the game. West Ham had been established in that philosophy. The Cearns family literally built the stands and created the physical setting in which the club performed. There was no impropriety attached to their activities. Cearns Ltd was a prominent, well respected local firm, the type of company to which a club like West Ham would be likely to turn for services. Cearns himself did not vote on matters affecting his firm or its contracts with West Ham. No major negotiations were conducted without bids being solicited. Cearns Ltd delivered on its promises. If anything, the close ties between 'the builder of stadiums' and West Ham United ensured that the club received special care in its dealings with the firm. The club showed many of the traits of the non-profit organizations that were the backbone of public services in the years before the creation of the welfare state. Its directors served West Ham as they did hospital and charitable boards, though football thrust them into the public spotlight.

Many normal business options were not available to the company known as West Ham United. It could not expand into other markets or significantly diversify into other product lines. Anything that detracted from football destroyed its *raison d'être*. Moreover it could not move to somewhere where it appeared that football might succeed financially. It is not clear which scenario sounds more ridiculous: West Ham moving its team or another community asking for the team to be moved. Can anyone visualize the crossed Hammers of Hampstead or the Camden Town Claret and Blue? Players could be sold, but the traditions of the team could not. The Hammers might cease to function for a variety of reasons, but moving the club was not one of them. Trophies and mementoes are portable, but they would not rest comfortably in a new setting. The site of the ground might be shifted as long as it remained within the general region, but even that kind of move would have to be justified to the public. The company could not be sold to anyone who would change its basic structure, its business, or its location. Why would anyone buy the company other than for the excitement of being involved with football?

Financial decisions taken by the board had to consider something much more important though ill-defined than either the bank balance or the club's performance on the field. The loyalty of its supporters was the glue that held the organization together. Club and supporters were in a symbiotic relationship; one could not exist without the other, and they acted as checks on each other's conduct. The directors appeared to have complete freedom of action, but the freedom was illusory. The club had become almost a captive of the community in which it existed and which the directors purported to serve. The directors' feeling of accomplishment would disappear if they alienated too many local men interested in football. The shareholders were names to whom the board owed their diligence, but the real owners were a much more nebulous group – the tens of thousands of people who talked about the club, gave vocal and emotional support and paid their money at the gate. It is absurd to think of the business of football without taking into account the emotional link between supporters and the club – just as absurd as it would be to equate the West Ham directors with Walter O'Malley, the entrepreneur who moved the Brooklyn Dodgers away from their home and relocated a team with the same name, but none of its traditions, in Los Angeles.

CHAPTER 3

The 'family club'

From a monetary point of view it might be better for the club to stay in the second division.

A. C. Davis, West Ham director, quoted in the *Evening News*,
20 April 1936.

West Ham has often been described as a 'family club'. The term comes easily from the mouths of men like Reg Pratt and Len Cearns; the former followed his father on the board, the latter served with his father. Four generations of the Cearns family have been board members.

However, 'family club' means more than the domination of the board by two families. Reg Pratt thought the phrase described a feeling that West Ham has consciously tried to foster the sort of loyalties that are involved in a family. There have been only five managers and five secretaries in the history of the club. Former West Ham players have filled almost all the slots as trainers, coaches and scouts. Many West Ham players who have gone on to careers with other clubs retain a strong sense of identity with the Hammers. Few of the individual attributes of West Ham are unique to the club, but they combine to intensify the sense of 'family'. Indeed, the family analogy has been applied to West Ham for so long by so many people who have no direct ties with the club that it is virtually impossible to convince anyone in football that West Ham is not a family club.

If West Ham United is a family, it is a patriarchy with a well-defined group providing the leadership and setting the standards of conduct. More accurately, the leadership of West Ham is a self-perpetuating oligarchy. The board has reflected the transformation of West Ham from an industrial team into a professional club. After 1904 the hallmark of the West Ham board was continuity. The nine-member board that made the decision to join the Football League in 1919 contained five men who had served on the board since 1904.[1] During the 15 years between 1904 and 1919, four members did not seek re-election, one member died and only one failed to be re-elected.

A football supporter might assume that being a director combines power and excitement. These men can spend time with great players,

The local businessmen who led West Ham United into profitability and laid the basis for its future success. Joseph Grisdale, a local coppersmith, became chairman of West Ham United in 1904 and led the board in its important decision to move from the Memorial Ground to the Boleyn Ground at Upton Park carry out their actions in the hallowed precincts of 'the board-room' and exercise control over the most important organization in the emotional lives of thousands. A football supporter might be excused for imagining the West Ham board to be a group of men whose actions take place in an atmosphere resembling that of the worlds of finance, politics and entertainment. It will be disappointing to the fantasies of outsiders, but most actions of the West Ham board are rather dull; they have little in common with the high drama of football.

The deliberations of the board include every aspect of the activities of the club. The board has, at one time or another, been involved in the choice of managers and staff, the selection and transfer of players and the terms offered to them, the renovation and creation of new facilities, and the operation of properties that have nothing to do with football matches. The board sets the tone for the way in which both the business and the team operate.

The first chairman of the board was Lazzeleur Johnson, a clerk who lived in Forest Gate. He worked at the Thames Ironworks and had been connected with its Football Club. He purchased ten shares of West Ham United in July 1900 when they were first issued to the public. He was succeeded as chairman in 1903 by Edwin Smith, a timber converter from Plaistow. Both men had been signatories to the Articles of Incorporation which brought West Ham United into existence. In 1904 Joseph Grisdale, a coppersmith from Plaistow, was elected as chairman. He served until 1909 and presided over the most important decision made by the board – the move to the Boleyn Ground. In 1909 William White became chairman. He was a barge builder, a resident of East Ham, and had been on the board since 1903. He had been one of the leading advocates of the move to the Boleyn Ground, even though that meant distancing the club from the site of his business in Blackwall. White remained chairman until his death in 1935.[2] The board had been in turmoil when White took charge. There had been deep divisions of opinion about the move to the Boleyn Ground, and there was uncertainty about the financial security of the club. White's report announcing a profit in 1906 was hedged with reminders about how novel this experience was for West Ham.[3] The club still lacked serious working capital and was able to sell few shares. That made it dependent on gate money for funds to provide the facilities and create a team to attract more supporters.

The 1904 election was the most contested in the history of the club. Three directors who resigned by rotation stood for re-election and lost, even though the board was enlarged by one member; Joseph Grisdale was elected and he also became chairman. The two defeated members, George Hone and J. W. Y. Cearns, lost despite Hone's ownership of 50 shares and Cearns's association with the club since its formation. Other new directors were Henry Carter of Barking Road, John Reeves of Canning Town and Henry Mattocks of Canning Town.[4] After 1906, every resigning director who put himself forward for renomination was elected. In addition, there were four nominees from the floor in 1906, 1907 and 1909, a figure only exceeded in 1904 when the board was in transition and six nominations were made.[5] In 1906, Henry Carter failed in his attempt to regain the board seat he had lost the year before and J. W. Y. Cearns was elected. This reversed the results of 1904 when Carter had joined the board and Cearns had been displaced. In the next eight years, Carter made three more unsuccessful attempts to join the board. Cearns remained until his death in 1934.[6]

From 1909 onwards, every chairman served in the office until he died or resigned from the board. A directorship was transformed into virtually a lifetime appointment. Elections to the board became a formality demanded by the Articles of Incorporation. Individual shareholders, however, still tried to gain seats on the board – and a local publican, G. H. Batt, was nominated five times in a six-year period. His final effort in 1914, along with two other candidates, marked the start of one of West Ham's most durable traditions: the absence of contested elections to the board. Since then, shareholders have never had to consider new candidates. 'Stability' and 'family' became the the the salient characteristics of the board: the former because of the small turnover among directors, the latter because at least one member of the Cearns family served as a director at all times.

The directors could plan for the future with the assurance that they could carry our their programme. Board members shared a similar background and status: they lived in the East End, most of them in the relatively more affluent area of East Ham, and Essex. They were self-employed businessmen or artisans whose socio-economic status was well above that of the players and the vast majority of people who attended matches. The composition of the board was not the result of a conspiracy by a small group of entrepreneurs to control an activity that engaged the attentions and passions of local workers. It simply continued a tradition that can be traced back to the Thames Ironworks when the club's affairs were run by a group of 'gentleman administrators'.

That they were doing the job for which they had been elected made it easy for the directors to secure re-election. From 1905, at each AGM the chairman could report on the latest successes of the club: the move to the Boleyn Ground, victories on the pitch and a profit. By 1910, the chairman had 'the pleasure to be able to state that the club is now practically free from debt, and the £2,000 which was a debit against the company in 1904 has been almost depleted'. Success was not limited to the balance sheet: the team had made more points and scored more goals than ever before.[7]

A fascinating aspect of the early history of West Ham United was the silence of Arnold F. Hills. There is no evidence that he attempted to exert any influence on the structure of the board or the practices of the club.

West Ham directors on tour with the club in Norway, May 1927. Vic Watson is at the far left of the front row, J. W. Y. Cearns at the far right, with his son W. J. Cearns next to him

After the move to the Boleyn Ground, Hills gave his unqualified support to the board. He exchanged occasional correspondence with Mr White and expressed approval of the way in which the club was run.

Between 1914 and 1923 there were no additions to the board. The retirement of a director was the occasion to co-opt A. C. Davis to the board in mid-year. This process enabled the board to bring in new members without electing them. It also enabled the new director to learn about the workings of the club and to stand for re-election. West Ham's directors were men of affairs in the community, but their public *personae* have often been identified with their positions as unpaid directors of a football club. When G. F. Davis died in 1934, the local newspapers praised him as 'a great sportsman' whose life had been dedicated to West Ham United. There were dozens of floral tributes, and the crowd was so large that traffic from the Boleyn Ground to the cemetery had to be regulated by the police.[8] When J. W. Y. Cearns died in the same year, his ownership of a construction company rated scant comment in comparison to his service as a director of West Ham. Other directors received the same kind of recognition over the years.

In 1924, the board underwent a great change. Two new members, W. J. Cearns and F. R. Pratt, were co-opted. Cearns was the son of J. W. Y. Cearns, and F. R. Pratt, a local timber merchant, was his friend and business associate. They and their families became the backbone of West Ham United. W. J. Cearns served on the board for 26 years until his death and was chairman from 1935 to 1950. F. R. Pratt remained on the board until his death in 1941, becoming vice-chairman in 1935; he was succeeded on the board by his son R. H. (Reg) Pratt. In 1948, Cearns's son L. C. (Len) Cearns joined the board. Since 1924 there has always been a member of the Pratt family and at least one Cearns on the board. They have not just been directors: between 1935 and 1986 the chairman and the vice-chairman were either a Cearns or a Pratt.

W. J. Cearns served on the board for a decade with his father. The elder Cearns had been associated with the Castle Swifts, St Luke's and the Thames Ironworks football clubs, the three leading amateur teams in the East End, and had been a founding member of West Ham. W.J. started his professional career as a junior clerk in an engineering firm in Canning Town. He became a travelling representative for W. Smith and when that firm collapsed he founded his own company, W. J. Cearns Construction and Engineering. Among the major projects in which the firm was involved were the greyhound stadia at Hendon, Southend and Wimbledon. Cearns built the first permanent building at the Hendon Aerodrome and his firm completed a stand for the Leicester City Football Club during one close season. The project that meant the most to him, both as businessman and sportsman, was the construction of the first concrete stands for West Ham. That was followed a few years later by the 5,000-person capacity double-decker grandstand, which was in place by the time of his death in 1950.

Anyone who enters the Boleyn Ground is surrounded by monuments to W. J. Cearns, but steel and concrete are only the most visible signs of his influence. He became a director when the board was still savouring promotion and the 1923 Wembley Cup Final. These events had brought West Ham United into a new world. The directors had to adjust to their new status and the responsibilities of the first division. W. J. Cearns and F. R. Pratt were the first directors not to have been associated with the pre-Boleyn Ground club. More importantly, they were the first directors to accept first division status as something more than a bizarre dream.

W. J. Cearns's personality dictated that he would be involved personally in running things. He attempted to maintain facilities equal to those of most of the so-called aristocratic clubs even when West Ham fell out of the first division. In 1935, at the first AGM at which Cearns presided, he began by reminding the shareholders that the club was facing financial problems and that it would be very difficult to raise the money to restore the club to its former status. This meeting included the unusual event of someone other than a director standing for election to the board. A stockholder, Mr H. S. Wray, nominated himself. When the chairman asked for a second there was none. Cearns thereupon declared the nomination rejected.

The following year, Cearns had to face questions about how the board was discharging its responsibilities. The team had finished just short of promotion to the first division and had transferred a popular player. When a shareholder asked about the latter, the chairman replied, 'David Mangall [the player in question] carried the best wishes of all at West Ham upon his departure'.[9]

Cearns was dealing with something more important than the disposition of one player. Events surrounding a late-season loss raised questions about the motives of the board. West Ham lost their last home match of the year to Charlton Athletic in a performance that the *East Ham Echo* labelled 'the worst of the year'. Messrs Cearns and Pratt publicly congratulated the Charlton directors on their victory and promotion, and were quoted by a reporter as stating, 'West Ham will try again.' It was an admirable sporting gesture, but this, unfortunately, was the occasion on which A. C. 'Bert' Davis made his famous comments to the press: he was quoted as saying that he preferred to have West Ham near the top of the second division rather than in the first division 'because it is a better paying proposition'.[10]

The *Evening News* report on West Ham concluded, 'He [Davis] is entitled to his opinion, but if I were a director I'd want to be at the top. Finances would balance out sooner or later.' In a final blow at Mr Davis the *News* reminded its readers 'that whatever difficulties there are at West Ham, they do not exist at Charlton'. Davis had certainly blundered. He had worried aloud more about the balance sheet that the League table, and he had made the comment in the hearing of a reporter. His remarks were such a public embarrassment that the incident became an issue at the AGM.

At a board meeting, a director, Mr Rooff, reluctantly brought up the subject of the *Evening News* story. He said he had expected to see a contradiction published by Mr Davis, but since that had not taken place, it was the responsibility of the board to do something. The statement 'purported to be made by Mr Davis was bound to have a bad effect upon the players and supporters'. Rooff's analysis raised issues that went beyond what his fellow director had said. Davis had spoken as an individual and should have faced up to the consequences of his words. But he was part of the board and it was up to the other directors to assume collective responsibility for the harm caused by one of their colleagues. Other directors agreed with Rooff about the damage that had been caused, but they wanted to counter it without criticizing Davis. They tried to put some of the blame on the press for misreporting what Davis had *meant* to say. The only criticism the directors were willing to level against their colleague, even in the privacy of the board-room, was that he 'had been unfortunate in expressing his thoughts so badly'.[11]

Davis concluded the discussion by telling the board that he shared their concern that his words had become a cause for many harsh comments about both himself and the board. He regretted the whole episode and assured his colleagues that it would not happen again. He also proposed a resolution to be passed by the board and distributed to all the usual newspapers. It was passed unanimously.

> The Board of Directors deplores the recent statement attributed to a Director of the Company to the effect that the West Ham United Football Club was not anxious for promotion. It must be apparent to all that the steps the Board has taken and the money invested by the Directors from time to time in order to improve the playing strength of the team, together with the degree of success which has attended their efforts, is sufficient indication to all West Ham supporters of this Board's determination and constant endeavour to place the West Ham United Football Club where we consider it rightfully belongs – back in the First Division.
>
> In making this statement they wish with the greatest possible emphasis to assure all who have the welfare of the club at heart that they will leave no stone unturned in their continued endeavour to achieve promotion and it is their fervent hope that their efforts may be rewarded next season.[12]

The effusive prose is out of character with the normal business of the board, but this statement was more concerned with public relations than with setting forth the facts. It met the issue obliquely, starting with the caution that the statement was 'attributed' to a director. It never hurts to plant the idea that the problem is really a product of journalistic excess. Almost all of the statement was an emotional appeal to believe in the good intentions of the directors with some vague mention of what they have done for the supporters in the past. There was no attempt to counter Davis's proposition that it made better *economic* sense to remain in the second division. The directors drew back from discussing the unthinkable, that winning football was not the purpose of their stewardship of West Ham United.

The published statement ignored Mr Rooff's original point that Davis must accept responsibility for his comments. The board chose to take collective action rather than allow their colleague to face the music. By putting the weight of the board behind the explanation, the other directors hoped to bury it. The directors must have realized that they would be held responsible for Davis's actions since they had elected him, but it would not do Davis or the board any good to hold him up to public ridicule. The best policy was to make a public show of unity, trumpet the concerns of the board and hope that the issue would soon be forgotten.

West Ham narrowly failed to gain promotion in 1935 and 1936. In 1935, the popular reaction was one of optimism, but in 1936 it became a combination of disappointment and outrage. The events of 1936 revived and gave new impetus to a feeling among supporters that the board was not much concerned with promotion. Versions of the story had been common within the borough for years. They attributed the lack of ambition to West Ham's unwillingness to spend money, the inability of the directors to function in the first division, and the comfort and security felt by the directors in the smaller pond of the second division. West Ham United remained in the second division for more consecutive years than any other club in history. The directors were the villains in a drama that ran for 25 years in the East End. Blaming the players would force supporters to undergo the emotionally wrenching act of disowning their alter egos. A knowledgeable supporter could 'prove' the charges against the directors by referring to the events of 1936 and the verbal ineptitude of Bert Davis.

Davis's real indiscretion was not his comment, but that he made it in the presence of a reporter. The story was too good for the newspapers to allow it to die. The 1936 AGM attracted press coverage and the board used the opportunity to try to retrieve its position. Davis stated that nobody was more keen for honours to come to West Ham than he.[13] An enthusiastic supporter might have seized on the relative nature of that statement to point out that nobody on the board seemed very much concerned with promotion, but the press ignored that interpretation. The chairman replied to a questioner that Davis had been quoted out of context and that the club had been unfairly stigmatized. The speaker thanked the chairman for his attention to the issue and took it no further. Davis merely commented that he 'had been misinterpreted and that his wish had always been to see the club in the highest place in football'. He was not challenged, no questions were raised, and the shareholders greeted his explanation with applause.[14]

The 1936 meeting tested Cearns's ability to deal with a problem that could not be handled within the inner sanctum of the board-room. Since it had started in the press, it would have to be overcome in public. Cearns chose to issue a statement on behalf of the chairman and board. He said that Davis had been misunderstood and had meant to say that 'from a monetary point of view it might be better for the club to stay in the second division, but it was not meant to convey that there was no desire for promotion. Their one desire was to return to the first division and they were striving for that end.'[15] After this, there were occasional newspaper articles about the lack of ambition on the part of West Ham directors, but the issue was closed as far as the board was concerned.

The primary responsibility of a director was to attend the weekly meetings, where virtually any subject could be raised. The majority of the discussion centred on details having little directly to do with the footballing aspects of the club, including weekly reports of cheques passed, income, and projected expenditure. The manager and/or secretary reported on the activities of the previous week and any special issues. Until the 1960s the board either named the teams for the next

W. J. Cearns, chairman of West Ham United from 1935 to 1950, ran the club with a strong hand

matches or gave its approval to the selections made by the manager. This approval was usually a formality, but the continuation of the practice showed that the board did not intend to relinquish any of its power. A match report was made by a member of the board who was charged with attending a particular match. At least one director travelled with the various teams to away matches and went to the Boleyn Ground for reserve matches; this responsibility was spread among the directors.

Board meetings averaged 48 per year, and it was unusual for any member to miss more than three of them unless he was seriously ill or away from London for a long time on business. There is only one instance of a member being reminded of his poor attendance and asked if he intended to carry out his obligation to the shareholders and the club. Service on the board became a matter of routine business. The directors knew they were responsible for the welfare of the club and did not neglect it. The board dealt with small issues to ensure that they would not reach crisis proportions. Each board member had an equal vote, but in practice a hierarchy was established. The chairman presided over meetings and gave the necessary orders and instructions to members of staff. He also spoke publicly on behalf of the board.

Most football chairmen have access to the press and can establish a public personality. In the case of West Ham, the chairmen have chosen to operate within the more enclosed context of the club. W. J. Cearns's approach was that of an activist patriarch. Before he became chairman in 1935 he had established a close relationship with many of the veteran players. His work with the players was not restricted to the time he spent at the ground. It was commonplace for the captain, George Kay, to phone Cearns at home to discuss the club and to be invited to the Cearns home on Sundays and during the close season. Kay spent enough time with the chairman's family to teach the next generation of Cearnses how to play tennis. Cearns also spent hours on the telephone with the secretary-manager Charlie Paynter. Although the chairman's part of those conversations was limited largely to, 'Yes, Charlie, No, Charlie', we can assume that he would have rung off if he felt his time was being wasted. Cearns also believed in going into the dressing-room on match days and during the week, and travelling with the players, but seems to have deliberately avoided any discussion with the players that even hinted at interference with the game itself. Pep talks and after-the-match praise for the players were his stock-in-trade.

Cearns was chairman when the maximum wage and lack of freedom of contract were accepted without question. The players were transitory, the board was the continuing aspect of the club. Cearns often offered fatherly – or worldly – advice to players, which ranged from suggesting ways in which they could plan for the future to reminding them of their social and moral responsibilities to the club and the game. When Jimmy Ruffell decided to refuse an offer from the FA to join the England side travelling during the summer, Cearns told him that he was afraid that such an action would have serious consequences for the future. Ruffell decided to go with his wife and children on a long planned holiday and was not recalled to the England side for several years.[16] Cearns did not chastise Ruffell, but he did remind other players that they must make sacrifices for the good of the game.

When Reg Pratt assumed the chairmanship in 1950 he tried to involve himself in some of the personal and financial problems of players. The dividing line between being paternalist and being patronizing is extremely thin and by the 1950s many players were rejecting both. Pratt's view was that players wanted little to do with directors: 'If the players thought at all about the directors, they saw them as a necessary evil... those upstairs who were not very interesting.' Given that perception of the players' attitudes, it was not surprising that Pratt retreated from W. J. Cearns's dictatorial approach. The most visible change took place in the early 1960s when Pratt stopped going into the dressing-room after matches. He was convinced that the players did not want him there when they lost, and he felt that he could not go into a winning dressing-room if he was not there at other times.

Changes were magnified at West Ham because of the personalities of the two chairmen involved. W. J. Cearns was the autocrat who expected his word to be followed. He had little patience with even a minor questioning of his writ. He represented a generation of employers who were convinced that their workers did not have to be told what was expected of them. Pratt preferred to work through the staff and allow the club to operate without direct regular intervention.

Reg Pratt and Len Cearns were West Ham directors for most of their adult lives and grew up with the club from childhood. They attended most home matches, and Pratt had vivid memories of the children's turnstile and the greeting of the gatemen. Like other boys, they had their heroes, and Pratt was in tears when his idol, Sid Puddefoot, was sold to

Reg Pratt, chairman of West Ham United from 1950 to 1979, was particularly proud of his role in creating the youth scheme at the club. He is pictured here with two top young players, Paul Allen (right) and George Cowie

Falkirk. Loyalty to West Ham and disappointment at the transfer of a great player were common to thousands of boys, but Pratt and Cearns were different because they had a direct relationship with the club. Some boys might wait indefinitely outside the ground for their heroes to emerge after a match; Len Cearns waited for hours outside the board-room for his grandfather to emerge after a match. He was never allowed in the board-room, but how many other boys knew where the board-room was, let alone thought about not going into it?

When F.R. Pratt died, his son Reg 'assumed that he would be invited'. Len Cearns's situation was different: he was asked to join the board by his father. In 1939, when W. J. Cearns proposed that members of the team should join the Territorials, his son joined up with them. The football games that took place during slack time were the only times that Len Cearns was on the field with the professional players whose fate he would one day determine.

Reg Pratt's and Len Cearns's conversations about their role as West Ham directors were filled with phrases that conjure up the Victorian heritage of the club – a strong sense of civic commitment by the middle class combined with paternalism. Cearns looked back to the days before sport became so commercialized '...everybody was more of a team... and there was more voluntary work thoroughout the community'. Pratt commented of the board, 'We're here to be shot at, and shot at we are.' Being a director was a serious and worrying job with the responsibility for decisions that affect the emotions of thousands of people. Pratt had few doubts that the club meant a great deal to the community and, in turn, the actions of the directors were open to constant public criticism. When the club did well in the League table, the directors were merely doing what they should, but when the club faltered they became targets for criticism. Pratt gave the strong impression that he would prefer anonymity for himself and other directors as this would enable them to 'get on with the job' and not have to think about public conventions. In Len Cearns's words, 'There are right reasons and wrong reasons to be a director and publicity is one of the worst.'

Pratt looked on his position 'as a heritage. I'm just following on a tradition.' It satisfied part of his 'bent for public service...an urge within me to do something for the community'. Not surprisingly, Pratt also served as a JP. Other directors served on the boards of hospitals, childrens' homes and other such institutions. Being a member of the West Ham United board did not convey status in the local community as much as it recognized that status.

Two features of the West Ham board made it very different from any other local charitable or civic organization: the product and the selection process. West Ham United had to display its wares before a critical public every week: its audience was made up of men who were convinced they knew more about football than either the directors or the managers. Hospitals and other social service organizations might occasionally be challenged for the inadequacies of their services, but consumers and the general public usually assume that the people running the institution are experts. The 'users' of the service provided by a football club think that it should win every week, should have the best players, and not put up admission prices. Failure in any one of these areas is the fault of the people running the club.

The leadership of the board was fully aware of what the public expected of them, but the board had to draw its own distinctions between what the supporters wanted and what the club needed. The business backgrounds of the directors could not be transferred directly to West Ham United. In football, management cannot exercise direct control over the end product. Even if the board acted in accordance with solid business practice and followed the pattern set by the best clubs there was no assurance that the product would be what the directors planned. The board could control expenditure but it could only encourage successful football. There is, however, no way to judge the success of a football club by its balance sheet, although failure is easy to see.

West Ham's years in the second division were testimony to the inability of the club to raise its performance above a certain level. But was that a fair measure of the success or failure of the board? The chairman's annual report always included a summary of the season's performance, but it was not the first issue: the financial situation of the company came before any talk about football. In his annual report, the chairman made another important distinction: West Ham was described as 'the company' when discussing its financial situation, and it was 'the club' in other contexts. What exactly was meant by the club? This is a question of more than semantic interest.

Len Cearns's response reveals some of the problems: 'We fall into the trap of calling it the company rather than the club, even though we like to think of it as a club. That's what keeps us interested in it.' Thousands are deeply involved with West Ham and support it. They have no role in determining the future of 'their' club. Chairmen speak in terms of their legal responsibility to the shareholders but at the same time claim that their 'main responsibility was to the supporters, to those people who thought West Ham United meant something'.

The leadership of West Ham has a constituency that extends far beyond the people who attend matches. West Ham United is an institution that gives people a sense of identity. For the past decade, historians and sociologists on both sides of the Atlantic have been engaged in an important debate over whether, and if so how, sports organizations reflect the society in which they exist. The leadership at West Ham has worked on the assumption that the club is a civic resource without parallel and the populace has responded in a way that reinforces that belief. Supporters would never envisage a referendum on how the club should act or the possibility of the directors loosening their control.

West Ham directors like to see the club as a link with the past. Even when other aspects of community spirit 'have broken down, the attitude towards the club has remained the same'.[17] The folk mythology surrounding the club is equally important. Does production rise at Dagenham when West Ham is doing better? Do schoolboys in the East End feel a sense of guilt when they go to clubs other than West Ham? Was football at West Ham one of the ways in which social divisions were ameliorated in the East End in the wake of the General Strike of 1926? Is West Ham football something special for the people of East London? Whatever the answers, there is no doubt that the board has always acted on the premise that the club's game is important to people. The mission of the board, *as defined by itself*, is to maintain the club and the activity.

The board is a 'closed shop' and conscious effort has been exerted to bring in men with close links to other board members. This guaranteed that they 'would be the right sort' and would 'know what the interests of the club are': the best way to ensure homogeneity has been to turn the club into a family operation in the truest sense of the phrase.

In the 1970s Reg Pratt recognized that 'it might look better if we had one outsider'. But that admission raises more concerns. To whom might it look better – other clubs, the directors themselves, the press, or the supporters – and what difference would it make? Clearly, the exclusive nature of the board has not troubled Pratt or other directors very much, for they could have changed it any time they wanted. Occasionally an outsider has made his way onto the board and had some impact. Dr Thomas, 'a great director who had a tremendous effect on the club', seems to have been that type of man.[18] That anyone could consider Thomas an 'outsider' shows the close-knit nature of the board. He was a prominent physician, well-known and well-liked in the district and an old friend of the chairman, Reg Pratt.

The men who ran the board saw nothing unusual about their actions; East Londoners tend to be 'family oriented' in their personal and business lives. Why shouldn't West Ham follow that pattern? Len Cearns viewed family ties and inbreeding as a danger in most businesses, but felt football was different. The club was much more than commerce: it should represent community standards and the way to ensure that was to have men on the board who understood tradition.

The directors have looked within the club for employees and have been most reluctant to discharge staff – managers, secretaries, coaches, scouts, or anyone else. Directors understand that they have been out of step with the majority of football clubs, but they take pride in being 'poor butchers'.

West Ham's directors have followed a policy of internal conservatism based on maintaining that which they have inherited, even if they can not define it. The board has looked at the rest of the world of football and decided what it does *not* want to happen at West Ham, especially 'the new breed of chairman', men who get on to a board by putting up money: '...especially in the provinces...being a director makes you somebody ...gives you a chance to strut around town showing how important you are...to be associated with a club and especially to be chairman is a step up on the social scale.'[19] It does not matter if this analysis is correct or not, for the philosophy it implies has governed the policies of the West Ham board for almost 50 years.

All the goals of the club, including victories and promotion, must be obtained within the traditions of West Ham. There have been few serious attempts by local businessmen or politicians to use the club or buy their way on to the board and these have not gone very far. West Ham might have been a natural target for men who wanted to enhance their status or popularity in the area, but there have been few attempts to invade the closed circle of the board-room: 'Even if outsiders wanted to have a go at this club they probably thought that it was tied up by the two families.' This is not precisely true, but the legend is stronger than the reality. The Pratts and Cearnses have never owned 50 per cent of the shares, but they have exercised effective control over the club. The largest single group of shareholders are the desendants of Arnold F. Hills and 'luckily they have been loyal to the board'. The chairmen 'do not know who runs the Hills shares...[they] never even ask for Cup tickets'.[20]

The hallmarks of the board have been its sense of tradition, its steadfast conservatism and the directors' belief that their role is one of public service. Indeed, one consistent criticism of West Ham has been the adherence of the board to practices that seem antiquated. The leadership admit that they are out of touch with many other clubs, but they claim proudly to be in the mainstream of their own history. This might be viewed as a form of special pleading, a way of covering their inability to win championships with a mantle of moral superiority, but the directors want success within their own traditions. The board defines the club and then has to live up to its own definition.

CHAPTER 4

It won't work without money

Barclays Bank has consented to loan us £1,000 for the July wages.

Report of the chairman to the West Ham board, June 1926

Even after professionalism was legalized in 1886 administrators and club directors continued to operate as if there was something tainted about money. The maximum wage and control over the registration of players created an artificial financial world for the club. The businessmen who ran the clubs might have been firm believers in capitalism, but they created a system for their 'other business' that violated their capitalist principles. This was supposedly done in a good cause – to encourage competition on the pitch and protect the spiritual purity of the game by limiting the influence of money on players who were assumed to have insufficient moral fibre to resist its blandishments.

Even if West Ham United made a profit, little of it could be channelled to the shareholders as dividends and none could go to the directors for their services, but this should not lead to the misconception that the men who were responsible for running West Ham United were not concerned about money. Approximately 48 times a year, the West Ham board assembled for its weekly meeting, in which one constant item was a discussion of financial affairs. At minimum, this meant the weekly income and a balance statement. The other extreme was lengthy discussion about how to raise money to meet the obligations of the club and plans for the future. The subjects in which money was a major consideration included virtually every issue affecting the club.

The long-time auditor for West Ham remarked that any analysis of West Ham that treats it just like a normal business would be in error, but any conclusions that did not take into account that it was a business would be absurd. The directors act as the representatives of the shareholders and are legally liable to them for actions taken on behalf of the company.

The investment of the shareholders is very small and monetary considerations are often swamped by the emotional aspects of the game. But the directors cannot abandon their sense of fiscal responsibility just because the amount involved is not very large. In financial terms, the directors could afford to let the company go into liquidation, but this would run counter to the emotional aspect. It might be impossible to ensure football success for the club by good management, but the directors could easily ensure failure by financial mismanagement.

Money has been of continual concern to the men who run West Ham United since 1900. The financial decisions they have made have created a sense of what the club stands for and have had an important effect on how supporters and other football observers have viewed events at the club. The projected capitalization of West Ham United was £2,000, 4,000 shares at 10s each.[1] In the years before the First World War, the board attempted to market the shares with disappointing results. The pattern of shareholding, including those purchased by Hills, gives the impression that many were purchased either out of some sense of loyalty to the old 'Irons' club or just from a desire to retain quality football.

In its first years, West Ham maintained its financial viability through a combination of loans from A. F. Hills and an overdraft. From 1905 the company showed a profit in its operating account, but it took five more years to bring the overall balance into profitability. By 1910, the company had eliminated an overdraft that had been as high as £568 the previous year.[2] Two years later, it paid off the outstanding balance of £2,500 on the loan of £3,000 that Hills had made six years earlier.[3] After seven consecutive years of showing a profit in the profit-and-loss account, the West Ham directors had cleared up all the financial encumbrances they had incurred in order to get the club operating and to set it up at the Boleyn Ground. The pre-1914 board set the pattern for its successor. Dividends were paid from the profit-and-loss account and profits went to pay off outstanding debts. Management was expected to run the club at a profit; there was no possibility of a wealthy patron supporting the club. Overdrafts and loans were considered unacceptable for anything other than emergencies or major capital improvements to the ground. There was to be no future Hills. None of the directors who joined the board after 1914 could support the club financially; they could handle the incidental expenditures that went along with carrying out their responsibilities to the club, but their main qualification was to bring solid business judgment to the board.

It is fatuous to think of the carnage of the First World War in terms of its impact on football. But for West Ham, the timing of the suspension of football could not have been worse. The 1913-14 season had been a business success. The balance sheet was a testimonial to the decisions taken by the directors three years earlier. The net profit had reached £2,200 and the chairman had the pleasure of announcing that the new stands had been paid for entirely from increased gate revenues. He then recommended, on behalf of the board, that additional facilities be built and contracts tendered for improvements to the enclosure and new stands. Based on the attendance of the previous year, the chairman predicted that the new construction would be paid for within three years.[4] The AGM of 1914 drew the largest number of shareholders of any meeting and they questioned the chairman severely about his report and recommendations. This performance was out of character, showing the board that financial success was not an unmixed blessing. 'After several questions, the report was carried unanimously', but then there was a move to appoint a chartered accountant as the auditor of the club. This, however, was defeated. Decisions on whether the new wealth of the club should be spent on facilities, players or set aside led to the dissension that surfaced in 1914. The board's plans were clear; its previous decision to put its money into bricks and mortar had succeeded, and it was recommending more of the same. The decision to spend more than £2,000 showed how serious the board was about spending money.[5]

The club took economy measures in May 1915 when it terminated the services of two of the groundsmen and changed the status of Charlie Paynter. His 'engagement as groundsman was cancelled and he was appointed as caretaker'.[6] This move was part of a broader effort by the board to bring down its expenditure. It also lodged an appeal against the rates. (During succeeding years, the directors battled regularly against the rate collector.) The board felt it had to demote Paynter 'in view of our appeal against the rates'.[7] Borough officials finally realized the hardships imposed on the club by the war; the rates were reduced substantially and terms of payment worked out.

Meeting the rent payments for the Boleyn Ground was a greater problem. The board approached its landlord and explained its financial problems. In 1915 the Archdiocese of Westminster reminded the board that a contract was not open to change because one party found itself in temporary difficulties. By the spring of 1916, the landlord realized that the club's difficulties were not short term and had been caused by circumstances over which it obviously had no control. The landlord's solution was to allow West Ham to pay only £300 in rent for the year 'if the war lasted' and to make a donation of £100 to the Archdiocesan charity.[8]

By the end of the war, the club had paid for the partial improvements made in 1914. As soon as plans were made to start football again, the board asked Cearns Construction Ltd for tenders and specifications for some of the additions to the ground that had been discussed five years earlier. The firm replied with a tender of £1,181, more than the board could afford with its diminished account. The board responded with a proposal to ask Cearns Construction 'to accept deferred payment for any future contracts'.[9]

If there was any construction company in England that knew West Ham was not merely pleading poverty it was Cearns. Ten days later the board's request was accepted and arrangements were made for the submission of specifications. The bidding process for the new work at the ground continued for more than a month. Four companies were invited to submit bids and specifications for various parts of the work. The combination of several projects discussed by the board over the past five years was reduced and consolidated in one set of contracts awarded to Cearns Ltd. The amount was £6,040, which was slightly less than the bid of other contractors but more than the board could finance with existing resources. Yet the board had reason to be optimistic about its investment. It had completed its first season in the Football League and had shown a record operating profit of more than £4,000. The chairman assured the shareholders that the record gate takings were proof of 'the popularity of League football'.[10]

The board was engaged in a two-pronged improvement plan for the ground – repairing the dilapidation that had taken place during the four years of non-maintenance, and adding to the facility. The financial future looked bright, but ready cash was still needed. At the end of the year the directors had to approach both Cearns and their bank manager, asking the former for an extension of bills that were due and the latter to allow the club to maintain an overdraft in its current account. Cearns Ltd and Barclays Bank consented to the requests of the board.[11]

The amount of money involved in the discussions of the winter of 1921 was fairly minor. The discussions took place against the background of two successive years of high profits. At the end of the season, the chairman did not think it was even worth mentioning the momentary financial problems. He stressed the club's growth and the investment the board had made in its future. Since the end of the war, the company had spent more than £21,000 on the ground, making a total of more than £35,000 since it had accepted tenancy of the Boleyn Ground. There was still more than £4,500 to be paid, but the chairman expressed complete confidence in the club's ability to liquidate the debt without resorting to any extraordinary measures. No mention was made during the AGM of a most important financial deal undertaken by the club – its involvement in the transfer market. The club showed a balance of £5,000 in its transfer account caused by the sale of its most famous player, Sid Puddefoot, to Falkirk for a record club fee of £5,000. Puddefoot's departure helped put the club on a solid financial footing and enabled the board to contemplate future expenditures, few of which involved acquiring players.[12] Puddefoot's departure was the spectacular off-the-field event of the 1921-22 season, but an equally significant move took place when in the spring of 1922 the club obtained a lease of 34 years on the ground. This ensured the continuity of the setting and that the club would continue to benefit from the expenditures it had undertaken.

April 1923 was the high point of West Ham's history – the club gained promotion to the first division and reached the Cup Final. From a financial standpoint, the year had been equally spectacular. The profits of £8,382 were almost 80 per cent more than any other year. The spurt in

The 1923 side put West Ham on the map by gaining promotion to the first division and reaching the final of the FA Cup

revenue was coupled with a drop in expenditure on maintenance and major work on the ground.

Outside comments on the West Ham board almost always involve one or more of the following epithets: careful, conservative, cautious, businesslike. These could be euphemisms for criticisms of the board's failure to act more decisively, but they are spoken by men who admire the way in which the club has conducted its business over the years. The directors were well aware that they were using other people's money. Their caution stemmed partly from their business background and also from an occasion in the mid-1920s when they decided to act as guarantors for the loans needed to pay for the new facilities that were started after 1923. From June 1926 the directors were not only protecting the investment of numerous small shareholders and the community resource that the club had become: they were guarding their own personal investment in the financial stability of West Ham United.

The success of the club in 1923 convinced the directors that they had a new status in football. They decided to invest more money to improve the product. This equation is simple in most businesses, but what did it mean in the case of West Ham? How could the 'product' be improved? Where could the money be raised?

In August 1925 the *East Ham Echo* featured a lengthy article about West Ham United in the news section headlined, 'West Ham's Achievement'. The story was an exercise in civic pride as well as reporting. It described a luncheon hosted by the club to celebrate its great success. The vice-chairman, Mr Johnson, presided and reminded the guests they were celebrating one more instance of West Ham living up to its policy of providing what its supporters wanted and the club needed. One director discussed the technical details of the new construction and reminded the audience that West Ham always stood for innovation. There were toasts from assembled members of the FA council and the press, followed by many flattering comments about the labours of Syd King, the manager, and his staff. The luncheon was celebrating a victory, not over a footballing opponent, but over West Ham's long-standing economic status as a fringe club with second-rate facilities. In the same way as a journalist in the 1980s might describe the physical attributes of a transferee, the *East Ham Echo* writer talked in glowing detail about the size of the new stand, the amenities it provided and the cost to the club. He mentioned that the supporters had gone through 'trials and tribulations with United', but now they 'can be proud of yet another splendid object accomplished by the energetic band of directors'. The decscription made it clear that the newspaper felt that supporters wanted the new comforts and would look at the stand with pride usually reserved for a victorious side.[13]

The directors were prepared to spend money and did their planning and spending with pride. In the midst of the euphoria, however, pointed comments were made that looked beyond the new facility. Although it was presented as a jest, a director's comment to the mayor that he should 'go easy' on the rates and remember how much local labour went into the building of the stand, showed that the board were aware of local political and economic sensibilities. W. F. White, the chairman, concluded the speeches by stating: 'Today is the second red-letter day in the history of the club...The fist was getting into the first division and the third will be when we win the English Cup.'[14]

A week later, the *East Ham Echo's* match report read more like a construction summary and appraisal of a building site than a football commentary. It went into detail about the number of bricks, the tonnage of steel, and the amenities, to include a refreshment room that accepted reservations by telephone. The unrestricted sight-lines and scoreboards were written up like stars of the new season. The construction was the biggest investment made by the board, a symbol of what the directors thought was important. In his speech at the luncheon Mr Johnson had taken the opportunity to remind everyone that the policy of the club had always been to put all the money it gained 'back into football' after it met certain obligations to charity.[15] His definition of football requires some qualification. Only once since 1919 had the club spent more in transfers than it had received. In six years it showed a balance of almost £13,000 in the transfer account. At the same time, the club had paid almost £48,000 for major work on the ground and had contracted for £26,000 more work to be done before June 1926.

Ten months after the opening of the grandstand the club accepted 'with thanks' the offer of the chairman to lend the club £1,000. A resolution followed that all future loans from other directors to the club should bear an interest rate of 6 per cent per annum.[16] A month later the board received notice that 'Barclays Bank has consented to loan us £1,000 for the July wages.'[17] The request was not unusual, because of the seasonal nature of football income. However, this was the first time West Ham had been forced to approach its banker for assistance in more than 20 years. The directors resorted to a new measure: the issue of 100 debentures worth £300 each. This occurred although the club showed a profit in its operating account of more than £6,000. The balance sheet between 1923 and 1929 showed profits ranging from the high in the Cup year of £8,382 to a low of £6,100 in 1925. The club was doing well at the gate and the board could count on relatively stable wages. The extraordinary expenses involved in the reconstruction of the ground had to be handled differently, however, thus the sale of debentures.

The holders of a debenture have first call on the assets of any company should it undergo liquidation. That applied as much to West Ham United as it did to any industrial firm, but the players were West Ham's only significant redeemable assets. The major expenditures had been made to improve the ground, but that would revert in 30 years to the Archdiocese of Westminister, the owner of the freehold. There was no overwhelming economic or business reason to buy the debentures; the interest rate was not excessive, certainly not more than could be obtained from similar investments in more solid companies. The project to which the funds were dedicated was meant to increase the club's revenue from its supporters. The board could charge increased prices for those who wanted to partake of the relative luxury of the new grandstand. This was reminiscent of 1905, when the board had looked to a prospective audience 'up market' of its traditional hard-core working-class supporters. The board was staking its economic future on improvements that had nothing directly to do with the club's performance on the field – the same board that took pride in having built a team at minimal cost. An article in the *East Ham Echo* pointing out that 'now a footballer can cost as much as £5,500 and the whole West Ham team cost less than £2,000. Watson cost £25, Ruffell and Tesadern nothing' inspired the board's approval and pride.[18]

A debenture for improvements to the Boleyn Ground was the kind of investment the board could appreciate. There was a permanence about the grandstand that could stand as a visible sign of the interest and foresight of individual directors; a good result, on the the other hand, was transitory. West Ham had never given the impression that it was competing for championships with the great established clubs. The club might be new to the first division but no one could deny the *East Ham Echo's* boast that West Ham now had the 'largest grandstand in London'.[19]

The board never discussed an alternative method of raising the money, even though 1,200 of the original shares remained unsold. Thus debentures enabled the directors to raise the necessary capital but not diminish their control over the company. The directors worked hard to reduce both the debt and the debentures. By 1929, only 47 of the debentures remained unredeemed and the debt had been reduced by almost £5,000.[20] The improved financial picture was the result of profitable seasons and the directors' willingness to negotiate a banker's line of credit. The individual board members pledged themselves to act as guarantors of the debts incurred to the bank up to £750 per man. This was not a close-season expedient: the directors were organizing the finances on the assumption that the bank would maintain the club's 'right' to run an overdraft.

The overdraft had the potential to cause problems for the club. In 1931, Lazzeluer Johnson sent in his resignation after more than 30 years on the board. He turned down the efforts of his colleagues to grant him a leave of absence until the 'present run of his business ended'. He also asked to be relieved of his liability for the overdraft of the club, to which the club responded with a 'regretful, no'.[21] Johnson's liability came up again a year later after his death and the suspension of Syd King (see Chapter 6). The board then named two directors as a finance committee, and decided on an audit and a discussion of the bank guarantees. The auditor's report was ready the following week and did not make pleasant reading. In the course of its discussion on finance the board requested the bank to release the estate of the late Mr Johnson from its liability for the overdraft.[22]

The board was trying to sort out its management problems and put the financial situation in order. A final audit showed that the overdraft had risen to more than £12,000. Each director assumed a liability of over £2,000 as part of his responsibility to the future of the club. There is no need to restate the reasons why the directors should accept these financial responsibilities. But why should the bank have been so willing to become a partner in the financial future of West Ham United? The overdraft exceeded the amount to which each director was pledged, but that was outweighed by the status of the directors. They were prominent local businessmen. They had the resources to cover the club's debts and the bank could count on the directors' sense of honour as well as their regard for their reputation to back up the debts. They were good customers of the bank, part of the local merchant class upon whom the bank depended for its expansion of business.

The concern of the club and its directors to protect their reputations accounted for the speed with which they dealt with Syd King (the team's manager) in 1932 (see Chapter 6). He was not only guilty in their eyes of insubordination and drunkenness, he was the cause of some of the financial difficulties. The board did not much care whether the financial problems were due to embezzlement or mismanagement, but it had to restore confidence in its ability to run the club, which meant the dismissal of King, the establishment of the finance committee and a rigorous system of bookkeeping and controls at the bank.

In three consecutive seasons (1931-33) West Ham United had disastrous results on the field: hovering near the bottom of the first division, being relegated to the second division and barely surviving the first season there. Gate receipts did not decline during that period, but profits dropped in the first two years due to a redemption of some of the debentures and increased repairs to the ground. The first year in the second division saw a dramatic rise in profit (almost £4,000) that can be attributed to a decrease in repairs and a sharp drop in the wage bill, from £14,226 to £12,299.[23]

The emotional hold that football has over its supporters has often been likened to the role played by religion in pre-industrial societies. One of the less obvious comparisons is financial. The unique situation of the Church as an institution that outlived its servants gave it a privileged legal status that sometimes translated into financial advantages. Bankers regarded the Church as much more than its tangible assets or the ability of its leadership. Even the most hardened businessmen saw that it served a social function important enough to be worth bending some of the rules of good business judgment in order to aid the institution. Likewise, West Ham's bank managers and directors sometimes seemed to act in uncharacteristic, almost unbusinesslike ways.

Experience of the first division had made an indelible impression on West Ham United. The supporters had tasted the glory of playing the best; their dream was to return to the first division. It was up to the directors; public opinion judged the board by an easily defined goal. After 1932, the board's decisions were scrutinized with that one objective in mind, and financial moves took on a new importance for the supporters. They wanted the club to acquire players to bring it back up; improved facilities were secondary. The board too had been affected deeply by the club's time in the first division. The directors had become used to the status and hobnobbing with the best in football. The other legacy of the first division was the building boom at the ground and the debt it caused.

The end of the disastrous 1933 season was a good time for the board to step back and take a long look at what measures were needed to put the club on a solid financial footing. West Ham was still running a substantial overdraft and there was approximately £9,000 in outstanding debentures. Mr F. A. Enders proposed a scheme to issue a second set of debentures that would carry special voting rights. They would be issued to directors and would provide them with collateral security for their bank guarantee. The proposal was complicated, and the resolution also called for a complete investigation into its legality and how the bank would respond.[24] It was necessary to amend some of the rules of the club in the light of the proposal, making it mandatory for directors to accept their share of the guarantee with the bank.

An extraordinary meeting of the shareholders approved a proposal to issue £2,000 in debentures, each of which had a value of 5s. They were to be issued only in multiples of 100.[25] A week later, the board met with Mr Crosbie, the bank manager, to get his opinion. 'He indicated the guarantees of £1,750 from each of the seven directors would be agreeable' and asked that the proposal be sent to him in writing. One director, W. J. Cearns, was exempted from the guarantee at the request of the other directors.[26] Five months later, the scheme was put into effect when the bank formally accepted the guarantees of the directors for a total overdraft of £7,000 with the debentures as secondary collateral. The directors agreed, in the chairman's phrase, to take the whole issue 'in order to put the company on a firm financial basis'.[27] The involved dealings in 1933 were meant to raise money, support the bank guarantee, give the directors more security, and make sure that the board retained control over the voting shares of the club. The new debentures and the co-operation of the bank enabled the club to reorganize financially and pay for the new construction. The financial integrity of the club was ensured when the board and the bank became virtual partners in support of West Ham United.

From 1934 to 1939, West Ham United stayed in the race for promotion until the last weeks of the season and showed profits based on a steady increase in gate money. One other important feature appeared on every balance sheet between 1934 and the outbreak of war in 1939: the club was spending money in the transfer market. This process originated with the manager or scouts, but the final decision was the directors'. At times, they discussed the footballing qualities of transfer-related players, but their major concern was based on economic considerations. Inability to buy players carried little weight with supporters, and the directors had to get used to their motives being questioned.

Supporters, and even the occasional spectator, could see the hand of the board at work in the players they obtained and the condition of the ground. Major ground improvements attracted temporary notice, but they quickly became part of the landscape and were taken for granted. The board could court popularity by purchasing players, but it remained cautious: it had to assume that any single purchase might not work out well, in which case the investment would be lost. There was more than money involved: even a good new player could not ensure success for the team. The failure of a publicized new player called into question both the football and business judgment of the board. One can almost hear the complaint of the disgruntled supporter: 'They don't want to spend money on players and when they do all we get is a load of rubbish like him.' Expenditures on the ground represented something solid and tangible, the type of decisions the directors made in the normal course of their business. They could evaluate what they were getting for their money. This investment could not backfire on them unless the crowds did not come, all too possible if the club failed miserably on the pitch. Thus the board was wrapped up in a circular series of considerations when they decided how to spend the club's money.

The directors knew that if the affairs of the club were terminated, they would operate under rule 43, section 6 of the FA, which gave the shareholders the right to the assets of a club only up to the par value of the shares. Everything beyond this had to go to charity or to the FA. The debentures gave the directors security that was translated into a willingness to spend money on improvements for the club; their investment was secured again by an asset that does not appear on a normal balance sheet: the players. They were a commodity that could be sold if the club floundered. The real guarantee of the club's financial stability was the willingness of members of the local business and financial communities to ensure that it would never be pushed to the point where it had to consider either selling off its marketable assets or going into liquidation. The bank manager could be counted upon to extend the overdraft, the Archdiocese of Westminster to renew the lease at fair terms rather than taking over the property and its improvements, and the board to stand behind the necessary financial obligations. None of these assumptions had to be stated, let alone written down. The men who handled the financial future of West Ham United all operated within a common set of values. They spoke the same language, moved in the same circles, and had common standards of conduct. The financial viability of the club was ensured because the men who controlled it were committed to continue the institution, for reasons that far transcended anything that could be put on an accountant's ledger.

CHAPTER 5

Spending money isn't always easy

What do people think we are going to do for that sort of money, sell the ground?

Eddie Chapman, West Ham secretary, commenting on the rumour that
West Ham intended to purchase Budgie Byrne, 1962

Raising money to support West Ham was a tiresome, sometimes risky business for the directors. Spending money should have been the opposite side of the coin, a time when a director could get pleasure and praise from his service to the club. The board's expenditures present a good picture of its priorities and attitudes towards success. Every expenditure had to be weighed against other uses for the money. After 1910 the board started on a long-term policy of improving and expanding facilities at the ground – the purchase of players was a minor concern. Two assumptions underlay that policy: that the personnel was adequate for the level of competition in the Southern League and could be improved without transfers, and that the facilities at the ground could not meet the needs of the club. Bricks and mortar versus players remained a major part of West Ham's policy decisions well into the 1950s.

It is difficult to show the impact of a newly purchased player on takings at the turnstile. A dramatic improvement in the playing fortunes of the club may take place on the arrival of a new player but that could be attributed to coincidence. An injury, bad judgment on the part of the manager and scouts or totally unforeseen circumstances could turn a purchase into something worse than a total financial loss: a bad buy was an embarrassment to the board, especially since a major topic of conversation among thousands of people was how West Ham spent its money.

Most self-respecting supporters were sure that they could pick a better team than the manager and buy a better team than the directors. It was easy to complain about the inadequacies of the players West Ham purchased and even easier to hold the club responsible for the players it did not purchase: there had to be players on the market that could help West Ham; why weren't they in the team? Two reasons presented themselves to supporters: the manager was not a good enough judge of talent, or the board was unwilling to put up the money. The club was particularly annoyed by the charges of running a cut-rate operation that often appeared in the press, for the directors regarded themselves as acting with fiscal responsibility. West Ham had always delighted in showing it could manage with less than other clubs. Most supporters, on the other hand, would have sacrificed this and the board's principles in return for a winning team. But there was not much money available, and the club resisted allowing 'the size of our purses to be the measure of our worth'.[1] On occasion, as we have seen, the press praised the club for assembling the team carefully and not spending money needlessly.[2] Success could go a long way towards making a policy look good. Ironically, the 1922-23 season was the only time between 1913 and 1933 when West Ham spent more on purchasing players than it received for players it sold.

A few years later the *East Ham Echo* was more critical of the board, claiming that, 'Depending almost entirely upon "local talent" and upon the cheese-paring methods of the directors is worse than useless – it is suicidal.' According to the same reporter:

> Other directors have seen the importance of spending money to improve their teams. If the Hammers' directors had done that, the team wouldn't be in such sad shape...directors pride themselves on their ability to run the club in the cheapest possible way, but the big gates they get at Upton Park and elsewhere do not justify such actions...Nowadays the cheapest teams cannot be the best teams, and there is no reason why the Hammers should not be a much better team than it is.[3]

Criticism of the board was not limited to the sporting pages. The author of 'Echoes of the Town' concluded by saying that the directors could 'pat themselves on the back and say how clever they are in having the "cheapest team" in the first division, but cheapness is not the way to win.'[4] Victory determined feelings about West Ham and the directors. One correspondent made the distinction clear: 'We have much admiration for the "Hammers", but precious little for their cheese-paring directors, and it is high time that the latter looked to the interests of the club.'[5] The club was not winning, and somebody had to be the cause of its slide down towards the bottom of the first division. Policies that had been admirable in the 1923 flush of victory looked hollow and unimaginative after years of bad results and less hope for the future.

Even after relegation, a syndicated columnist writing under the title of 'Ex-International' appealed for sympathy for the West Ham way of doing things. He used the club as an example of what was right in the game, especially the 'Hammers' wise management'. The board kept out of the transfer market and gave promising young players a chance to show what they could do. However most supporters believed that the glories of 1923 would 'not be repeated until the club buys good, hard-working players'.[6]

The club's financial reports show that West Ham spent little on players. Between 1919 and 1932, the club showed a yearly balance in the transfer account ranging from £608 in 1919 to £5,000 in 1922. These figures need explanation: 1919 was the first season of post-war football, and 1922 was the year in which Sid Puddefoot went to Falkirk.[7] In normal seasons, profits in the transfer account were usually in four figures and twice exceeded £2,000. The directors made little mention of profits from transfers, choosing to ignore the subject at the AGM. At first glance it seems strange that a business should choose not to discuss a significant part of its yearly profits, but the chairman preferred to talk about expenditures, especially improvements to the ground.

In 1913 the club had entered into contracts to build a new stand and enclosure and do additional work on the south bank. This cost more than £4,000, a sizeable sum for a club that had cleared its debts only two years earlier.[8] The chairman reported to the 1914 AGM that the construction had been an unqualified success; the stand was comfortable and had attracted larger crowds. The stand was entirely paid for and the whole construction project should pay for itself in less than three years. The First World War ended any hopes the chairman might have had of paying off the previous expenses even though West Ham continued to show a profit during the war years.

The profit reached £2,000 in 1919 when the board took a decision second in importance only to the move to the Boleyn Ground. West Ham applied for admission to the Football League, a decision not entered into lightly. The ambition of the directors was met by resistance from the Southern League. The latter naturally saw West Ham's departure as part of a growing trend that would deprive the Southern League of its most important clubs and consign it to a 'minor league' or nursery club status. West Ham's directors decided to fight the Southern League, but an arrangement was worked out between them when it became clear that West Ham had the support of the major League clubs.[9]

There was no question but that West Ham was set on a new course, one that was supposed to take it into the first division. As soon as it was accepted into the League, the board authorized spending over £2,000 to clean up the ground and repair damage. That was just the first step in an ambitious scheme to bring it up to the level of most first division grounds. A 'record profit for the company' during its first year in the League was testimony enough to the wisdom of the board in abandoning the Southern League for better competition. A £4,700 profit enabled the club to pay off its few debts, take care of the repairs, and think about how to spend its money. In 1920 the board began rebuilding at the ground, adding stands and increasing the ground's capacity. Contracts worth more than £6,000 were entered into and over the next three years West Ham spent more than £15,000.[10]

In 1920 the chairman informed the shareholders that the club had spent more than £35,000 since beginning its tenancy and had been able to pay off all but £4,500 of that amount. But that figure was to look almost puny within a couple of years. A new 34-year lease in 1922 meant security of tenancy, and promotion in 1923 meant that West Ham could expect bigger crowds. The 1923 profit of £8,382 dwarfed the former record of £4,727.[11] The following year, a profit of £7,139 (without a very successful Cup run) gave the board some indication of what it was like at the top.[12] The *East Ham Echo* estimated that West Ham's grandiose plans would cost £40,000. By the end of 1926 the club was pledged to spend more than £56,000 on the ground.[13]

The great new west stand with its terraced enclosure was the visible sign of the club's new status and hope for prosperity. It was the proudest possession of the board, and the chairman spoke of it in glowing terms. Local newspapers followed the course of its construction, and the unveiling of the completed grandstand was a civic event.

The stand was 'christened with its first match', with over 30,000 in attendance. The programme gave various details about it, ranging from the 780 tons of steel, 840 tons of cement and 18,000 bricks that had gone into its construction, to the fact that the roof shielding the supporters from the elements weighed over 300 tons. The board congratulated itself on the stand, Mr Davis reminding everyone that West Ham 'had always stood for innovation, off the field as well as on it'.[14]

In its first year playing before the new stand, the team finished eighteenth in the first division, barely avoiding relegation. Its record improved over the next few years, finishing as high as seventh in 1930, but the performance on the field never lived up to the boasts made by its directors or the hopes of its supporters. West Ham dropped into the second division in 1932 after years of near misses. During the struggles against relegation the press began to complain about the spending policies of the board. West Ham did not buy players and there were no important projects at the ground after the grandstand was completed. The club drew large gates, but appeared unconcerned with putting any money back into the game. It had built a winning team without buying players. By the time West Ham was fighting relegation, there was no money to make immediate buys. The tradition about how they did things at Upton Park stood in the way: the board had become as much a captive of its own mythology as it had of its temporary depressed finances.

The directors were often criticized for not having bought players, but the transaction that impressed itself most deeply on the memories of West Ham supporters was the sale of a player whose *departure* coincided with the onset of the best years that West Ham enjoyed in its history. Sid Puddefoot was the stuff of which heroes are made: a local lad, good-looking, soft-spoken, modest and a scorer of goals. When West Ham entered the League, Puddefoot was the player whose talents would be on show. In 1920, West Ham supporters looked forward to recognition of their local hero, but would have reacted with dismay if they had known

Syd Puddefoot, West Ham's great hero. His sale in 1922 for a record fee helped to lay the basis for the feeling that the club was more interested in money than success

why he would become famous. Puddefoot's sale to Falkirk in 1922 set a record for any player moving from England to Scotland – £5,000.

There were reasons other than financial ones for the sale. Puddefoot stood in the way of the talents of Vic Watson. The club became more successful with Watson, whose record outstripped that of his predecessor. However, despite West Ham's success and Watson's heroics, Puddefoot assumed a major place in the club's mythology. His career coincided with the post-war revival of football and West Ham's move into the League. For a generation of supporters who had grown up during the First World War he remained someone very special. Almost 60 years after Puddefoot was sold, Reg Pratt, who as a boy had 'worshipped him like a hero...still had trouble forgiving the directors for sending him away to Scotland'. Pratt's memory of his feelings about Puddefoot made it easier for him, years later, to understand supporters' bitter feelings about some of the actions he took when he ran the club. Another of Puddefoot's admirers, the actress Anna Neagle, tried 25 years later to show her appreciation. She was doing a show in Blackpool and introduced Puddefoot from the stage. True to form, 'he was too embarrassed to stand up' to take the plaudits of the crowd.

Puddefoot put West Ham on the front page of the sporting press. The club had a player good enough to bring a record fee that reversed the trend of big money going north. There was some pride among supporters that West Ham had produced someone so valuable, but that was overriden by the feeling that the directors had taken the first available opportunity to cash in on the market value of their top player, and Puddefoot's move to Falkirk provided some foundation for a belief that the directors' main interest was the cash box, not the performance of the team.

The rumour ran that Puddefoot had been sold to help balance the books. Clubs are jealous of their privacy, supporters adamant in their belief that there is something to hide. A look at the club's books shows that it needed money before Puddefoot's move north. In May 1921 the board took some of the financial responsibilities for the work on the ground on its own shoulders. The chairman and Mr Handley acted as personal guarantors for £900 each of projected expenses; two months later the chairman made a loan of £500 to the company.[15] The board's ambition perhaps outpaced its ability to manage the club's finances. The new year brought the need to pay Cearns Construction's overdue account. The only way to do that was with a loan of £2,000, payable at 5 per cent interest per annum from Mr Iggulden.[16] A week later the club accepted another loan of £500 from Mr White. The directors had moved on from being administrators to passive guarantors to active investors in the future of West Ham United.[17] They needed money for the future success of the club. The club's most convertible asset was its players and Sid Puddefoot was the most valuable of them. The transaction was so important that the directors took the unprecedented step of paying a bonus of £300 to Syd King, the manager, 'for his action in connection with the transfer of Puddefoot'.[18] King had managed to get top price at a time when money was the most important consideration for the directors.

The sale of Puddefoot was a short-term solution to West Ham's problems. The club continued to haemorrhage financially and the directors stepped in to keep a respectable account available. The chairman lent the club another £1,000 and throughout 1922 the directors continued to make loans.[19] The board tendered an offer of £20,000 for the freehold of Boleyn Estate. The offer was refused, so Puddefoot became the man who helped balance the books rather than providing the down payment for the home of the Hammers.

Puddefoot was gone, but certainly not forgotten. Local papers continued to feature stories about him even though the Hammers were playing better than ever. A rumour that he might be going to Tottenham Hotspurs for £5,500 appeared prominently in the *East Ham Echo* and the same paper extolled his five-goal performance at Falkirk in January 1923. Nothing showed the lingering influence of Puddefoot better than the marvellously ironic accolade paid to Vic Watson. In March 1923 when Watson was capped for England he was identified by the *Echo* as the 'man who took the place of Puddefoot'.[20]

Within months after the 'White Horse Cup Final' 'Puddefoot's flying visit' was in the local press: the 'famous Hammer for whom Falkirk paid a record fee' would have liked to return to football in England. He visited his team-mates, employers and the ground.[21] There never appeared to be any sense of bitterness on his part, and the board seemed totally unconcerned about charges that the directors were more concerned about money than victory. 'Sid Puddefoot coming back?' asked the *East Ham Echo* in January 1924 after his most recent visit to London when he had 'a round of golf with Syd King.'[22] 'The confessions of Sid Puddefoot' was tame stuff compared to later memoirs, but it showed how disenchanted he was in Scotland. He had 'learned the lesson that money was not everything' and 'spent most of his time sighing for London'. He felt a complete outsider and hardly ever got the ball. He was busy dodging serious injury because Scottish football was much rougher that the game he had left behind him. 'My offence as far as I can see is a English accent. I assume that this is the case because in all the abuse screamed at me by spectators the word English is employed as an adjective.'[23]

Puddefoot did nothing to discourage the rumours that he might be returning to West Ham. He visited West Ham while Falkirk was negotiating with other English clubs. His move to Blackburn for £4,000 in 1925 was featured in Essex newspapers; 'Puddey's success at Blackburn' drew headlines, and he continued to be a part of the local sporting pages throughout most of his seven-year career with Blackburn. His eventual return to West Ham had a bitter-sweet quality about it. He arrived late in the 1932 season, just in time to play in a couple of matches in West Ham's forlorn bid to escape relegation.

The 1932-33 season was probably the most tumultuous to date for the club. Events on and off the field left management and supporters uncertain of what might happen next. West Ham had almost left the second division, but going the wrong way – the club had finished only one place above relegation. Attendance decreased slightly from the previous year and the balance sheet showed a profit five times what it had been in 1931-32. This was due to a great Cup run that took the club to the semi-finals. It helped the bank balance and brought some excitement to the supporters, but could not mask the problems facing West Ham.

At the 1933 AGM the chairman informed the shareholders that 'bearing in mind last season's difficulties we are making every effort to strengthen the club's playing staff'.[24] West Ham's deficit of £1,985 in the transfer account was scarcely a fortune, but it was a start. During the years when West Ham chased an elusive promotion the board reversed its long-time policies about spending. The balance sheet tells the story. The club made no investment in facilities and cut back on maintenance at the ground. Each year more money was spent for players than received for sales. The figure dropped to £2,500 only once and twice it exceeded £8,000. The purchase of players like Marshall (from Arsenal for £2,000 plus another £750 if West Ham gained promotion to the first division for 1935-36), Mangall (from Birmingham for £780), Dell (from Dartford for £1,000) and A. Walker (from Arsenal for £1,000) are examples. Transfers which cost the club more than £15,000 in a three-year period did not take West Ham back to the first division, but they kept the team in a competitive position and sustained the interest of supporters.

What accounted for these new financial policies? The obvious reason was the drop down the table and the public discontent it caused. The directors had no desire to be criticized for standing in the way of the success of the club. The shift towards a more aggressive policy of buying players was made easier by Syd King's departure: he had grown up with an impoverished West Ham United and enjoyed telling stories about how close the club had been to financial disaster. King liked to point out that it had remained true to its old traditions. His successor, Paynter, had been at West Ham over the same period, but he had not been in charge and could thus become part of a new policy more easily.

Large expenditures on players had public appeal, but the board had to explain itself to the shareholders. In 1935, the chairman reminded them that trading figures for the previous year must be understood in light of the considerable payments for players.[25] Things had certainly changed at West Ham United. Before 1934, if the chairman discussed transfer fees at all, he pointed to profits. In 1937 he took an almost apologetic tone for having spent much less money that year on transfers than in the previous year, 'but we now have a nucleus of a very strong team with thoroughly capable reserves'. The club would sign further new players to bring it up to the 'very highest level'. The chairman made a direct correlation between results on the field, gate money and the need to buy new players. Attendance would increase if the team came close to promotion or if the supporters thought it was good enough. New players, especially those who commanded a high enough price, showed that the club was trying to get back into the first division.[26]

At the 1936 AGM the chairman announced that the club had spent a record sum, more than £8,000, to improve the playing side of the club. Profits were down partially because of the 'extra cost of transfer fees', which had 'been fully justified...since our League side has been strengthened to enable us to make another very strong bid for entry into the first division...and the foundation of a playing staff has been laid that promises well for the club's future.'[27] Cearns's assertion about the impact of new players was what the shareholders needed to hear because in May 1936 the board had suffered a public relations disaster, the occasion on which 'Bert' Davis commented before a reporter that it was a better paying proposition to be successful in the second division than unsuccessful in the first. As we saw in Chapter 4, the repercussions of this remark were considerable.

Despite winning seasons after 1936 and the large sums spent on new players, the residual effects of Bert Davis's moment in the glare of publicity refused to die away. The belief that West Ham didn't really want to be in the first division haunted the directors and became part of the folk mythology surrounding the club. West Ham looked even worse the following season when Charlton, the team West Ham 'should have beaten out for promotion' challenged the leaders throughout the season and ended up in second place. The board may not have reacted consciously to this, but its buying policies were affected by it.

In 1939, when West Ham finally had a side good enough to challenge for promotion – a team that Charlie Paynter and others often described as the best he ever managed – the team got to Wembley again. Unfortunately, the Second World War ensured that West Ham would be unable to gain promotion. The War Cup has a prominent place in the club's Trophy Room, but it was a poor substitute for the victories that supporters thought would have taken place if the board had done its job.

During the First World War, the landlord of the Boleyn Ground, the Archdiocese of Westminster, had been unsympathetic to West Ham's lost revenue and had dropped the rent only marginally. In 1939, however, the landlord took the initiative and made an interesting proposal to West Ham. The club could have the ground at a rent of £1 per annum and would be responsible for preparing the ground as a military training area. The forecourt provided space for drill manoeuvres, and other areas for shelters and practice ranges. West Ham accepted the terms, which also included a small fee to be paid to the Boleyn Social Club and an implied promise that favourable terms would be negotiated when the lease was renewed in four years.[28]

It was not as easy to deal with the rate collector as with the landlord. In the midst of the blitz, West Ham received a shock when the bill from the Borough of East Ham arrived. There was an increase of more than 50 per cent in the valuation. West Ham appealed, and there was an exchange of letters followed by a series of meetings. West Ham's representatives formulated a case for a rate reduction, but its best approach was the simple statement that 'our gates were exceedingly small and we would no doubt be trading at a loss' until the conclusion of the war.[29] The Borough Treasurer agreed to postpone the collection of the new rates and a month later the Rate Assessment Committee upheld West Ham's appeal and lowered the rates from £1,350 to £200 for the year ending 31 March 1941. It also agreed that the next assessment would be reviewed before it was sent to West Ham and that it would take into account the circumstances of the new football season.[30]

West Ham's decision on how to spend money after the war was made for the club by the Luftwaffe. The roof and the Boleyn Castle were damaged severely by bombing. However, money was not so great a problem as red tape and the unavailability of materials and men to do the work. West Ham tried to start repairing the Castle as early as December 1944. The Castle was unimportant to the football ground, but it was a local curiosity, and had been listed according to the Ancient Monuments Act of 1931, which made it easier to obtain a licence from the Ministry of Works to go ahead with the preliminary repairs. Work on the ground itself was a very different question. It was badly damaged, but still adequate for the small crowds that attended war-time football. The Ministry of Works would not approve any work to go ahead without weighing it against the thousands of other requests.

The government had encouraged war-time football, and the directors could not understand why they were denied local permission to begin repairs, especially 'in view of similar work being carried out to the local cinema'. The board wanted 'to enquire of our local authorities, why the differentiation'.[31] The local authorities merely replied that 'some set of priorities had to be established'.[32] The ground was damaged, but it was no worse than the somewhat primitive conditions that had been normal at many grounds before 1939. The size and reputation of the club might have worked against its efforts, since West Ham had not gone out of its way to make itself popular with local officials. It was easier for the local authorities to understand the plight of cinema owners or shopkeepers who derived their livelihood from the business. It was harder to sympathize with West Ham, especially when the club could manage without the repairs.

When a request to repair the roof was turned down for the second time, the directors tried to put their claim forward in greater detail: there was no covered accommodation for patrons in the cheaper part of the ground and the wooden east terrace was deteriorating quickly. This was supposed to show that the club was interested in its most ordinary supporters. Also, the materials for the repairs, mainly corrugated iron, were not used in housing construction. Finally, they asked why Clapton Orient received permission to work on their ground, especially since they were using asbestos sheeting, 'which is used in houses', and the structure to be covered was a simple concrete terrace.[33] Ironically, the club's attempt to spend money, after years of being accused of meanness, in amounts that dwarfed any previous expenditures, was blocked for months by the local authorities and the Ministry of Works. In the autumn of 1947, the club was finally given permission to start repairs, and contracts were signed with Cearns Ltd. By 1950 West Ham had spent more than £165,000.

The club tried to cope with the post-war problems with the same small, untrained staff and the minimal financial resources it had always used. The broad scope of the board's concerns became clear at such times as the meeting of 21 December 1948, when the directors considered restructuring that would give a new face to the ground and cost close to £100,000, and a bill from a Mr P. Taylor, for £1 7s 9d, for spectacles that were broken when he was hit in the face by the ball.[34] It would be interesting to know the outcome of a request from a Mr King who 'was unable to pass the turnstile to the stand owing to his being rather corpulent...and he hurt his groin'. There is no further reference to it or how Reg Pratt dealt with the matter.

When the board decided to modernize and repair the ground in 1949, there was no turning back, for more than money was involved. The plans for the Boleyn Ground showed that the board thought it would be necessary to provide better accommodation for spectators to keep them coming despite the steady growth in attendance and the increases in gate money.[35] West Ham was ploughing back the profits into the facilities, and not spending on players.

When Reg Pratt became chairman in 1950 he soon took the opportunity to make a public statement about the 'Hammers' future' in two articles in the *Stratford Express*. The second article principally discussed finance and how West Ham intended to spend its money. This type of publicity was almost unheard of at West Ham. Pratt's articles in the features section of the *Stratford Express* were in reply to critical letters about how the club operated. He wrote in a conciliatory, sometimes condescending tone, and the series showed clear memories of 'Bert' Davis's 1936 remark and a distrust of sportswriters.

Pratt reminded his readers that the club was still paying off some of the debentures for the 1924 construction. Serious war damage had to be repaired. The board planned more changes for the comfort of the spectators, but he could not go into detail until the club knew it had the money. He assured everyone that the directors would not benefit financially from the club, their only interest being to bring in 'the success that the supporters deserved'. He repeated the accusation that the press distorted the facts about football and West Ham.

Pratt knew that his readers were interested in knowing when West Ham would improve the playing side. He could only ask them to be patient and trust the steady policies of the board. There were no short cuts to success; the great West Ham sides of the past, 1923 and 1939-40, had cost very little. The club was spending a lot of money, but this had to go into facilities. Some improvements would have to wait until West Ham achieved first division status. This argument was supposed to disarm the critics who claimed West Ham was more interested in bricks and mortar than in playing success. The chairman tried to clinch the argument by pointing out that it would cost £10,000 to make repairs 'to the old castle and the buildings near it'. 'Bang goes another player.'[36]

As we know, decisions to spend money were never made easily at West Ham. In May 1959 the club received a bank loan of £30,000 and an increase in the club's overdraft.[37] The money was needed quickly so that the club could take advantage of a coup by its chairman. After four years of desultory negotiations concerning a new lease for the ground, Reg Pratt entered an agreement with the Archdiocese of Westminster to sell the freehold to West Ham United. Two quasi-public institutions like the club and the Church found it difficult to keep their negotiations secret for very long. It was unseemly for them to be involved in wrangling over rent for a piece of land that had such an emotional hold on thousands. The sale of the freehold would solve the problem, by giving the club security in its planning for the future, and ending charges that the Church was making unreasonable demands. The sale had been Pratt's idea and he retained the initiative throughout four months of negotiations. He let the Church negotiators ponder over the public response if the price were so high that West Ham could not afford to buy it, or only at the cost of future players.

The Church accepted the figure that Pratt proposed even though most

The Boleyn Ground in 1968 before the east stand was built

outside observers thought that £30,000 was a very good bargain for West Ham. The club made commitments beyond freehold: a contract for 'the construction work that was necessitated by the purchase of the Boleyn Ground…at the cost of £35,269 9s 10d'.[38] In the six years after buying the ground, the club spent £94,000 in construction and improvements. It had literally mortgaged its future.

The burden imposed by the purchase of the ground and the improvements stretched West Ham's finances, but the club handled the situation with little difficulty. A year after the bank had extended the credit it expressed 'satisfaction with the progress made' in reducing the debts of the club.[39] West Ham had paid off £6,000 of the loan to buy the ground; three months later the debt was reduced by a further £5,000, leaving a balance of £19,000.[40]

The purchase of Boleyn Ground will always be associated in the minds of the supporters with one player, Harry Hooper Jr. He certainly had not reached the mythic status of Sid Puddefoot, but there were some similarities between the two men. Both provided glamour and goal-scoring skills while playing for a mildly successful but undistinguished club. Both had the misfortune to leave the club when it was creating a team that would gain promotion. Both brought large transfer fees when the club needed the money – money to pay bills that were in danger of becoming long overdue. There was no dramatic symbol of what had been purchased with the £5,000 for Puddefoot; Hooper, on the other hand, was known as the player who financed the ground. A sign scrawled on the entrance put it simply: 'Sold to the Wolves for £20,000.'

After 1958 the board's commitment to expensive projects was based on a dramatic rise in gate money and bright prospects for the future. Promotion was the reason for the optimism that pervaded West Ham United. It could be said that the board's willingness to spend tens of thousands of pounds stemmed from a shrewd investment of £10,000 made in October 1957: the purchase of Vic Keeble. It was a reversal of the 1956 sale of Hooper. When Keeble arrived, the club was drifting in its normal place in the second division. He was not a great player, but he came to the right club at the right time. Keeble was an instant celebrity, being that rare commodity, an expensive purchase. His first appearance was in the Dick Walker testimonial, and he almost upstaged the star of the evening. Newspapers reported that the crowd reached 20,000 because so many wanted to see Keeble.[41] A few months later, when a rumour circulated that Keeble had been killed in a car accident, the switchboard at the ground was flooded with calls.[42]

When local papers ran lengthy articles applauding promotion, Keeble's arrival figured prominently. His skills and role in the promotion accounted for much of the publicity, but he was originally important because West Ham had been willing to spend a lot of money for him. Ironically, the newspaper article that paid special tribute to Keeble went out of its way to point out that promotion 'was a tribute to the long-sighted imaginative policy adhered to by the men in charge of the club – often in the face of fierce criticism'.[43]

Two years after West Ham and Vic Keeble had celebrated the victory at Middlesbrough and the second division Championship, a series of injuries ended Keeble's role as an active player. How would a balance-sheet-oriented business evaluate the £10,000 West Ham had invested in Keeble? Was there any way to evaluate the excitement caused by the promotion, to quantify the euphoria of the ride home from the station or the borough-wide celebration that followed? How much was it worth to Reg Pratt and the other directors to think that their stewardship had been vindicated? On the same day that Reg Pratt informed his colleagues that Keeble's career was over, he told them that the bank had increased their credit and that the club had exceeded all expectations in its ability to repay the loans.[44]

After promotion it was imperative to stay in the first division. The club did not have the money to spend indiscriminately, and the team had enough good young players to be selective in the transfer market. The board's philosophy showed itself early in its first division life. West Ham would spend a lot of money for a player who served a particular purpose. When Phil Woosnam arrived in 1958 the £30,000 fee represented what the *Ilford Recorder* described as 'a milestone sum'.[45] The club record fee singled him out for the rest of his career at West Ham. His performance was always evaluated against the expectations of him, represented by the size of the fee. Woosnam was proof that West Ham would spend money and act like the clubs it admired. He was an easy target for any discontented supporter who complained that the club wasted its money, the same supporter who would have complained earlier that the club was not willing to spend any money.

Most consumers are not interested in balance sheets and the financial transactions of companies, but this is not so in football. At West Ham, the years of being a marginal club and not spending money for players had left its mark on supporters. Expenditures were supposed to be an indication of how much a club wanted to succeed, and it did not take much adversity to resurrect the criticism of how West Ham operated. When the club started badly in its second season in the first division, the West Ham manager, Ted Fenton, attempted to use the press to quieten critics. He said that the Hammers were playing in bad luck, but admitted 'that I need a goal-scoring forward'. He anticipated the response and went back to a familiar theme:

> The sort of man we need is in the £25,000 bracket. If we had that sort of money, *and you know very well that we haven't*, and could find the man, we would have to be certain he was the right one. If we bought and then the player did not come off, we could not be like some clubs and say 'Oh, right. Put him in the reserves and we'll go out and buy another one.' No, we've got to be right the first time.[46]

The *Ilford Recorder* published a reply to Fenton in the form of a 'letter from a supporter'. It was a demand for change and consideration for the paying customer. The author 'anticipated that management will bring up the question of money again' when trying to explain why we have not rectified the obvious weakness in the playing side. But they should be reminded that 'for what the club offers they must be amongst the highest priced grounds'. He did not object to increased admission fees, but he expected West Ham to live up to its share of the bargain. The club had stated in the programme that 'the building up of a reserve' is an important task for the club, but the playing staff had been reduced from 38 to 30. There had been no important additions to the club, in fact 'you have not spent a penny in the transfer market in two years and have got £8,000 for Nelson and £3,000 for Dwyer'. So much for the lingering effect of the record fee paid for Woosnam! What had West Ham done for the supporters lately, except lose matches?

Attendance was very good; West Ham was eleventh in home

attendance with an average of 28,078 and sixth in away crowds with an average of 31,373. The criticism of the management of West Ham was an overestimate, but it was prophetic. The author 'warned' the Hammers to look around them at the falling gates throughout football. 'You are a business selling entertainment and the way to succeed is to have a successful team. The onus is now on you.'[47]

Woosnam became the subject of widespread rumours when the 'Woosnam-for-transfer controversy' started in the press in 1950.[48] West Ham needed money to buy a goalkeeper and other players. If Woosnam was worth £30,000 to West Ham, what was his value on the transfer market? Negotiations had been going on with Wolves about a possible deal that would bring Finlayson, a fine goalkeeper, and Murray, a better-than-average centre-forward, to West Ham in exchange for Woosnam. When news leaked, Woosnam went to the chairman and asked for an explanation. Pratt told him to forget about it, that the deal was off, and Woosnam left to 'think about it'.[49] A few days later, Woosnam asked to move. The chairman 'was shattered', and had to work out what to do in these unexpected circumstances. He agreed to try to make arrangements but stressed that 'my first concern must always be that of the club'.[50] Talks started with Arsenal for a deal that would have brought Herd and Bloomfield to West Ham, but the latter refused to move and Arsenal would not transfer the former. Woosnam was playing under a stronger microscope than usual, pestered by the press and unsure of where he might be at any day. When news about negotiations concerning him became public, the situation became impossibly complicated. The public was treated to a very rare look at how the club operated. Details were published in the *Ilford Recorder*, in the form of a statement from Reg Pratt, which also appeared in the programme the following week. Copies were sent 'to each of the many fans who had written protesting against the deal'. Pratt tried to avoid publicity, especially about private talks. The statement was published because Woosnam symbolized past actions of the club. One section of Pratt's statement was capitalized so that no reader could miss it: 'AT NO TIME WERE WE EVER PREPARED TO LET PHIL GO FOR A FEE, JUST LIKE THAT.'[51] Woosnam never had the white-hot loyalty of Hammer supporters as had some of his team-mates. The deals proposed for him seemed to make sense to help the club. Why, then, was there such an uproar about the possibility of moving him? Because he was a symbol that West Ham had to spend big money to help the team, and now the board was trying to sell him. Was he to be the latest version of Puddefoot and Hooper?

Woosnam might not go for cash, but less than a week after Pratt's statement Noel Cantwell was on his way to Manchester United for £30,000.[52] No publicity had surrounded the deal for Cantwell even though he was a popular player with a successful career at West Ham.

Many supporters may have shared the opinions voiced in letters to the *Ilford Recorder*: 'We have bitter memories of the star players the board has sold, Goulden, Macaulay, Hooper, Smith, etc. Now Cantwell and how can that be explained?'[53] But there was little of the emotionalism that had surrounded the talks about Woosnam. The Cantwell transaction was evaluated by what it did to improve the club. Cantwell's own analysis mirrored general feelings: 'It was a good deal for West Ham, they got £30,000 and had John Lyall ready to play in my place.' Cantwell almost decided against accepting the transfer: 'There were many reasons for wanting to go to Manchester United, but behind it all, was the question of did I want to leave West Ham...I had been so happy there...and I don't throw things like that away easily.' Cantwell is convinced 'that the club would have respected my opinion and there would not have been any trouble there. They just would have realized that I didn't want to go.'

The week the board ratified Cantwell's sale, it heard the bad news from Eddie Chapman that after nine matches home attendance was down 68,000 from the previous year and receipts were down by £1,978. Two weeks later 'plans for new floodlighting which will cost between £15,000 and £20,000' were announced. No one labelled the floodlights as 'paid for by Noel Cantwell'.[54]

Cantwell's departure helped balance the books for the 1960-61 season. It had not been a success on the field, at the gate, or in the office. The departure of Fenton, the manager, was the first step in restructuring West Ham. Before his first season, Fenton's successor Ron Greenwood purchased Lawrey Leslie, the Scottish goalkeeper, for £14,000, most of which was balanced by the sales of Smillie for £7,500 and Obeney for £2,000. But the real shock came towards the end of the season when West Ham bought Budgie Byrne, a third-division player, to the club. This time, the club tried to keep details of the negotiations under wraps. When Eddie Chapman was asked about Byrne, he 'laughed off the story'. The secretary responded to rumours that figures ranging from £50,000 to £70,000 were involved: 'What do people think we are going to do for that sort of money, sell the ground?'[55] West Ham did not sell the ground, but it did buy Byrne, paying £58,500 in cash and a player valued at £7,000.[56] His arrival ended weeks of speculation during which the club had been in the national spotlight. The board had given tangible evidence of the confidence it placed in Greenwood and his plans to strengthen the playing side. The purchase of Byrne was an investment in improving attendance. It was another symbol that West Ham was prepared to pay the same as the big clubs. Supporters did not need to feel that the club was outclassed in the board-room any more than on the pitch.

Setting a fee and finding money were sometimes the easiest part of a transaction. West Ham saw deals break down as both potential seller and buyer when players baulked. John Bond refused to move to Queen's Park

Rangers in 1962 after the price had been set; he preferred playing in the reserve side to leaving.[57] John Lyall turned down a chance to move to Brighton three months later.[58] The club's efforts to purchase Terry Venables and Alex Stepney fell apart over the question of signing-on bonuses and Peter Bonetti turned down the opportunity to move to West Ham United.[59]

Even when all the usual problems of a transfer had been resolved, something else could go wrong – witness the case of Peter Brabrook. Less than six months after purchasing Byrne, West Ham paid another £35,000 to obtain Brabrook from Chelsea. Negotiations took more than two months. There was an ironic touch to this, since West Ham had missed the chance to sign Brabrook in 1953 when he was a schoolboy star on their groundstaff. In 1962, Brabrook refused a move to Everton and expressed 'a great desire to play for West Ham'. He was seen often at the ground, 'sometimes acutely embarrassing the club'.[60] This report was published a month after West Ham's offer of cash and players had been rejected by Chelsea. When Brabrook refused to sign a contract with Chelsea, the club claimed, in a 'bombshell accusation' that West Ham had illegally approached Brabrook.

Chelsea implied that Brabrook's intransigence had been caused by statements made by Ken Brown and Greenwood, and that West Ham had not made an acceptable offer because they believed that they could get Brabrook cheaply. The allegation was extremely serious because it involved a practice that could undermine the whole contractual structure of football. It was compounded since it came in the wake of a threatened strike by the Professional Footballers' Association.

The charges were received with surprise and cynicism at West Ham. The club reacted publicly with a claim of innocence: 'We have a complete answer to anything that Chelsea may allege.'[61] Privately, many observers remembered how promising East London players had found their way to Chelsea amid rumours that the inducements had been more substantial than a promise to play in a good side before appreciative crowds. A League tribunal cleared West Ham of all charges and left it to the two clubs to set a fee for the transfer of Brabrook. A few weeks of 'haggling over small sums' followed, but Brabrook finally came to West Ham at the end of October 1962.[62] The uproar had obscured the fact that the board had once again been willing to open its wallet for a player.

The purchase of Byrne and Brabrook showed the great faith that Reg Pratt and the other directors placed in Greenwood's ability to judge talent. They were paying huge fees for a third-division player, and a player whom they had not signed years earlier when they had had the chance. There would be more than the normal criticism if the deals went sour. The importance of the purchases was summed up by a local journalist a year later.

> Some knowledgeable people think West Ham has spent too much money to
> keep up with the Joneses...Just the opposite is true; the bank balance is
> positive...and the only reason for transfers will be by request.
>
> The days of the overnight transfer of star players to keep the finances
> straight – Harry Hooper and John Smith are cases in point – are over at
> Upton Park. The club showed this when they spent £100,000 on Byrne and
> Brabrook, a change of policy which could not have announced the
> Hammers' top flight aims more patently.[63]

West Ham broke a 25-year run when it gained promotion and had
shattered an older tradition to bring in a new manager. The reluctance of
the board to spend money dissolved as a result of these changes. A
parallel can be drawn with West Ham's previous promotion to the first
division in 1923, when the board had spent large sums of money on the
ground to show itself and others that it belonged in the first division.

The purchase of Byrne and Brabrook ended questions about West
Ham's willingness to enter the transfer market. Nothing could end
criticism of the judgment of the manager and the board, but such
complaint is endemic to football. West Ham had finally lost its
reputation for being tight-fisted and using the sale of players to pay the
club's bills. By their new spending policy, especially in the transfer
market, the West Ham directors gained national publicity and attracted
some floating supporters. After 1962, the success of West Ham's youth
development scheme added a new problem. West Ham had good quality
young players who attracted the attention of clubs with better prospects
and fuller wallets.

'NO COMMENT is the official West Ham line,' was the angry
response of Ron Greenwood and Eddie Chapman in 1963 to newspaper
reports that Bobby Moore was heading for Tottenham Hotspurs.[64] The
brightest young star of West Ham United supposedly asked for a
transfer. The club denied the story and said there was no way that it
would release him. The newspaper battle of words symbolized the
responsibility of Reg Pratt and Bobby Moore: the former to his vision of
West Ham, the latter to his future in a business where his career could be
ended at any moment. Pratt's first response was a combination of
incredulity and anger. Why should Moore allow himself to be associated
with statements of this type? Why should he be disruptive 'when he is
earning as much as anyone can pay him and he got a £750 benefit last
year? I can't understand why Moore said these things. He has no right to
say them.'[65] Reg Pratt had dealt with strong-minded players like Allison,
Cantwell and O'Farrell, but Moore's challenge to authority seemed more
pointed.

The public discussion carried on for weeks. Moore attempted to be
conciliatory and leave open the possibility of his transfer. He 'was
complimented' by West Ham's stated objective to use him as the
cornerstone of a great team, but he was dubious about the possibilities.

He was ambitious and thought it unlikely that West Ham would ever become a 'super club'. He had to consider his own future: 'Long before this week's headlines I made it clear to West Ham that I had ambitions. I told Mr Greenwood if the chances came for me to join a larger club, I would like the opportunity to do so.'[66]

Pratt's response was described by one newspaper as 'angry' and that is exactly the tone that comes across from the printed word. The chairman was a quiet man but ex-players remember his temper, and that he was a 'bad loser'.

Moore's comment about his own ambitions touched a nerve in Pratt because it gave the impression that West Ham did not share that feeling. The 'super club' remark reopened old wounds: Pratt stressed that West Ham didn't want or need anyone else's money. Almost 30 years of frustration were behind his concluding remark: 'It makes me mad that people expect us to part with our best player at the drop of a hat.'[67] It is not clear to which 'people' he was referring in that statement – Moore, Tottenham Hotspurs, the press, or the public, but all of them could have qualified. Less than a year after West Ham had spent more than £100,000 on two players it was time for Pratt to try to exorcize the ghosts of the past 30 years.

No serious negotiations were taking place about Moore, but the rumours were important because they went to the heart of the mythology surrounding the club. That is why Reg Pratt could not afford to ignore them. The transfer would have created a fascinating situation: the fee for Moore would have surpassed what West Ham had paid for Byrne. What would the club have done with the money? Less than six months later, the chairman made the flat assertion, 'We will need every penny!' He was talking about grandiose plans to continue improvements at the ground. The setting for these remarks was the celebration to honour the proudest moment in West Ham's history – winning the FA Cup.[68]

Moore was too valuable both on the field and as a symbol of the club to be allowed to go. Plans to improve the ground made it unthinkable for Moore to leave West Ham. How would supporters have responded to a new stand paid for by the proceeds of the Bobby Moore transfer? This would have destroyed all the efforts Pratt and Greenwood had made to exorcize the ghosts of the club, including memories of Puddefoot and Hooper. The board expected to charge first-division prices for first-division-sized crowds. Moore's sale might have led to more requests for transfers. If the management seemed to think that the club was going nowhere, why should the players have more faith than their bosses?

Reg Pratt did not let West Ham's spending policy in the early 1960s speak for itself. He opened the 1964 AGM with a lecture about 'the various ways of running a football club'. It was more satisfying to develop players than to buy them, but 'nine years ago, however, having seen the cream of that talent lured away before our very eyes, we decided to do something about it'.[69] He spoke in glowing terms about the youth scheme: the Youth Internationals it had produced and the playing staff who had come up through the ranks. West Ham was willing to spend money, but was not going to brag about it or condition people to think that purchasing players was normal. The transfer of seven players and a successful Cup run were signs of the manager's skill. Greenwood had been brought to Upton Park to produce a winning team and the directors would help him as much as they could.

Pratt stressed that 'No one can accuse the club of not making strenuous efforts to improve its amenities.' The major items included £45,000 for the main entrance, £14,000 for covering the north bank, £17,000 for new floodlights, £5,000 for new toilets for seatholders and more that £3,000 for other miscellaneous facilities.[70] By 1964 West Ham had spent more than £100,000. Since its promotion, the club had dug deep into its profits and increased its overdraft, but could not bear the total cost of repairs out of its own resources. The need for additional funds brought about a relationship between West Ham United and the Supporters' Club that led to the West Ham Building Fund. In 1962 West Ham received approximately £4,000 from competitions and pools run by the Supporters' Club, and the estimate was that this figure could be doubled. The 1964 FA Cup victory brought out thousands of supporters who wanted to do something for West Ham. The board planned improvements that would more or less remake the ground, but the new block of seats and other changes would take more money than West Ham was willing to raise. The Building Fund came to the rescue and turned over more than £23,000 to the club in the next 18 months.[71] The east stand, improvements to the training ground at Chadwell Heath, and 'A' block in the west stand were made possible by co-operation with the Supporters' Club. The arrangement had come a long way from the half-time scoreboard, the first project of the development fund.[72]

West Ham United's directors never had enough money to spend it lightly. Spending decisions were the most public action taken by the board and represented the public image the club wanted to present. Expenditures were taken against the backdrop of available funds and how any specific expenditure might bring in new revenues. When West Ham was relegated it bought expensive players in an effort to regain its position in the first division. During its long stay in the second division, the board returned to a policy of trying to make money in the transfer market. It also stopped spending on the ground after the improvements planned while West Ham was in the first division were completed.

West Ham's last-minute failure to gain promotion in 1936 did more to shape the post-1945 policies of the board than anyone at the club realizes or wants to admit. 'Bert' Davis's disastrous statement ensured that until the club gained promotion the board would always be under a cloud of distrust. Nothing until the purchase of Vic Keeble in 1957 could wipe out the effects of 1936.

Twenty-five consecutive years in the second division did much to shape West Ham's attitude when it was promoted in 1958. There had been a complete turnover on the board, but the leading members were carrying on from their fathers. They understood the popular distrust of the board's spending policies. It is logical to assume that the board hoped the size of the fees for Woosnam, Byrne and Brabrook would put an end to the complaints about their refusal to spend. At the same time, Reg Pratt's public statements denied that the club had ever been unwilling to spend. He worked hard to convince outsiders that nothing much had changed at West Ham while highlighting what was new. He was caught in the dilemma of being the heir to a tradition that he admired and the guiding force behind ending it. Fortunately for Pratt and West Ham, his actions were judged by results on the pitch and not by the contradictions and inconsistencies in the rhetoric he used to explain them.

Traditions died hard in the conservative atmosphere of the West Ham board-room, and few were engrained as deeply as the reluctance to spend large sums for players. In 1963, Pratt had the best of all worlds: the club had bought the players it needed and showed a 'healthy surplus'. West Ham maintained its tradition by dedicating much of its new revenue to projects to improve the Boleyn Ground. It learned to cope with the pressures of being in the first division. No aspect of the club's policies better demonstrates the change than the way in which the board and its chairman chose to spend money.

Pratt was proud of how the club performed, both on the field and at the box office. He could take credit for encouraging his managers to become involved in the transfer market. In 1963 he summed up his philosophy to the shareholders, saying that he would spare no effort to enhance playing strength, especially through transfers, and that the club had gone into the market 'in a way which I humbly suggest was as bold as it was brave. The fact we were involved in a record Football League fee staggered most people, but recent events have, I am sure, shown you what we had in our minds at the time.'[73]

CHAPTER 6

Managers need not apply

Syd King laid down the law thick and heavy.

Jimmy Ruffell, West Ham International and member of
1923 Cup Final team.

'Fenton replaced' was the headline on the sports page of the *Ilford Recorder* in March 1961.[1] The story stated that the West Ham manager had been allowed to resign rather than being sacked. At most clubs, the dismissal of a manager would not cause much surprise: the football manager's security is best described by an American baseball manager who pointed out that 'there are two types of manager – those who have been fired and those who will be fired'. That Fenton's departure caused a great stir was indicative of West Ham's record with managers and the newspaper's recognition of it.

Ted Fenton became only the third manager in the history of the club when he took the job in 1950. His tenure in that job has been the shortest of any manager in the club's history. The unwillingness, or as some would describe it, the 'inability' of West Ham directors to replace managers has been a distinctive feature of their stewardship. It is one of the first things that outside observers point to when they describe West Ham as different from other clubs. It is easy to name the managers of West Ham between 1900 and 1986: Syd King, Charlie Paynter, Ted Fenton, Ron Greenwood and John Lyall. They all stayed with the club long enough to outlive directors, impress their personality on the club and give West Ham its public face.[2]

In 1923 West Ham United finally achieved success. It led the second division and played in the first division Cup Final held at Wembley Stadium. The London and national press reported on the players and other aspects of this somewhat unfashionable and little-known club. The *East Ham Echo*, the paper that knew the most about the club, did not feature the captain, star players or directors in its Cup Final issue. The manager was the star: 'West Ham is Syd King.'[3]

E. S. 'Syd' King had played for the Thames Ironworks Club and continued as a West Ham player until the end of the 1902 season. That year, he took over as secretary-manager, and for the next 30 years he guided the fortunes of the club on the field and in the office. King's responsibilities and powers can be summarized simply – he ran the club as long as he operated within the financial constraints imposed by the board, informed the board of what he had done and did nothing of a public nature to embarrass the board. The board never considered dismissing him on the basis of the won and lost record of the team. The strength of King's position was his long association with West Ham and the bond of trust that existed between him and the board. Once that trust was shattered, though, there was no way of repairing it.

Beside his duties in running the club, King was also its public relations department and best asset in signing players. He became the flamboyant public face of West Ham, enabling the board to operate in a quiet, self-imposed isolation from outside pressures and notice. King's appearance was almost the personification of 'East End flash', in which so many residents took pride. He made no effort to hide the status or relative prosperity of being connected with professional football. His taste ran to expensive bowler hats, well-cut suits and diamond stick-pins. He made a point of attending fetes, charity dances, festivals, openings and other local events. 'He was a local celebrity, the manager of West Ham United' and he played the role to its hilt.[4] King was the most visible member of the club, his face was better known in the borough than any of the directors and most players. He was more public that the former, more permanent than the latter.

King knew that his image could be useful to West Ham. When he approached a potential player, the boy felt a sense of pride, if not awe at being asked to the ground for a trial. One example was Jimmy Ruffell, a winger for the 1923 Cup Final and England, who was playing for a company team when he came to the attention of King. When Ruffell was called up to King's office after two nights' training, his reaction was a combination of apprehension and pride. 'After all, it was a big thing for a 20-year-old to go to see such an important person as the secretary-manager of West Ham United.' Ruffell was not an awestruck young supporter but a mature young man with a steady job who had never seen West Ham perform. When King asked Ruffell if he wanted to become a professional footballer, the young man replied 'Yes, if I am good enough' and left everything in King's hands. There were no discussions about the contract or its implications. Ruffell knew nothing about the procedure for becoming a professional – that was King's job. He received a £10 signing bonus and a wage of £4 per week for the whole year, which compared well with his previous wage of £2 17s 6d. He was being paid to do something 'I used to do to amuse myself'. King could use his charm, but he also understood the importance of keeping the players in line. After Ruffell had been training with West Ham for a fortnight, he was again called into the manager's office. This time, there were no questions or compliments. King 'laid down the law thick and heavy...telling me your job is here' and said in no uncertain terms that Ruffell had to give notice to his employer. Players had to realize 'we were professionals' and had to live up to the standards of other professions.

King's first important exercise in public relations had nothing to do with the performance of the team. In May 1904 he held court for the press at West Ham's new home, the Boleyn Ground. He described at length the comforts of the new ground, emphasizing that it had seating for 2,000, covered areas for 3,000 more and could comfortably hold 20,000. Refreshment rooms would be added and dressing-rooms for the players, 'Indeed, nothing that was likely to add to the comfort or conscience of the spectators and players would not be provided.' King affirmed the desire of the club to begin a 'bright new era' and concluded his comments by informing reporters that 'Many new players including some internationals were being brought in – most of them from the north.'[5]

The inaugural season at the Boleyn Ground did not live up to the expectations of either the supporters or the manager, but at the start of the following season King was once again extolling the virtues of the club and its bright future to the press. He emphasized the same features he had a year earlier – the wisdom of the move to the Boleyn Ground and the dedication of the board to providing a first-class operation. He would have other opportunities to talk about events on the pitch. His comments about comfort, facilities and access made it abundantly clear that the club was marketing something in addition to possible success on the field.

King's initial contribution to West Ham United was to provide administrative stability and a personality with which supporters and local residents could identify. It was not by accident that King became 'Mr West Ham United', a role he assumed with the willing support of the directors. Despite this, King is not the manager that the club honours or older supporters remember. King led West Ham to Wembley and into the first division, but it was his assistant and successor, Charlie Paynter, who became as much the symbol of West Ham as the Cearns and Pratt families, the Boleyn Ground, or the singing of 'I'm forever blowing bubbles'.

Paynter was a local boy who trained as an electrician and worked for the Thames Ironworks before joining West Ham in 1901 as a player. By 1905, his participation had been severely limited by injuries and his main role was that of coach and scout. His familiarity with local football and his outgoing personality suited his job as talent hunter. Thanks to Paynter, the club got the opportunity to bring local talent on to the books, especially young men who had shown to advantage with one of the many local industrial or church clubs. He filled many roles: assistant trainer, assistant manager and scout. He was one of the three full-time employees of the club, very much junior to both King and Tommy Robinson, the trainer.

When Robinson retired in 1912 a newspaper writer thought that 'West Ham without him is like Hamlet without the prince.' He had been involved with football in the East End for almost 50 years, having been associated with St Luke's, the Castle Swifts and the Thames Ironworks club. He had been part of the Ironworks club committee and the consultative committee that brought West Ham United into existence, and honorary trainer for a few years before accepting the paid position in 1904.

The press was unanimous that 'everybody liked Robinson', but ambivalent on his role as trainer. No one commented that he would be missed by the players, and one writer went so far as to point out that the club's recent run of failures might be laid to the outdated practices of the trainer. When Paynter was named as trainer, the top sportswriter in the East End wrote: 'Whether this is the best choice that could be made is extremely doubtful, especially if up-to-date methods are required.'[6] Little public notice was given to Paynter's promotion and no reference was made to it at the AGM.

After the 1923 season, everyone tried to find explanations for the new success of East Ham and what made it different. What emerged in the press, and quickly became part of the accepted mythology surrounding the club, were the linked ideas that West Ham had been built on a solid foundation of local players and that the team was 'marked with a special sense of togetherness'.[7] These could have been convenient clichés to describe a team that did not have a tradition of victory. But in West Ham's case, there was some truth in them. The use of local players had not been a question of choice for King, however: the board could not afford to buy players, so he had to find them.

Paynter was responsible for bringing many players to King's attention. The trainer would give his opinion on a player, but the decision and the offer were strictly up to King. Once a player joined West Ham, he had a well-defined relationship with both men. No junior player would think of going to the manager's office or approaching him at the ground. In the eyes of many players, 'Charlie was our dad, he was the man we went to talk with about things.'[8] Paynter acted as intermediary between players and the manager; King played the same role between players and the board.

Public recognition and praise from the board were good for King's self-esteem, but he also received more tangible recognition. By 1914, the club had raised his salary to £5 a week. His top player was making a wage of £4 during the season and £3 during the close season. King also received yearly bonuses, which started at £50 per annum and rose to £100 by 1914. Mr Fundell, the assistant secretary who handled the administrative details of the club, was paid £3 per week, as was Paynter.[9]

The outbreak of the First World War forced the football clubs to make important changes. By the spring of 1915, West Ham was in financial difficulties. Players were dropped from the books and West Ham continued to pay for medical treatment for some of them only 'as an act of grace'.[10] The assistant secretary was put on part-time wages and other economies were made.

However, no matter how tight the financial position of the club became, it kept King, Fundell and Paynter on the payroll. Paynter received £2 15s per week as caretaker, and Fundell's wage was cut back to £1 per week to act as part-time assistant to the secretary. King continued to earn £5 per week throughout the war, and all three men received annual bonuses. These *ex gratia* payments were more than trivial gestures of appreciation: Paynter received £10, Fundell £25 and King 100 guineas at the conclusion of the 1916 season.[11] The board may have felt some sense of obligation to them, but the directors were also planning for the future of West Ham. They wanted to keep King and his assistants ready for when football resumed at the end of the war.

In addition to financial considerations, the board had other ways to reward loyal service. In May 1917, Mrs King and Mrs Fundell were nominated by the board to be life governors of the West Ham Hospital, one of the many local charities to which the club was a regular contributor.[12] Board members and their wives had been long-standing members of local organizations, and the inclusion of Mrs King and Mrs Fundell showed that the board thought their husbands worthy of representing the club in its broader civic context.

A direct consequence of West Ham's application to the Football League was a series of changes in the staff. Three new men were hired and Paynter was reappointed to his former position as full-time trainer and coach. The biggest change was in the salaries paid to the top men: King went up to £10 per week and Fundell to £4 10s per week. Paynter's re-employment by the club on a full-time basis was more complicated than the other arrangements. The board originally decided to offer him £5 per week plus the same bonuses as were paid to the players.[13] That would have amounted to considerably more than the assistant secretary. The offer was changed before it was tendered to Paynter. The new terms were £4 4s per week 'to be employed on the ground to the end of June and £5 5s per week from 30 June to the end of the season as trainer'.[14] He thus filled two different posts, one during the season, the other during the close season. Players also drew two different wages, but they were expected to do little or nothing for the club during the close season. Paynter's contract paralleled those offered to the players, rather than that of the assistant secretary. The other distinction between Paynter and Fundell was that Paynter received a bonus of £25; while Fundell's bonus was £100.[15] The bonus had nothing to do with their wages, it reflected the status of the jobs held by the two men.

The distinctions between the staff were important signs of the social

West Ham supporters on their way to Wembley for the 1923 Cup Final

structure of the club and the hierarchy that ran it. King was in a class by himself. He had enormous decision-making power and was the only one who spoke directly to the board on his own initiative. In return for these responsibilities, he was handsomely rewarded.

In April 1920 the club completed its second season in the League. It had been a very successful year and the team finished fifth after a seventh place result the preceding year. The board lavished praise on King and also went out of its way to recognize the anniversary of his twentieth year with the club. His salary was set at £10 per week, the same as the previous year, but he was presented with a cheque for £1,500 tax free in appreciation of his service to West Ham.[16]

Until 1923 King had been nothing more than the long-serving secretary-manager of a good second-level but undistinguished club – the classic big fish in a small pond. His personality and activities on behalf of West Ham had equipped him to show his worth on a larger stage, and West Ham's spectacular 1923 season gave him that opportunity. In the articles about the club leading up to the Cup Final, King was often the featured personality. He provided good newspaper copy and had a natural flair for providing quotable remarks. Throughout West Ham's drive to promotion from the second division title and its unlikely

The scene just before the first Cup Final to be played at Wembley in 1923. The finalists were West Ham and Bolton Wanderers; Bolton won 2-0

appearance at Wembley, football observers kept waiting for the bubble to burst. King understood the reaction and knew how to play up West Ham's role as an underdog. He could talk about how the club had risen from obscure roots: he was the man who had been with West Ham when it barely survived. Far from making any effort to hide the bad old days at the Memorial Ground, King went into great detail about the club's problems. On the eve of the Cup Final, how many managers would talk about the time 20 years earlier when the total takings at the gate for his club had been £12? King reminded everyone how close West Ham had been to insolvency when a few civic-minded individuals had saved it. In 1903 the club 'was on the threshold of extinction'. In 1923 'it is on the threshold of the Double'.[17]

For many in England, the 1923 Cup Final will always be known as the 'White Horse Final', but to East Londoners it was the year of the illuminated tram. A week before the final, King announced that there would be civic receptions at the West Ham borough hall on the Saturday evening and on the Sunday in East Ham and borough-wide parties, win or lose. What mattered was that West Ham United had made it to the Final. That night the club travelled through the borough on a tramcar completely decorated with light bulbs spelling out its name and displaying its crossed hammers. The board and civic officials organized the reception, but it had been King's idea.

The electric tram decorated in West Ham's colours to celebrate the 1923 Cup
Final

King was in his element when West Ham went up to the first division.
He reminded the players that they had nothing to be afraid of; their
success was a sign that they were as good as anybody. He got the
directors to put some paint on the ground, improve the changing-room
and buy new strips. King's talent for publicity and creating an image for
West Ham was important, but there was more than this to competing
successfully in the first division.

After a few years, the novelty of first-division play had worn off and the
club settled into a pattern of mediocre finishes. Criticism began to mount
about the team's poor performance. Newspapers called for changes in the
playing staff, criticizing specific players and the directors. Yet,
throughout West Ham's slide down the first division there was little
direct criticism of the manager, and the board showed its faith in King;
his yearly bonuses were continued and in April 1931 at the conclusion of a
poor season he was given a dramatic vote of confidence. Ten shares of
stock were transferred to King from F. C. Johnson and the certificates
were signed and sealed in the presence of the entire board at its weekly
meeting.[18] This was much more than a business transaction concerning
£5 worth of negotiable paper: the shares meant that King was something
more than a long-serving employee.

Less than two years after King was welcomed as a shareholder, his
whole world fell apart. A terse notice in the minutes of the board for 7
November 1932 summarized the end of King's career in football and the
end of an era in West Ham's history: 'It was unanimously decided that
until futher notice C. Paynter be given sole control of players and that E.
S. King be notified accordingly.'[19]

It is important to note what did not happen at that meeting: King was not sacked and Paynter was not named as manager. The action was not taken in response to poor performance by the team. If that had been the case, King would have been replaced years earlier and since Paynter was in charge of training the players he would have been shown the door with his boss. The crisis that took place at the end of 1932 went to the core of how the board viewed their role and the responsibilities of the manager-secretary.

There was nothing special on the agenda for 7 November. However, during the discussion on the team, King was drunk and insubordinate. Consumption of large quantities of alcohol was nothing new to him. He was a regular at many of the local pubs and one of the duties performed by young players was to fetch him cases of bottled beer from the local at the end of Green Street. At the meeting of 7 November at least two members of the board questioned whether King had been supervising the activities of the players and whether he was paying attention to the affairs of the club. King replied in a manner that was insulting to the questioner and proved the charge against him. Any chance that the board would overlook King's problems ended when he walked into the board meeting drunk, and then refused to assume the role of a repentant employee.

The next night, there was an emergency meeting of the directors, only the third in the history of the club. (The other two had been called to decide on the move to the Boleyn Ground and on how to raise the money to keep the club solvent). The directors met to discuss King's future and decide how to clear up the problems he had created for them. The formal resolution of the board stated that 'owing to his insubordination and drunkenness [the discussion showed that the phrase was not limited to the events of the previous night], Mr E. S. King be suspended for three calendar months from 9 November 1932 without salary, and further stipulate that he shall not visit the ground during this period.' The resolution of the board left open the possibility that King might be reinstated at the end of that period if the directors were satisfied with his conduct. However, his salary would be reduced to £8 per week and his position would be that of secretary.[20] The resolution was precise in its wording and left no question that King's role in directing the players at West Ham was over. Members of the board might have anticipated that King would not return to the club in any capacity, but had no way of knowing that he would commit suicide barely two months after his suspension.

The board also expressed concern about King's honesty in the business of his performance. Alan Searles was appointed secretary *pro tem* and authorized to 'collect all keys, documents and property' of the club from King. Two directors were appointed as a finance committee, the first time this institution was used.[21] A week later the finance committee and

Searles reported that the 'company's affairs would be run more efficiently' in the future. Searles informed the board that in future all goods 'would be ordered through the company's regular order books'.[22] The businessmen who ran the board acted with dispatch in a presumed case of employee dishonesty or insubordination. They were more at home with that than trying to allot the blame for the dismal performances of the team and its slide towards relegation.

A couple of weeks later a major row developed over Paynter's competence and whether the club should appoint him as the permanent manager. No questions were raised about Searles's ability to replace King as secretary.[23] In fact, Paynter served the club for another 20 years and was identified nearly everywhere as the embodiment of West Ham United. Searles, the honest bookkeeper, was sacked by the club 15 years later as a result 'of his defalcations' in swindling the club by cooking its books.[24]

When King left, the only public announcement was that Paynter was taking his place temporarily to direct the team. The board gave no reason for its actions. The final decision about King took place at a very heated board meeting on 3 January 1932. The resolution passed was to the point. After reviewing all the circumstances that had led to King's suspension the previous November, the board concluded that it could not re-engage him in any capacity. The secretary was instructed to advise King of the decision and add the regrets of the board. No director suggested that either the chairman or the board should inform King personally, or that he should be given the courtesy of a letter from them. Appreciation of his long service to the club (pre-dating that of any of the directors) was summed up in the offer of an *ex gratia* payment of £3 per week to be paid to King 'as long as the company shall see fit'.[25]

King's dealings with the club after his dismissal were limited to one request for match tickets. The chairman also received a letter from Mrs King asking for tickets for her husband. Less than a month after his dismissal, King committed suicide by drinking a corrosive liquid mixed with an alcoholic beverage. The inquest into his death found that he had committed 'suicide while of unsound mind' and noted that he had been suffering from persecution delusions for some months. His son testified that King had become very depressed while the team was falling out of the first division and his paranoia had started then; he made a special note during his testimony that his father had been satisfied at the way the club had handled his retirement and had been grateful for the £3 weekly pension.[26]

The club's response to King's death was a model of understated grief. A formal resolution of their regret was placed in the board minutes, the directors ordered that flags at the ground be flown at half mast, and the team wore black armbands for the remainder of the season. The club forwarded the letters of sympathy it received to Mrs King and sent her a cheque for £40 to assist in buying a grave. Finally the minutes of 3

January were revised to note that a £4 per week *ex gratia* payment should be received by Mrs King. It must be noted that the directors were careful to refer to the money as an *ex gratia* payment and never used the term pension, which had been introduced by King's son during his testimony at the inquest.[27]

West Ham was not free of the problems King had left behind him, either in the office or on the field. A new accounting system was introduced within a few months intended to shield the new secretary from temptations that had faced King. The problems with the team were more severe and more complicated. Charlie Paynter was the natural choice to take over from King, at least as a mid-season replacement: he knew the organization better than anyone and had close ties with the players. If those qualities recommended him to the board, he had corresponding liabilities: he was the trainer and had assumed the role of manager when King was incapable of functioning. Thus Paynter was as responsible as King for the poor seasons.

Charlie Paynter assumed control of the playing side of West Ham in November 1932. The length of Paynter's tenure and his personality colour any discussion of his role within the club. Almost everyone who had any dealings with him or West Ham had their 'Charlie' stories. His long career with the club transformed him into a ubiquitous figure, 'the man who was always there'. It is hard to accept that his appointment as manager was marked by controversy and uncertainty. Paynter was given temporary control over the players at the time of King's suspension. A week later, the directors had some second thoughts. Replacing a manager was a new experience for them and they had to improvise. The directors tried to keep their affairs out of the public gaze, but how could any reporter help but notice that Paynter, not King, was running the team? Rumours that surfaced immediately about Paynter damaged his position and threatened to tear apart the unity that had always been the hallmark of the board of directors.

During a normal business session of the board, a director raised a question about Paynter. Other members of the board were very upset by an article in *The Star*, which quoted Paynter as complaining about the dimly lit dressing-rooms and other bad conditions at the Boleyn Ground. Mr Cearns reminded his colleagues that there had been other articles about Paynter and the 'better part of the interviews were both beneficial and valuable'. Nevertheless, an impression emerged in the press that the board was either trying to hide something or that it did not know what it was doing. The board 'regretted the surfeit of publicity given to the club's recent events' and resolved that additional publicity should be avoided and no future statements made. This meant that everyone, especially Paynter, should avoid talking about the changes that had occurred.[28] This might put a better face on West Ham's problems, but it did not resolve Paynter's status.

Paynter had requested a clarification of his position and asked to appear at this meeting. The board approved a motion that the issue was too complex to be handled now and should be carried over to the following week. How did the board expect Paynter to understand what was happening or explain it to others when the board itself was unsure of what it was doing? There was a possibility that King would return, and the directors did not want to give Paynter any more power or status than was necessary to handle the immediate problem. They avoided making any decision that could break apart the structure of the club.

The board's unwillingness to make a firm public decision about Paynter put him in a very difficult position. He was questioned by the board about the newspaper articles, and admitted having spoken to the press, but suggested that the statements attributed to him were 'journalistic inexactitude'. Having accepted this explanation, the board turned its attention to Paynter's performance. In the previous week's match, he had not gone on to the field to attend an injured player. When questioned about his conduct he replied 'To have done so with recent events in mind would have been an embarrassment both to the club and to myself.' His reply ended the questions but did not solve the problem. Until the board could make up its mind about what to do with Paynter, the club would suffer; the players were uncertain and Paynter, the faithful servant of 30 years, was left in limbo.[29]

The next discussion about Paynter's position was one of the few times the board had an extended debate on any issue. There was a rare division between directors during which they set forth their views on how the club should be operated. G. F. Davis had been the author of the original resolution to give Paynter sole control. Two weeks later, he explained that he had 'no suggestion of giving him more power, but of safe-guarding him from interference by Mr E. S. King'. He reminded the board that the action had been taken before it had suspended King. Davis thought it appropriate to reaffirm Paynter's control over all matters dealing with the team, but to leave the power to engage players in the hands of the two scouts, Messrs Liddell and Leafe. Davis was trying to get his colleagues to see how their inaction had put both themselves and Paynter in uncomfortable positions.

Mr Pratt spoke against limiting Paynter's role in the engagement of players, fearing that restrictions of this type 'might dampen Mr Paynter's enthusiasm'. Once again, the hard-headed businessmen who ran West Ham were confronted by the anomalies of the football business. It is interesting to conjecture how many directors, Pratt included, would have raised the consideration of employee enthusiasm before deciding how to handle employees in their own businesses. The directors were trying to live up to their two primary responsibilties: to protect the economic integrity of the company and to provide a viable football organization. In the past they had deferred to King's experience and position. Now they had to make some fundamental decisions about their role in the football and administrative side of West Ham.

A. C. Davis brought the attention of the board back to the question it had been trying to avoid: what should be done with Paynter, and how long could he be expected to perform the duties of manager without the title and authority? Davis rephrased the question and asked if West Ham needed a manager at all. After all, 'two weeks earlier he had asked if the board intended to appoint a manager and the answer had been negative'.[30]

Davis wanted decisions made that evening about the future of the managership and Paynter. The two questions had become inextricably linked. Davis proposed two possible solutions and invited the other directors to make a decision based on them. One alternative was to 'appoint a manager – a stranger, because it is necessary to have someone to deal with all matters concerning the team, etc.', another was not to have a manager at all. Both ideas flew in the face of West Ham traditions. A club without a manager might seem like a contradiction in terms, but Davis's exercise in hyperbole made the point: what were the directors doing running West Ham during King's absence? A new manager would run the team and take the burden off the board, but it would not be an unmixed blessing. If Paynter was not appointed he would probably leave West Ham. If he were appointed he would assume a new role. One director pointed out that no matter what happened, the same negative effect on the club would apply: 'we would lose the services of one of the best trainers in the country.'

The priorities of the board were obvious. They wanted to retain Paynter in his valuable role as trainer. Given King's recent performance, the board might have concluded that a manager was more trouble than he was worth. Paradoxically, the final argument against appointing Paynter as manager was that there were 'many cases where managers had to relinquish their positions owing to the failure of their teams. [The directors] had no wish to see such a valued servant as Mr C. Paynter similarly placed.' We can assume that the directors were speaking frankly since their comments were not meant to be repeated outside the board-room. They were ostensibly protecting Paynter from himself by ensuring that he was not promoted to a more important position: a striking example of the paternalism which marked so many of the actions of football management.[31]

Davis's fear that Paynter might have to be released ignored one critical point: there was no reason to expect Paynter to 'relinquish his position'. Managers did not usually resign, they were sacked, and the board had complete control over that. If the West Ham directors did not want Paynter to leave after an unsuccessful season, they merely had to renew his contract.

The directors had not replaced King because West Ham had played badly. They took action against King only when his conduct showed that he was incapable of carrying out his duties. Apart from having been insubordinate to the board, King's drinking problems had reached the stage where he might become a public embarrassment to West Ham and the directors. The next time it might be harder for the board to keep King's indiscretions within the family.

The chairman attempted to resolve matters by suggesting that Paynter be paid a bonus of £4 for a win and £2 for a draw, in addition to his weekly wage as trainer. That would give him a wage almost equal to that of Syd King. It was a hard-headed economic answer calculated to show Paynter that the club valued his services and knew that he was taking on a new responsibility. W. J. Cearns's reply to this brought the issue into sharp focus: 'It was not a matter of monies, but prestige.' Cearns knew why Paynter had wanted to appear before the board and had asked for a clarification of his title, and it was not for a rise in wages.[32]

After a 'long discussion' Pratt moved a motion, seconded by Cearns, that Paynter should continue his duties as trainer and be appointed trainer and players' manager at a salary of £10 per week and his match bonus be discontinued. He would 'look for players, when free if he so desired'. In an accompanying motion, Liddell and Leafe were made responsible directly to the board. The meeting ended with a formal resolution that 'The directors felt sure that there would be harmonious workings amongst Messrs C. Paynter, Liddell and A. R. Leafe which would prove beneficial to the club.' Paynter was asked back into the room and told of his appointment. He thanked the directors for their confidence in him and assured them that he would do everthing possible to further the interests of the club.[33]

The confusion over Paynter's position with West Ham was a product of the directors' previous policy of giving Syd King almost free rein to do as he wished. When the board was forced to make changes it wanted to avoid bringing public attention to the unfortunate circumstances of King's suspension. The board's desire to avoid possible disruption and change ran counter to the desires of its faithful employee. Paynter refused to accept this treatment. His stubbornness forced the board into making a decision; he also understood his value as a trainer, and probably knew that the board did not want to give the slightest public impression that they were not in control.

Paynter settled for the somewhat ambiguous title of players' manager. In the context of the previous two weeks, it was clearly a victory for him. He had a title that corresponded with his responsibilities and a salary commensurate with the work. He was no longer a worker partially dependent on weekly bonuses; he had become part of the managerial structure of the club. The board's decision in January 1933 not to re-employ King consolidated Paynter's position. There was no longer any question that he was an interim appointee. Charlie was 'the guv'nor'.

King's death ended an era in the history of the club and changed Paynter's life. The circumstances surrounding King's suicide brought renewed interest from the press and the public in the way the board had handled him. It might have caused bad publicity for the team. West Ham needed someone to act as its spokesman. When Paynter was approached by the press for comment on the impact of King's death on West Ham's future he still had fresh memories of the board's displeasure at previous dealings with the press. His first response was to define more precisely his role. The board reaffirmed its earlier statement that 'there are no objections to Mr Paynter giving information to the press. It was left to his discretion to choose the right matter.' They added a provision to the resolution, which stated: 'Mr C. Paynter should be the sole member of the Staff whose duty it is to give and see Publicity on *Team* matters.' Paynter was asked to come into the board-room, where he was informed of the board's latest resolution and told that the board expected that he 'would collaborate with the secretary' on matters dealing with the press.[34] When Paynter assumed his new position, the board made a distinction between the manager and the secretary. Paynter was taking on only part of Syd King's responsibilities and power, but the new manager stamped his personality on the club even more than his predecessor. The transition had not been as easy for the board or Paynter as it might have been. Once he took over there were few difficulties between him and the directors, and no reason for anyone else to apply for the position of manager.

CHAPTER 7
Who is running the club?

Paynter was so distinctive, a real personality, the kind of person you never forgot.

Dame Anna Neagle talking in 1980 about going to West Ham matches as a girl.

King's sudden dismissal in 1932 left West Ham without the man who had monopolized its management, on and off the field, for 30 years. During the transition from King to Searles, the new secretary, and Paynter, the players' manager, the club was held up to public scrutiny. Relations with the press were an integral part of the job done by the new administration. In this area, any parity between Searles and Paynter disappeared. Newspaper readers were not interested in the inner workings of the club, even though they might have got some perverse enjoyment from learning about the possible fiddles worked by King. The directors did everything possible to keep out of the papers; no news was most definitely good news from their perspective. That left Charlie Paynter as the public persona for the club, and very few men in football, or any other occupation, were better suited than he to step straight into that role.

When Paynter retired in 1950 he was honoured by his club, the League and the Football Association. His testimonial match attracted the aristocracy of football. Arsenal performed on the field against West Ham and Mr Paynter sat in the directors' box flanked on one side by Mr Arthur Drewry, president of the Football League, and on the other by Sir Stanley Rouse, secretary of the Football Association. The whole evening was a festive occasion and Paynter received many valuable gifts. The proceedings were bathed in sentimentality; members of former West Ham sides were present and Paynter received best wishes and gifts from them as well as from the 1950 side. At a surprise ceremony following the match, Dick Walker, the captain, gave Paynter a gift and then told him, 'I don't want you to thank us, we thank you for what you have done for us.' Other guests at the match included Viscount Alexander, political dignitaries, local football officials and Vera Lynn, who had once been a neighbour of Paynter's. In the board-room ceremony following the match, Paynter was honoured by a series of speakers in a 'room crowded

Charlie Paynter, the 'Grand Old Man of West Ham', served the club for 50 years as assistant trainer, trainer, manager and secretary

with nobilities from the football world...occupying a prominent place was the FA Cup, which the holders had brought along to add distinction and colour to the occasion'.[1]

The presence of Arsenal, the Cup and the leaders of English football showed the regard in which Paynter was held. During his tenure as manager, West Ham had remained in the second division, finishing in the top four only twice. The club's record in the Cup had been generally undistinguished, with one noticeable exception when it returned to Wembley on a warm June afternoon to win the 1940 War Cup Final. Only the most diligent football fans or West Ham supporters remember that match. As Paynter looked around him at his testimonial match it must have been a cruel irony to remember that the most talented side he had ever managed played in a season that lasted only three matches. If results had been the basis for retirement honours there was little reason to expect that outpouring for Charlie Paynter. Longevity, especially in a business like football management, might be reason enough for a spectacular farewell, but that does not explain why Paynter survived so long, and why he left 'at the top of his form'. His reign as manager is more remarkable when we remember that when the directors appointed him they were not sure that he was capable of doing the job.

When Paynter left the field at half-time and at the conclusion of his testimonial, the large crowds broke into repeated choruses of 'For he's a jolly good fellow'.[2] Paynter was a product of an age in which footballers remained part of the class and neighbourhood in which they were born. He was intensely proud of having been a professional footballer and trainer. It was Paynter who enforced a dress code on West Ham players before 1914: a player could come to the ground for training in a coat and muffler, but he had to leave wearing a collar and tie because he represented the club and football. Syd King's admonition to the young Jimmy Ruffell that he was a professional footballer was echoed by Paynter's insistence that players live up to the standards that he set for them.

A high point of Paynter's testimonial was the appearance of many players who had been on the 1923 Cup Final side. The attention paid to that glorious moment in West Ham history obscured the fact that the team had been Syd King's, not Paynter's. The players had strong feelings for Paynter, who had discovered many of them, recommended them to King, and controlled their training. As long as King had been the 'guv'nor' Paynter received less public attention and credit than he deserved. The presence of the 1923 team at his testimonial was a long overdue honour, although in the meantime he had made up for the years in which he had laboured in the shadow of Syd King. Paynter was the quintessential 'club man', the faithful employee who understood the importance of submerging his self-interest or making sure it coincided with that of West Ham. Footballers in the 1930s lived near the ground, took local buses and trams or walked to training sessions. They were part of the local landscape, as was Paynter. He lived off the Barking Road, spent his time with his neighbours and became a visible sign of West Ham's ties with the community.

Paynter is an important part of West Ham folklore, but almost no one talks about him in terms of tactics, success, or specific teams. He was much more than a manager to most supporters, much less than a successful manager to those whose main interest lay in results. Paynter was first and foremost a great character, known by sight throughout the neighbourhood. He was 'almost larger than life'. One of his long-time admirers, the daughter of a sea captain from Forest Gate, remembered that he 'looked more like an office worker than a footballer'. The young Anna Neagle was not alone in being impressed by Paynter's appearance. The flair with which he acted was all part of a conscious effort to give the impression that football was a game in which men could become successful and respectable. Maybe Anna Neagle recognized another performer in Paynter. However, it was one of his former players who identified the trait most directly. Dick Walker knew how to play to the crowd himself, but recognized a master at work in Paynter: 'I loved the old boy...Sir Laurence Olivier had nothing on Charlie when there was an audience.'

Paynter transformed West Ham United into a reflection of his vision of what the club could be. He was operating on more than one level at a time. His public personality was a walking advertisement for West Ham United; he talked constantly about the desire of the team to perform for its supporters and the close ties that existed between them. He was an optimist; he believed in the future of the club and its ability to come back. His relationship with the directors was less flamboyant: he knew his place and he also understood the paucity of resources available to the Board. As manager, he had to inspire the players, and became a combination of friend, 'uncle' and boss. Paynter never backed the directors into a corner by making demands on them. He knew his place and he was aware of the paucity of resources available to the board. He stood between the board and the players, and no player, with the exception of the captain, dealt directly with the board. The exception was when the chairman wanted the personal privilege of telling a player he had been selected for the national side – something that did not happen often at West Ham. The players knew that Paynter could be a disciplinarian and they knew the board would back him up on such matters, including fines and suspensions. He made the yearly recommendation to the board about the retention of players and the wages they should be offered. The playing career of each man was short enough without endangering it by violating Paynter's rules. Players were informed in no uncertain terms that demonstrations of dissent on the field to officials would not be tolerated; nor would fouls be treated as a necessary part of the game. Paynter wanted a team willing to play hard, but 'putting the boot in' ran counter to his ideas of the game. He did not lecture on abstract ideas like 'good sportsmanship' or 'playing the game'. His approach was simpler – he expected players to do as they were told.

Paynter's dealings with his players were part psychology, part performance, and part authoritarian. The players remember him for an arm on the shoulder and a fatherly chat. When he criticized them, he did so in the privacy of the manager's office. The players had self-imposed team standards. Distinctions were obvious between younger players and veterans, and new players did not have to be told that they were part of a lower caste. Established players had nothing to do with newcomers and showed little, if any, desire to help younger players. That was understandable: any new player threatened their jobs and those of their friends. The young players also would 'get the old rubbish' for gear at the start of each season. This was encouraged by Paynter; there was no doubt in his mind that football was a hard game and the newcomer had to show he could stand up to its pressures. The difficulties facing younger players also gave Paynter the opportunity to exert his considerable talent for showing how interested he was in his players. Once a youngster had shown he was good enough to stay at West Ham, he became part of 'Charlie's team'.

Like any performer, Paynter developed a collection of useful tricks. After each game, he would go around and pat each of his players on the back. Spectators and officials saw this as a sporting gesture, further proof of the close ties between him and the players. It took players some time to realize that it was also the manager's way of seeing if they had worked up a sweat during the match. Paynter's early experience as a trainer with players who could not be trusted to give a week's worth of work for their wage died hard.

Paynter knew that he could discipline players, but he preferred to persuade them to do things in a certain way. He listened to questions and complaints, which gave the player the impression that he had been given a fair hearing. These interviews also gave Paynter the opportunity to exercise his considerable skills as a talker. Occasionally, he pushed too far. A promising young player approached Paynter to ask why he was not in the first team after a series of solid performances with the reserves. Paynter took the player aside and told him that he had shown steady improvement, but unfortunately, 'You don't have any experience at top level.' The answer was correct, but the logic and the fairness of it did not impress Frank O'Farrell. 'I felt it was a diabolical answer...how did I get experience if he wouldn't let me play? I lost a lot of regard for Mr Paynter from that time.' Ironically, it was in Paynter's 1950 testimonial match that O'Farrell attracted the attention of the new manager and moved into the first side.

When a player objected to the wage set by the board, Paynter was put in the middle. In 1933, four leading players refused the terms offered them for the following season. One, Jimmy Ruffell, sent a formal request to the board for an increase in wages, 'but it was resolved [by the Board] that the terms remain as offered'.[3] Paynter was instructed by the board to play two of the dissatisfied players, including Ruffell, in the next reserve match. Even though Paynter did not agree with this assessment of Ruffell's value as a player, he did not question the board's action. The dispute over wages continued into the summer by which time three of the players, including Ruffell, had been given better terms. Throughout the 1930s the board regularly gave Paynter instructions about specific players.

Paynter's ability to get on with people served him well in his relationship with the board, especially since each director felt the need to deal directly with Paynter on occasion. In any case, the whole administrative operation at West Ham was so small and informal that it would have been absurd to establish a highly formal chain of command. This arrangement continued even after W. J. Cearns became chairman in 1935. Cearns was a strong personality, a man who wanted to exercise personal supervision over many activities of the club. In his business, he was used to giving orders and having them followed, but he was astute enough to understand that Paynter brought a special talent to his job and that the club was well served by him. Paynter took great pains to let the chairman know what he intended to do, especially if it involved any changes. In this way, he enlisted the chairman's support and protected himself against suspicion that he was trying to usurp the powers of the board.

Paynter's status at the club changed quickly. In May 1933 he was given shares in the club. At the start of the 1933-34 season the board passed a formal resolution asking that Paynter be present at board meetings during his 'report' to the directors.[4] This meant that he would be there to answer the directors' questions and to argue for his position if that became necessary. His weekly appearance showed everyone that his position was no lower than Syd King's had been.

When the need arose, the directors showed their support for Paynter. In January 1936, West Ham became embroiled in a controversy with the Dartford Football Club. Paynter had set up the transfer of F. Dell to 'take place immediately after the Dartford Club had ceased to be interested in the present season's FA Cup competition.'[5] A few weeks later, Dartford officials informed the West Ham chairman that they 'intended to repudiate the arrangements...because they had received larger offers...and had been advised that the agreements entered into with us were not binding with the Football Association'. Cearns insisted that his colleagues take every step possible to make Dartford live up to their bargain. He praised Paynter and pointed out that he had resorted to somewhat unconventional practices only to preserve the interest of the Dartford supporters while their club remained in the FA Cup competition. There was no question in the chairman's mind that 'the agreement was binding'. Paynter's method caused inconvenience and expense to his club. West Ham agreed to pay Dartford an additional £250 in lieu of playing a match for their benefit. Despite this, the board commended Paynter for his conduct. The tone of the discussion with Dartford made it clear that Cearns was incensed at the attempt to impugn Paynter's competence and honesty. Dartford gave West Ham a chance to disown Paynter's deal and to use him as a scapegoat. The response was the opposite of what they had expected.[6]

The directors involved themselves with Paynter's responsibilities when the assistant manager and coach, S. G. Gibson, died in 1938. The board considered applications for the position of coach. The best candidate appeared to be Mr R. John, formerly of Arsenal, and a special board meeting was held to interview him.[7] Paynter was not invited to the meeting, but was asked to make himself available later in the day. The directors questioned John about the role of a coach and discussed salary. They had a brief private discussion, after which John was brought back into the board-room and offered the position at a salary of £6 per week. Before John accepted the offer he was assured that he would be answerable to the board only and 'would be responsible for players on the field and during coaching, but that in the dressing-room, Mr Paynter would be "in charge".'[8]

Paynter was present when the offer was made. Both men knew exactly where they stood and what the board expected of them. At the end of the meeting the chairman stated that the board hoped that co-operation between Paynter and John 'in their different duties, would bring about a distinct improvement where needed – in the individual fitness, skill, knowledge of the game, and the general advance, as regards the tactics of the three teams'. In response to the chairman, 'Paynter assured the board of his whole-hearted assistance in making the venture successful.'[9] The new arrangement was a remarkable contrast to the terms upon which Paynter had become manager.

The cancellation of regular League football during the Second World War brought new problems for Paynter, but the most dramatic development had nothing to do with the nation's crisis. On 2 July 1940, the chairman informed the board that Mr A. N. Searles had been dismissed three days earlier. Cearns could not find an accountant willing to accept the appointment as secretary *pro tem*.[10] Nine days later, Paynter was named as secretary *pro tem* and the board was informed that the auditors had discovered the method by which Searles had been defrauding the club. The loss would be noted as a 'bad debt' and the club would not take action against its former employee.

A strange sense of symmetry, almost *déjà vu*, surrounded Paynter's situation. He had become manager because of King's drinking and petty larcenies and was confirmed in the post because of his ability as a coach. By 1940 Paynter had the administrative duties that he had not wanted, and the board had appointed someone else as coach.

Paynter continued as manager-secretary throughout the war. His primary tasks were to find enough players for each match and keep the ground in serviceable order. He had little interest in the duties of secretary and had part-time clerical help; even members of the board assisted him. The most valuable legacy Paynter received from Searles was a young player who worked in the office rather than on the groundstaff. He had taught himself some clerical skills and learned office practice from Searles. Paynter developed a close working relationship with the youth who had been predicted to become one of West Ham's top young players but instead became its long-serving secretary, Eddie Chapman.

At the end of the war, the directors realized that Paynter could not handle both jobs. Their decision to appoint a secretary took into account the fact that both King and Searles had mishandled the club's finances. The new secretary came with the best credentials for honesty and diligence: he was a member of the Cearns family. Frank Cearns's appointment as secretary in November 1946 was made with the stated objective of allowing Paynter to spend all his time with the players.[11] Paynter had been at West Ham so long that most people took it for granted that he would be there indefinitely. Players came and went, the staff changed, directors resigned or died, but Charlie was always there. When he informed the board of his plans to phase himself out of his job, Paynter stayed in character and ended his days as manager without disrupting the club.

'At the completion of the ordinary business' of the board meeting of 24

June 1948, the chairman reported that Mr Paynter had discussed with him the difficulty he was experiencing in carrying out his duties 'owing to advancing age particularly in respect of managing the team regarding tactics, etc.'[12] There is no evidence that Paynter was under any pressure to end his career as manager; the team had finished sixth, up six places in the second division table from the previous season. We can only take Paynter's announcement at its face value; a conclusion supported by the way in which he made it. Paynter discussed the matter with the chairman and laid the basis for the next couple of years when he 'suggested that Mr E. Fenton be engaged to assist him until he retires when Mr Fenton would, no doubt, be fully qualified to take over the management of the club'.

Paynter's successor could learn on the job, but would not have to cope with all the daily responsibilities at the same time. Fenton could acquaint himself with the players and the League.

The scenario had been arranged ahead of time with the chairman and some members of the board. Fenton attended the meeting and was asked to make a few comments. He expressed his 'great pleasure in obtaining the appointment that he always hoped would come his way'. He informed the board that he would commence his duties as soon as he could leave his present contract at Colchester. Paynter's opportunity to choose his successor was, in many ways, the highest compliment the board could pay him: the assumption that he represented something about West Ham that they wanted to continue after he left.[13]

Fenton had completed a couple of noteworthy seasons at Colchester, a club that was scarcely more than a decade old. He had had a fine Cup run and had attracted good publicity. One of his talents was for playing up to the media. He had a sure eye for the journalists' need for good quotes and 'hooks' for the next day's story. His success at Colchester did not create the opening for him at West Ham but it accelerated an offer that might otherwise have been a few years in coming. Fenton received an offer to manage West Bromwich Albion. That meant stepping straight into the first division and joining a club with a great tradition. According to Fenton, he immediately contacted Paynter for advice about how to handle the offer. Paynter had been Fenton's manager and had developed him from an apprentice into a veteran player, and Fenton realized that the West Ham manager might be contemplating his retirement. Paynter advised Fenton to decline the offer at West Bromwich and come back to West Ham on the understanding that he would take over when Paynter retired. This meant giving up the chance to be boss at a first-class club in order to become an assistant manager in the second division. His starting wage at Colchester had been £15 and by 1948 had risen slightly. He would have received an increased amount at West Bromwich Albion. His starting salary at West Ham was £15: clearly he did not go there for the money.[14]

Why did Paynter offer Fenton the job? Why did Fenton accept it? Why was the offer made when it was? Fenton's success at Colchester reinforced Paynter's feelings that his former player had the makings of a manager, and made it easy to convince the board that Fenton was the right man. Conversely, that success brought Fenton to other people's attention and pushed West Ham into making the offer in 1948. Thus Paynter had to make his decision to retire in order to get a commitment from the board that Fenton would become the next manager.

Fenton's willingness to become heir apparent at West Ham was not surprising. He had, after all, spent most of his life with West Ham; he was a local boy made good, one of eight children of a Forest Gate policeman. His father took him to West Ham for the first time as a child and hardly ever went to see another club play football. 'After all, West Ham was our club, East London's club. I'm a Cockney, not a proper one, but still a Cockney and that's what West Ham is.' Fenton left school at 14 and was pushing a cart for a living when he got the chance to play for West Ham. He was 'amazed' to be offered a contract. When he got 10s for playing in a practice match with West Ham he thought, 'I would have paid them to let me play.' He had dreamed of playing football for West Ham, but had not thought of football as a profession, and got a thrill from showing off the shiny leather bag with 'West Ham United' on it at stations when travelling to matches. Fenton stayed at West Ham for 16 years with time off for military service. He had no training for another occupation and gave little thought to his future, but that was common in players of his generation.

If Paynter had said, 'Go and get Fenton' when announcing his choice of a successor, the phrase would have struck a responsive chord. Fenton had been the first youth to be signed as a groundsboy by West Ham, a post that was anything but a sinecure for young players: the club got work out of them. Fenton's strongest memories were the 'flair' with which Syd King seemed to do everything, the bowler hats and the army-style inspections of Mr Pierson, the assistant manager, and Charlie Paynter being almost everywhere. There were the repeated trips to the local pub to buy cases of beer for King, a chore that carried a 10s tip from the manager. Above all, there seemed to be the constant cry of 'Go and get Fenton' for the next task. Everybody ranked over him and they could all find things for him to do.

Fenton's decision to go to West Ham as manager was a way of avoiding the challenges of the unknown: the prestige of West Bromwich and the pressure of the first division. Colchester had provided Fenton with the comfort of the small-time, local club – a version of West Ham. His willingness to entertain other offers showed that he was ambitious to leave. The offer at West Ham gave Fenton the best of both worlds.

Paynter must have known that the conduct of the new manager would affect his own reputation. He had spent too long at West Ham to see his work ruined by someone about whom he was unsure. He respected Fenton's dedication to the game and his performance at Colchester, and Fenton also had a sense of what the club meant to Charlie. He was not expected to be Paynter's clone, but the older man could assume that his former player understood how a West Ham manager acted in public and how he related to the board and the community.

A football club is a product of its own mythology. Why should Paynter go outside 'the family' to find his successor? Fenton had the qualifications that mattered to Paynter including the willingness to be Paynter's number two for an unspecified number of years. The arrangement worked because of the relationship between the two men and because everyone involved knew that Fenton would eventually take over.

If football careers are judged by statistics and records then Paynter's claim to fame as a manager was his length of service. For 50 years he was part of West Ham and for almost 20 years he was manager. He never put the board in the position of having to react to something he had already done or promised to do. His dealings with other clubs were preceded by discussions with his own board. Any important changes made in the team were announced to the board before they happened.

Paynter was the public face of the club. His style was that of an avuncular elder statesman rather than the flashy 'operator' that his predecessor, Syd King, had been. The board felt comfortable with Paynter; he had been at West Ham for nearly all his adult life. Directors saw Paynter rather like one of the concrete pillars at the ground. The board indicated that it wanted to take few chances and make no serious changes, preferring to concentrate on the financial crises endemic to West Ham. This was easier to achieve if they were sure that no explosions would occur on the managerial side of the operation.

Observers of football have drawn different conclusions about why West Ham has acted as it has done about managers. Not unnaturally, club officials like Reg Pratt and Len Cearns see it as a sign of loyalty, an admirable absence of the cut-throat instinct that marks the operation of too many other clubs. Many supporters have been proud of being identified with an organization that stresses loyalty. The distinguished journalist, Bernard Joy, saw West Ham as an anachronism in modern football, a place 'where loyalty is all important...[but] not enough ambition at the club until Ted Fenton came along'.

Former long-serving players have very different ideas about why West Ham has not become part of the managerial hatchet game, commonplace elsewhere in football. Noel Cantwell thinks 'the club reflected how important it was to have a sense of loyalty to people...they kept people around, but after all, some in-breeding isn't a bad thing. It gave you a sense of roots. There were people around like Paynter who could tell you what West Ham is like.' The negative side of that approach was 'The club didn't have character of steel...that probably came from the easy-going directors...and was the same reason they didn't sack managers.' Cantwell's friend and contemporary at West Ham United, Malcolm Allison, looked at the same facts and came up with a markedly different interpretation. Anyone who has followed Allison's career will not be surprised that he has strong, negative feelings about the style at West Ham. The board's 'play it safe' approach towards the appointment and retention of managers was just one reason why West Ham 'was just another unsuccessful football club...where everybody hides from the situation and doesn't accept responsibility for anything.'

Allison arrived at West Ham two months after Fenton became manager and while Paynter was still a consultant. Allison's opinion of both of them was simple: 'They were incompetent, neither had any idea of what a professional football club was...it was a pathetic club, [the board] didn't have any idea what to do.' Many people see West Ham's reluctance to sack managers as a sign of strength, but Allison saw it as proof of the lack of ambition and steel in the directors: 'The directors had no sense of how to achieve anything or to be successful. The club was like the poor who always make excuses for not improving their situation...It's an excuse to call it [retaining managers and players] loyalty because it really means they're afraid of outsiders. They're people who live in an iron village all their lives and appoint their own people.' The appointment of Fenton signified a malaise at Upton Park, the 'fear of the club's leadership to appoint anybody they think might be better than they are'. In one small respect Ron Greenwood, who became manager of West Ham in 1961, agrees with Allison: there had been a danger of in-breeding at West Ham. 'One of the things wrong with this club is an over-abundance of loyalty...But what's wrong with that?' Greenwood is convinced that the alternatives to loyalty are worse than the harm it might have caused. 'This country wouldn't be in the bloody state it's in right now if there was a bit more loyalty...Society wouldn't be so sick if there was more loyalty like there has been at West Ham.' Greenwood was vehement in his contention that West Ham's 'family-club approach' might 'be out of place' in modern football, but it has not been the cause of West Ham's relative lack of success. He sees the policy as a sign of strength, not weakness or lack of ambition. It would be easy for the directors to show the supporters they are trying to do something by sacking a manager. That would also make sure that the chairman got his name in the newspapers.

Paynter avoided the temptation to try to transform himself into an *eminence grise*. Fenton had a strong sense of himself, but he had the dual problems of impressing his own personality on the players and supporters and bringing some success to the club. The latter was the best way to achieve the former: he did not have the years of goodwill to draw upon nor the assurance of long-term support from the board. Success on the pitch was essential to Fenton, but West Ham had finished only two places above relegation. The playing staff for the 1950-51 season did not hold out hopes for great success.

Fenton also felt that the club had not been sufficiently publicized. They 'might have taken supporters for granted...I wanted them to do more public relations.' 'You had to notice Ted Fenton because he was always grabbing publicity,' is how Trevor Smith, the astute football correspondent on the *Ilford Recorder*, describes the actions of the new manager. He signed players on television, started rumours about potential signings, and coined terms to describe what was going on at West Ham. It didn't matter if he changed his stories from week to week – who would remember the first version? The important thing was to get people to start thinking that something new and exciting was happening at Upton Park. It might translate into more people coming through the turnstiles, and publicity might make it easier to start signing the players that were needed to turn the Hammers into a winning side.

Fenton had to face the problem of all new managers – how to assert his authority over players who had grown accustomed to the previous regime. Dick Walker, the captain and the most popular player, was the first to have problems with Fenton. Walker's description of the situation is simple: 'I didn't like him and he didn't like me.' It was a clash between very similar men. Walker saw Fenton's actions as 'a matter of taking over from somebody popular and wanting to show you're in charge'.

Fenton's problem was how to back up his own publicity: how to provide entertaining, winning football. This challenge was also an opportunity. The club had almost nowhere to go but up. For decades, East London had prided itself on being a breeding ground for footballers, but West Ham had attracted neither the best nor enough good local players. Fenton set out to improve the scouting system. He and Wally St Pier, a former player, begin to attend as many local matches as possible and did everything to ingratiate themselves with schoolmasters and football officials. They emphasized that things had changed at West Ham and that the club was once again really interested in local players. The men who ran West Ham might have been guilty of taking their fans for granted for years but were even more culpable in not cultivating the community as the natural area from which they could attract young players.

The changes Fenton instituted were to provide the basis for West Ham's success over the next decade, but he is the first to admit that he was working from necessity more than anything else. 'The only way to build the club was youth. There were lots of good players around, but I had no money to buy the key players we needed...There were always the problems of running a club on a shoe-string.' Fenton and St Pier used local pride as a selling point for young players, but they also pointed to 'the lowly status of the club as a way to show boys and their parents that

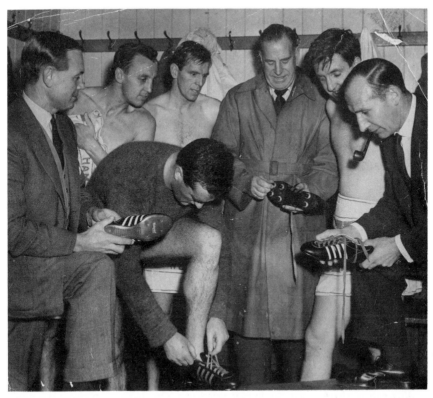

West Ham was one of the first clubs in England to wear continental-style boots. Noel Cantwell tries them on surrounded by (from left to right) Jack Turner, Vic Keeble, John Dick, Bernard Joy (football correspondent of the *Daily Express*), John Bond and Ted Fenton

they could advance in a hurry'. Again, Fenton turned necessity into a virtue but at the price of admitting that all had not been well with the Hammers.

Ted Fenton is known to people interested in football for three things: he succeeded Charlie Paynter, preceded Ron Greenwood, and took West Ham into the first division. The club holds the record for the longest continuous run in the second division, although it is hardly the achievement of which it is proudest. Since football managers are usually saddled with the blame for their teams' failures it seems appropriate to give Fenton credit for the successes. Ever since 1958, his exact role with the club has been the cause of constant and sometimes heated discussions by the men who played for him, the board that employed him, the journalists covering the team and the supporters. Fenton's contribution to the victorious club raises questions about the role played by managers.

Noel Cantwell, Malcolm Allison, Frank O'Farrell, Dave Sexton, John Bond, Andy Malcolm, Ken Brown – these names are only a few on the list of men instrumental in developing the style that brought West Ham its second division championship. They represented a new approach to football, a sense of tactics and a 'thinking man's game'. Their type of football was a product of their own ingenuity, the willingness of their manager to let them experiment. It produced what Bernard Joy called 'West Ham's tradition of playing colourful football as a way of getting away from the drabness of life in the East End'. Behind the changes was the destruction by Hungary of the England side in 1953 and the blow to English pride. Even conservative managers and clubs were jolted into thinking there might be another way to play the game and West Ham had less to lose by experimenting than most clubs. Any changes that took place in the training regimen or the style of play would either be made by Fenton or at least would have to gain his approval.

West Ham prides itself on playing 'entertaining football', a description that is heard constantly from club officials, supporters and even journalists. Although it is difficult to establish what the term means, it is clear that it entered the West Ham vocabulary between 1953 and 1957. Until the mid-1950s West Ham was 'known as an old-fashioned club'. No one would have pointed to West Ham as a model for innovation and forward-looking ideas either on or off the field. Paynter's demand for 'character on the field as well as off', translated into avoiding excesses rather than creating something different. Real change at West Ham could only take place when the man at the top was replaced.

The supporters were, in many respects, the last to appreciate what happened on the pitch. In the afterglow of the praise enjoyed by West Ham it has been easy to say that the supporters were always interested in entertaining football, and victory was almost incidental. But, according to Dick Walker, during the early 1950s 'the idea of West Ham being more interested in football than in winning is rubbish: winning is what managers, players and supporters all want. The only difference is that West Ham wouldn't stand for winning by kicking people.' Upton Park crowds appreciated skill and wanted to see a well-played match but not at the cost of victory.

Dick Walker's career with West Ham marked a transition: he ended an era while his replacement, Malcolm Allison, heralded the new. There is still uncertainty about the extent of what happened, why it happened, and what role was played by the management. The manager or the board might not have had the foresight or the ability to create positive changes, but they could have put the kiss of death on anyone else's attempts to change things.

Reg Pratt JP, a local timber merchant with strongly conservative views on politics and social issues, and Ted Fenton, long-serving player at West Ham, seemed an unlikely pair to preside over what John Cartwright

West Ham United, 1952-53 season

describes as 'a form of communism at the club. The players really ruled it.' That is the strongest description of what happened at West Ham in the mid-1950s, but is not much different from other versions. Looking back 25 years after the event, Cartwright remembers that the club he joined as a boy gave the impression of being 'the modern set'. There was a 'West Ham run', a kind of arrogant strut started by Noel Cantwell and emulated by other players.[15] Most of all, there was a sense that something was happening. The players were thinking about the game and talking about it among themselves. Most of them are still convinced that they developed a new kind of football and that the supporters had little idea of what was happening. Supporters, for their part, talk with pride about the 'West Ham academy of soccer', which was graduating students before their very eyes. If the 'Academy' existed, the headmaster was Ted Fenton, but the school was being run by the 'head boy', Malcolm Allison. There remains tremendous disagreement about Allison's conduct and how Ted Fenton reacted to it, but no one denies that Allison was the focus of the changes.

Allison's version of what happened is direct and exhibits the lack of modesty and understatement associated with him. 'Paynter was there as a consultant, Fenton was the manager. Both of them had no idea what a professional football club was. They cared about winning, but didn't know anything.' Allison reached an unspoken agreement with Fenton which gave Allison the right to organize training. Although it was only his second year at the club he was 'already running a good share' of it. 'I just told them what to do. It was my determination and aggression that made other players fall into line and realize there was more to the game than they thought.' Many of the other players had strong personalities of their own and some were certainly more talented than Allison. Older players

Malcolm Allison brought enthusiam, an excellent knowledge of the game and an insatiable desire for success to West Ham when he joined the club in 1951

were not prepared to be bullied or convinced by an upstart, especially one who was talking about Continental tactics and having West Ham wear the silly little boots and kit that he had seen in Europe.

Allison got his opportunity because a new generation of players was coming through, who were willing to listen to almost anything that might lead to success. He could convince other players how badly he wanted success for them, as well as for himself. His confidence and enthusiasm were contagious. He was contemptuous in his rejection of almost everything at West Ham, from the kit, to the atmosphere, to the chairman, to the manager, but he had enough sense to keep his views within the confines of the club. Allison knew Fenton could sabotage what he was trying to do. 'I was going to make the club a success in spite of itself. I blanked out the board, the manager, everybody who might get in the way. [I was] not sure of what Fenton was doing, I think he kept out of the way.'

The classroom for the 'Academy' was the Cassatarri, a café round the corner from the ground where the players went each day. They talked mostly about football. The talks were not a break from the routine of training; they were an intensive football education. Allison claims, 'We were like any revolutionary group. We got excited and built up a good feeling...didn't think it was anything special, it was just right for us.' The players must have reacted positively because there was no compulsion for anyone to keep coming. O'Farrell marvelled at how unique it was to get a group together that wanted to talk about the game. The sessions created a strong sense of identity among the younger players. They took themselves and their football more seriously. They had different personalities, ranging from 'Dave Sexton, Jesuit-educated, who used to draw up quizzes for everybody, to John Dick, who would bet on anything'.[16] What held them together was their interest in football and being part of West Ham United.

The players who met at the Cassatarri did not come there by accident. Allison may believe that 'West Ham was nothing more than our name. The identity was wanting to be a success...There was nothing there for the players...no feeling in the club among the players. It wasn't a club.' But the players were not a random group brought together at some neutral site like the FA coaching clinics at Lilleshall. They were at an obscure café in the East End because they were West Ham players and they were at West Ham because Ted Fenton and his staff had brought them there. O'Farrell's version is that 'It mattered to us that we were part of West Ham. We had a sense of loyalty.' Allison and O'Farrell thought they were doing different things. O'Farrell was part of an organization made up of players and the club. Allison 'wanted success, wanted to win, wanted to be famous, to be good at what I'm doing'. The paradox in Allison's situation is that the only way he could achieve his personal success was in the context of a club that meant nothing to him, but which allowed and encouraged the kind of innovation he wanted.

No one feels more strongly about Allison's positive influence than John Cartwright. He was trained at night as a youth player by Allison and was flattered by the chance to learn with the senior professionals. 'Malcolm Allison should be revered. They should have a statue to him at West Ham...He laid the foundation for the success of the club, not by what he did on the field, but what he gave to other people.' Over the years, there has been little agreement among journalists, players or supporters about how much credit should be allotted to Allison or Fenton for the changes.

The value of what happened at the Cassatarri had to be shown on the field, which meant producing winning, as well as different, football. For the first few years reception of the new style was lukewarm at best. Much of what the players had created seemed strange. The way they played with the ball, especially at the back, made it appear as if they were trying to bait both their opponents and their supporters. These were not the solid, hard-working footballers that East Enders had come to expect. It would have been easy for the club and its manager to put a stop to the experimenting that was taking place at training and on the field and go back to basic football, thus avoiding any possibility of having the worst of both worlds – being unsuccessful and different at the same time.

The changes were initiated and fostered by the players, but the survival of the innovations must be ascribed to the leadership of the club. West Ham did not change its style and gain promotion 'in spite' of Fenton. Even Allison's back-handed remark: 'I could take over because they were so confused that any strong personality could' does not explain why the players were given the latitude to succeed. One journalist, a close observer of West Ham, contends that 'The players ran the club. Fenton probably never knew what they were doing, but he knew he shouldn't interfere with what was happening.' If that was meant as a criticism of the manager, it was tempered by the conclusion that 'Fenton had the good sense not to interfere.' That might be the best analysis of what the West Ham management was doing throughout the period of 'player power' – not getting in the way.[17] 'Anything was possible,' according to John Cartwright. 'I'm not sure why, but the board let us run things. Maybe they were afraid of us. Maybe it did have something to do with the changes, [although most of the] players had little or nothing to do with the board. Players were players, the board was the board.'

There was a significant change in the board-room that paralleled what was going on among the players. When Reg Pratt became chairman he made some attempt to understand the players. If nothing else, he did not have the same gruff demeanour as his predecessor. Some of the players felt they could talk to him about the club. According to Noel Cantwell, there was a 'change in outlook at the club...Pratt becoming chairman might have been what allowed more worker participation.' In any case, players started to give their views at meetings and the manager listened. 'We were a new generation of players coming along...We [had] a good relationship with Pratt...He was a very bad loser.' This might account for his willingness to allow the team to take chances, even when it appeared to slip out of the control of the manager. Many of the players agree that Pratt made a difference: he gave the impression he cared what was happening, both to the club and the players.

Fenton was the key to what was happening at West Ham in that he could have sabotaged the changes. According to Cantwell: 'He was a good manager with a fair knowledge of the game. Won't go down as one of the best managers West Ham had, but he could take credit for the rise. He scouted good young players. We needed him to guide more, but he *might* have realized that he had keen and dedicated players and let them have their way.' Fenton would argue points with players, and once in a while Allison or Moroney would show him why he was wrong. In any case, Fenton tried to convince the players. It is difficult to picture Charlie

Paynter involving himself in sessions like that, and even harder to imagine W. J. Cearns encouraging his manager to sit down to talk with the workers. Allison's opinion that Fenton 'was promoted out of his depth' is in keeping with his feeling that Fenton was, at best, 'a necessary annoyance'. But John Cartwright, who is a great admirer of Allison, has finally concluded that 'The manager was willing to let people do things.' O'Farrell looked back on the situation and concluded that 'When Malcolm is critical of Ted, I think it served to make us more self-reliant and turned us into managers...If we'd have had a strong manager, we wouldn't have blossomed the way we did. That's why so many of us succeeded. Maybe Malcolm knew things already, but I learned some of it from Fenton.'

Fenton's job was to produce a team that would represent the standards of the board and win matches. In those terms, he was a successful manager. The club gained promotion in 1958 along with a reputation for playing good football. Fenton's role in the development was both crucial and ambiguous: it might be described as passive encouragement. In that respect, he reflected the most conservative traditions of the board and the club.

One consistent feature about West Ham has been the way in which the board and chairmen have refrained from taking actions that would give the impression that they knew more about football than the manager or players. The board's tradition has been to do little even when supporters demanded changes. It is not surprising that Fenton, the manager raised within the West Ham system, should also have acted almost passively in a situation in which his players were doing part of his job for him, and probably doing it better than he could have done.

The changes at West Ham depended on the unique personalities and talents of its young playing staff. They had a leader who had no interest in coming close either to the manager or to the board, a man who left no doubt that he was concerned only for his fellow players. They had a manager who was secure enough in his job to let the players go their own way. They had a chairman who would not sabotage what was taking place among them. They were playing for a club that could afford to be different because West Ham United had very little to lose.

CHAPTER 8

Bring in the outsider

West Ham suited me. It wasn't slick or smart; it was honest and sincere.

Ron Greenwood, West Ham manager, 1961-77.

'What's Going On?' asked the headline on the sports page of the *Ilford Recorder* on 16 March 1961. The article featured a photo of Ted Fenton with a huge question mark in the background.[1] The size of the headline and the picture of Fenton were reminiscent of another article that had appeared less than three years earlier when the *Recorder* ran a special sports section. That picture of Fenton had been next to a headline proclaiming 'Division One Again – After 26 Years.' There were action photos of first-team players and another picture of Fenton sharing champagne with Vic Keeble and Ken Brown.[2] In 1961 no one was pictured with Fenton; he was alone on the sports page as he was soon to be at the club. The two articles represent the most dramatic points of Fenton's career as manager of West Ham United: the triumph of promotion and the blow of resignation.

In 1958 the *Recorder* went to great lengths to point out that promotion 'was a tribute to the long-sighted, imaginative policy adhered to by the men in charge of the club often in the face of fierce criticism...Ted Fenton was fortunate in having the backing of one of the youngest and smallest boards of directors in League football at Upton Park.'[3] What happened in the ensuing three years to end his career with West Ham? In modern football there is an obvious answer: managers are admired when they win, sacked when they lose. Few professions are as liable to the 'What have you done for me lately?' approach. But that does not seem to have been the cause of Fenton's resignation. The 1961 record of the team, finishing sixteenth in the first division, was only marginally worse than the previous year, when the club had finished in fourteenth place with two more points.

The high point of Fenton's career in the first division had been in 1959 when West Ham had finished sixth. After that, the team had not challenged the leaders and appeared to be moving backwards, but there had not been any serious complaints, either within the club or in the press, about how Fenton was doing his job.

The timing of Fenton's resignation and the probable cause are the most dramatic evidence of how West Ham directors ran the club. Managers often receive an inordinate amount of credit for a successful team and similarly attract blame when their team is doing less well. An American baseball manager summed it up: 'If I was a genius last season, how come I got so dumb so quick?' In Fenton's case, what happened to make him so wrong so fast?

Ironies abound in Fenton's managerial career at West Ham and none is stronger than the mystery surrounding his departure. The press had little to say about the details – a remarkable situation considering that he had been so much of a public figure ever since he arrived as Paynter's assistant in 1950. He had made a conscious effort to dispel the club's reputation as 'an unfashionable middle-of-the-table second division club not wanting promotion from second division security'. Fenton used West Ham's return to the first division as a springboard to increase his public presence. In 1960 he published a book, *At Home With the Hammers*, part autobiography, part West Ham folklore. The book was an example of what the great American sportswriter, Red Smith, labelled the 'gee whiz' school of sportswriting. The book did not contain a negative word about anyone or anything. But there was some substance to it and it offered interesting commentary on the future of West Ham. In the book Fenton made an effort to convince the reader that West Ham was the equal of any of the great clubs. This carries a note of special pleading, a sense of the poor boy made good trying to claim that he has always belonged with the elite.[4]   Fenton was effusive in his affection and admiration for Charlie Paynter. He owed a great debt to his manager and patron, but he probably found a model in the more flamboyant Syd King. When Fenton wrote about his respect for King's contribution to West Ham, he remarked that King was 'personality plus and adored by the players. He was the Herbert Chapman of his time'. Chapman, the hugely successful manager of Arsenal Football Club, revolutionized the game, while King was only a mildly successful manager of a fringe club with no claim to tactical innovations. What therefore was the basis of Fenton's remark? It must have been that King had thought in terms of putting West Ham on the football map. Chapman had accomplished this with Arsenal; he had established a tradition that saw the club through even when its performance on the field fell below standard. Fenton shared a feeling with many of his players that Arsenal was *the* London club. It 'was always something special' to go to Arsenal's ground at Highbury for a match. No one at West Ham would admit they wanted to copy Arsenal, but they certainly wanted to be like it.

It does not matter whether Fenton was being unrealistic or pretentious in his plans to make West Ham United another Arsenal. He thought he could change West Ham and he worked on that premise. He used a variety of methods to get publicity for West Ham. Each spring, Fenton would approach the board with a list of possible tours in Europe and matches that could be arranged with sides visiting England. He took it upon himself to make contacts and arrange matches. He became the most vocal advocate of a scheme by the directors to enlarge and improve the ground. He lobbied for this expenditure, claiming that it would both increase attendance and enhance the performance of the club. In his book he described the plans with the usual hyperbole: 'Our plans for Upton Park...want to make West Ham a glamour club and Upton Park London's jewel of the east...I want to make us so ritzy that we will get the kind of reputation Arsenal had in the 1930s.'[5]

Fenton could not have any player he needed or wanted. He had to find the 'best players available', and did not have the money to acquire the top players on the open market. As so often happened at West Ham, Fenton turned necessity into an asset by creating the scheme to develop young players. Opinions differ dramatically about how much West Ham had depended on local players before the mid-1950s. It is not a question that can be answered just by referring to the statistics. The memories of the supporters are very subjective. Peter Lorenzo, the sportswriter 'who was born about 200 yards from the ground' saw his first match in 1936: 'It always mattered that the majority of the playing staff was local...It gave you an affinity and you like to think it wasn't a chequebook club.' Jack Turner, who saw his first match in 1920 and worked at West Ham from 1950 to 1966, had completely different impressions. 'The "tradition of local players" never existed...The teams I watched as a young man were made up almost completely of imports. The club had more success finding players in Ireland than it had in West Ham.' Malcolm Allison's analysis is more succinct: 'The idea that it was built on local talent is bullshit. They never had anything...youth team or anything else until 1956. Even then they were copying Manchester United and Chelsea.'

Allison's assessment of West Ham's move into player development may be correct, but it is also self-serving, since it coincides with his role as a youth coach. The comparison with a great club like Manchester and an aggressive recruiting club like Chelsea was in character with Fenton's public pronouncements that he intended to build West Ham into a team capable of challenging the best. From the mid-1950s the management of West Ham began a concerted effort to scout, sign and develop young players, most of whom had their roots firmly based in the excellent schoolboy football that had been a hallmark of the East End and Essex for decades. An ambitious chairman, Pratt, and manager, Fenton, took control and used established players to help bring youth to football maturity.

The foundations of the West Ham development scheme were a scouting staff that covered the region, and Fenton's ability to make young prospects believe that West Ham would be the best place for them. The diligence and personality of the scouts gave West Ham an edge in the competition to sign local players. When the scouts identified

Wally St Pier, the West
Ham scout with the mem-
orable handshake and
principles to match,
holding the 1975 FA Cup
at his testimonial match

a likely prospect, they contacted the lad's teacher and then went to see
his parents. Fenton was brought into the process as soon as the scout
thought he had a serious prospect, and often went himself to see the
player and his parents, a direct indication of how much West Ham
wanted the boy. If the boy and his parents consented, he would come to
training at the ground where he would be introduced to some of the
'household names' like Allison, Cantwell and Brown.[6] This might be
followed by an invitation to a home match, where the parents would
often be in the directors' box, and have drinks afterwards with Pratt and
Fenton.

   Wally St Pier had more friends in the East End and was better known
in footballing circles than any member of the West Ham organization.
He had had a short playing career with West Ham, after which he was
retained to scout players and act as assistant trainer in the late 1930s.
When West Ham started to scout aggressively, this large, avuncular man
seemed to be everywhere. He cultivated schoolmasters and developed a
unique personality. Whereas other scouts seemed 'a bit sneaky or
shifty...Wally was an honest sort of guy'. Wally 'gave you the full

message. He was a gentleman.' St Pier almost 'became part of the [boy's] family'.[7] He could feel at home with people and give them that impression. His approach was simple: it was not his job to 'sell' West Ham, as much as to convince the player and his parents that the club wanted him. He even put West Ham's mediocre record to good use. It enabled him to tell a boy that there was a good chance of playing in the first team. When West Ham moved into the first division, St Pier pointed with pride to the club's success and the skill of the players in it.

There were two boys who got away and caused bruised feelings throughout much of the East End – Jimmy Greaves and Terry Venables. Both were great schoolboy players, and too many people, including West Ham officials, assumed they would come to Upton Park. Persistent rumours circulated about the inducements that led them to Chelsea. Venables's recollection is that 'Wally was like a smashing grandad...When I signed with Chelsea the only thing that bothered me was that Wally would be upset.'

The distinctive features of St Pier's approach were his handshake, 'quite famous, or infamous [for its power] if you like', and his transparent honesty. Teachers, parents and boys shared a faith in what he was telling them. But he could not promise anything – that was the province of the chairman and the manager. St Pier would probably have left a club that did not back him up, but Fenton and Pratt made good his word. When Fenton visited a player, in one case spending days parked up the street from his home, it meant that he wanted him badly. Failures in cases like Venables and Greaves might have led Fenton to adopt other tactics, but that would have destroyed the influence that St Pier had meticulously created within the footballing community of the East End. Straight dealing was the best policy for West Ham.

Even a cursory look at West Ham United after 1950 shows the significant changes that had taken place on and off the field. Promotion was the culmination of a long series of less obvious moves by the club: changes in personnel and tactics, the improvement of players' conditions, and the introduction of skill-oriented training. The youth scheme fed players into the first team; Ken Brown was one of the first to make his presence felt. The manager was either involved in all of these or at least gave his sanction and approval. Even during the 'players' revolution', changes had occurred in the responsibilities of the manager. Fenton was trying to emulate the success of other clubs within the West Ham tradition of operating on a shoestring and within the board's strict sense of propriety and control. He and Pratt were fighting the widely shared belief that the club was unambitious and wanted to avoid the perils of success and top-quality football.

Fenton made one very significant departure from the past. His stewardship at West Ham initiated a new role for the manager: his primary concern was to manage the men who played for him rather than just being concerned with their training and how they played on Saturdays. Fenton changed the manager's role, but did not attempt to alter the way in which the board operated the club. Nothing in Ted Fenton's career as manager of West Ham United is as significant for analysing the nature of the club as his departure: how and why it happened and its immediate consequences.

Fenton's last days at West Ham were in marked contrast to the way he had sought press coverage. The first public notice of anything happening was a report in the *Ilford Recorder* that Fenton had disappeared from the ground, and no one at the club was saying anything more than the prepared statement to the Press Association.[8] Three days before the *Recorder* story, the board had given its approval to the following statement by the chairman: 'For some time, Mr Fenton had been working under quite a strain and it was agreed that he should go on sick leave. For the time being, we shall carry on by making certain adjustments in our internal administration.'[9] The *Recorder* stated that there was no certainty if or when Fenton would return. Pratt added that the decision to take over the team 'was made after a great deal of thought'.[10]

A local reporter pointed out that he had seen Fenton on Monday, the day the board took its decision, and he 'had looked quite well', but Fenton had left the ground the following day after a meeting with Pratt. There had been a terse comment by the secretary that Fenton 'had been sent home on sick leave' and 'no further comment' from Pratt. The timing and the haste of the action puzzled both the reporter and his readers. It was known that Pratt had discussed the matter with the players, but none of them were talking. The *Recorder* concluded its article by reminding its readers that 'The Upton Park club are proud of their tradition of never having sacked a manager. The present position gives a distinct and undeniable impression that a compromise has been attempted to preserve that tradition.'[11]

Trevor Smith, the sports editor of the *Recorder*, was correct in pointing out that the club had traditions to protect, but not necessarily those to which he was referring. What was at stake was not the mythology of never having sacked a manager, but the reality of the club's being unsure whether or not the present manager was acting in accord with other traditions of West Ham.

The board was acting rather as it had in 1932 when Syd King had been replaced. King had been relieved of authority for reasons that had little to do with the performance of the club. He was unable to reform conduct which the board found objectionable. His suicide was so traumatic that everyone forgot that he had been sacked. In 1961, sick leave was used once again to buy time until matters could be settled in a fashion that would enable both sides to avoid publicity and give the impression of an amicable, if somewhat mysterious, parting of the ways. The board was interested in accomplishing two things: it wanted Fenton to leave, and it wanted to keep knowledge of what caused the break within the close family of the club. Fenton was prepared to let the matter drop and assume his role as an ex-manager with some grace. He left football for outside business and preferred the whole issue not to be brought up again. The board and its ex-employee were in agreement on at least one point: that there was no reason to enlighten the public on what had happened.

If the board 'gave a great deal of thought' to their decision about Fenton, they certainly kept their own counsel.[12] The manager had attended board meetings regularly until the one at which he was put on sick leave. Five weeks earlier he had submitted the retain and transfer list to the board, and in early February he was instructed to make arrangements for a visit to the ground by Inter-Milan and for a proposed tour of Israel. When he went on sick leave, everyone outside the club claimed to have been taken completely by surprise. Most of the board did not know that there were reasons to consider dismissing Fenton until the weekend before the Monday board meeting. The players seemed genuinely shocked by Fenton's dismissal and unaware of the reasons for it. They did not talk about it to the press after it happened. The public were also in the dark, for even writers who had established very close ties with the club had written nothing about a possible shake-up.

A year earlier, the *Ilford Recorder* had approached Fenton to write an article about why West Ham had dropped so quickly from first to ninth position in the table. Even someone with Fenton's nose for publicity had enough restraint to avoid the invitation, stating that 'he was too busy to give the matter his attention'. We can assume that 'the matter' was writing the article, not the decline of the team. The article was written by a staff reporter, who returned to a familiar theme: how could West Ham succeed on a shoe-string? The writer asked whether 'West Ham is seeking men of established repute, or are they persisting with the "empty-kitty" policy?' Maybe the team had been playing over its head, but 'only one man knows the answer AND THE MAN ON THE SPOT JUST NOW IS TED FENTON'.[13] Talk about Fenton disappeared over the following months while the papers concentrated on which players might be coming or going. By January 1961 the club was stuck near the bottom of the table, but there was no public talk about Fenton's departure. The big rumours were that John Bond might be leaving, as was Phil Woosnam, the Welsh International, who had been West Ham's most expensive purchase.[14]

The atmosphere in the offices and board-room at West Ham belied any long-term dissatisfaction with Fenton. There was no need to call an extraordinary meeting. This leads one to assume that Reg Pratt handled the matter on his own and then informed the other directors. Pratt had not involved himself in running the team, and the logical inference from the method of Fenton's removal and the role played by Pratt was that the manager violated sensibilities of the chairman that had nothing to do with the everyday operations of the club. A manager could survive failure on the field and even the unfavourable public reaction that might reflect on the directors, but he could not hold his position if the directors thought he was acting in violation of their standards. The worst offence against the club was doing something that gave the appearance of cutting corners or using the club as a vehicle for self-aggrandizement.

Less than a week after Fenton left West Ham, Pratt issued another statement to the press, in which he said that the board had no plans to name a manager and that no one was being considered at that time. The club 'would be managed by the board' with advice from Albert Walker (one of the trainers) and Phil Woosnam.[15] This statement was not completely inaccurate. The board was not talking to anyone specific, but Pratt and others had started to make enquiries about potential replacements for Fenton. There was no need to rush someone into the job before the end of the season. West Ham's lowly position was certain as was its survival in the first division. Fenton had put together the transfer-retain list, and the only major step for a new manager would be to recommend acquisitions. In any case, the board did not anticipate spending much money immediately.

Fenton's departure came less than two weeks before the AGM of the shareholders. The significance of the events of mid-March was clear at the AGM, for no manager was in attendance. The meeting attracted 15 shareholders, normal attendance for the past decade. The chairman, after making the financial report, summarized the season and gave the normal thank-you notices to the staff and players. There was not a word about the managerial situation: no comment on Fenton, the board's new role or possible successors. No questions were raised from the floor. It was almost as if nothing had happened.[16]

The way the board structured the job of Fenton's successor may throw some light on the reasons for his departure. On 13 April Ron Greenwood was named manager. The board announced to the press that Greenwood's job would be 'concerned solely with coaching and training'. All administrative work would be in the hands of Eddie Chapman, the secretary, and his staff. The latter would also take care of all public relations for the club.[17]

From the moment Ron Greenwood appeared at the club he became a subject of controversy. Before he had done anything, he was already the centre of a revolutionary change; he was the first important figure in the West Ham hierarchy ever to be brought in without having any ties to the club. Thirteen years later, he still described himself as 'the new boy around here'. Over-statement and self-deprecation are not part of Greenwood's normal conversation; his description shows that he understood how he was perceived by people who identified strongly with the club.

WEST HAM UNITED F.C.
Formed in 1900

Football League (Div. II): Winners 1957-58 Runners-up 1922-23
F.A. Cup: Finalists 1922-23 Semi-Finalists: 1922-23 1932-33
Football League War Cup: Winners 1939-40
F.A. Youth Cup: Finalists 1956-57 1958-59 Semi-Finalists 1952-53

BOLEYN GROUND, GREEN STREET, UPTON PARK, LONDON, E.13

Directors:
R. H. PRATT, J.P. (*Chairman*)
L. C. CEARNS (*Vice-Chairman*)   W. F. CEARNS   R. G. BRANDON
Manager - Coach: R. GREENWOOD   *Secretary*: E. CHAPMAN
Medical Officer: DR. J. C. BELL, M.B., Ch.B.
Honorary Consultant: W. ALEXANDER LAW, Esq., O.B.E., M.D., F.R.C.S.

Nearing the Finish . . .

Our last but one home match of the 1960-61 season brings the players
and officials of the Manchester City club to Upton Park, and we again
extend to them a hearty welcome.

The City are not at present in a very happy position, and a declara-
tion by their chairman last week-end highlighted the disappointment which
has resulted from the situations in which they have found themselves
during the past three seasons. The purchase of players amounting to
over £100,000 in under two years has not halted the decline, and although
a victory over Chelsea last Saturday eased the tension, points are still
required in order to safeguard their First Division membership for another
year.

The task awaiting the Maine Road club here today is not made any
easier by the fact that they are deprived of the services of " star " inside-
forward Denis Law who is playing for Scotland at Wembley this afternoon.

Law made his City debut against us just over twelve months ago at
Maine Road, scoring one of their three second-half goals after we had
held a single-goal interval lead. We had earlier beaten the Blues here by
4—1, and on the occasion of our visit to their enclosure last November
secured our only away victory to date in the current campaign.

We shall, of course, be hoping to complete our first 1960-61 " double "
this afternoon, especially as we can also do with extra points to safeguard
our own status. Naturally we shall be just as keen to send the Mancunians
home empty-handed as they will be to annex the spoils, but whatever may
be the outcome we hope that the game will be of a higher standard than
we have seen here of late, despite the fact that " near relegation " duels
are notorious for " desperation rather than soccer."

Part of the program for Ron Greenwood's first match as manager of West Ham,
April 1961

Ron Greenwood

We are pleased to announce the appointment last Tuesday of Mr. Ron Greenwood as our Manager - Coach and know that he will carry with him the best wishes of all Hammers' fans and his many other friends in soccer.

Ron Greenwood needs little introduction to Londoners, for until a few days ago he was Assistant Manager to Arsenal F.C. In addition, he has played for three other London clubs—Brentford, Chelsea and Fulham—as well as for Bradford (Park Avenue)

RON GREENWOOD
Photo: Ilford Recorder

When still playing as a centre-half Ron qualified as an F.A. coach, and upon retiring from League soccer became manager of Eastbourne United in the Metropolitan League ; during his spell at Princes Park he was also appointed manager of the England Youth Team in September 1957. His immediate success brought him an offer from Arsenal, and three months later he became chief coach at Highbury. Within twelve months Ron's status was raised to that of Assistant Manager, and when Billy Nicholson gave up the position of Manager to the England Under-23 Team (to take his present job at Tottenham) Ron succeeded him there.

In both these national team appointments and on several F.A. coaching courses Ron has become acquainted with West Ham United players, so he is no stranger to the Hammers' playing-staff while our administrative side of course knows him very well.

Therefore it was not as a stranger that we approached Ron with a view to him becoming our Manager - Coach, and we are very pleased to record our thanks to those who assisted us in doing so, especially to Arsenal F.C. who readily released Ron to take this appointment. We feel sure that this step will be to mutual advantage.

Ron will be solely in charge of the playing-staff and will be freed of administrative duties in order to give him full scope in that direction. This entails certain internal administration adjustments, and as a result our Secretary, Eddie Chapman, will now deal with the whole of this part of our set-up.

EDDIE CHAPMAN

The decision to employ Greenwood was accomplished quickly, but it was not a snap judgment by Pratt. The board was making a statement about how it wanted the club to develop. Greenwood's qualities and beliefs coincided with the new direction the board wanted to take. The appointment surprised most of the supporters but came as less of a shock to the leading players or close observers of the club. West Ham was in transition. No one already there could step into the position, and none of its former players was a likely candidate.[18]

Greenwood's strong point was his consuming interest in the tactical side of football. His work as a coach at Oxford University and Arsenal fitted the recent changes at West Ham. Trends in football enabled West Ham to portray Greenwood and the club as the cutting edge of the future of the game. There was a feeling among the players that Greenwood had been advocating the same things at Arsenal as they had developed on their own; now that he was boss, he could put his plans into action with a willing crew of players behind him. John Cartwright described the situation: 'We needed somebody to conduct the orchestra...but unfortunately I didn't stay long enough to be conducted.' Cantwell saw Greenwood as the hope for a new future at West Ham, and Ken Brown goes even further, claiming that if Greenwood 'hadn't come, we would have been relegated'. Brown was not the only player to feel that Fenton had taken them as far as he could: Greenwood would give them the next boost. He 'knew we were fit; so he gave us the chance to play with the ball'. Malcolm Allison had left the club some years before, and had seen little to praise since then. He viewed Greenwood's appointment favourably; Greenwood brought good ideas and a concept of good football to West Ham, 'when the drive and fire was already there in the players'.

Pratt and his colleagues undoubtedly thought of Greenwood as someone who would build a solid football operation on the existing foundation. But they also saw something more in him: a manager who was interested only in the footballing side of his work, who would not detract from how the directors wanted to see the club. Pratt approached Greenwood on the basis of his reputation as a coach. He told Greenwood that West Ham had some very good young players, and said that he wanted someone to mould them into an aggressive, attractive, winning side. He gave no reasons for Fenton's departure.[19] Greenwood insisted on control over the football side of the club, which meant a free hand with preparations for matches as well as training and control of the players. He also obtained a commitment from Pratt that West Ham would go into the transfer market. The purchase the following season of Johnny Byrne for £65,000 from a fourth division club showed Greenwood that he could take the chairman at his word and show the rest of the football world that a real change had occurred at West Ham.

According to Greenwood, when he first arrived he 'didn't know anything about West Ham, either as a boy or as a player'. It did not take him very long to decide that he liked West Ham and the people around the club. 'It suited me. It wasn't slick, smart, it was honest and sincere. I felt a part of it...It became my cup of tea, since I'd been brought up in the north...and was a victim of good manners.'

If Greenwood felt at ease with the club, he was not comfortable with the supporters and the people who surrounded it. Fifteen years later, he reflected on his lack of empathy with many of them: 'The club is un-Londonish, although the spectators are not. They want the club to be as ruthless as any other, to spend money and sack people. They just have no knowledge of what really goes on at the club.' He pointed out the difference between the people who were part of the club, whose 'strong point was a sense of respect for one another', and the supporters who lacked that quality almost completely. 'Football is a reflection of life...unfortunately, there's a lack of respect in life in general and that all shows up in football.' He never tried to address the paradox of how the club could operate with a set of standards that, by his own reckoning, were out of touch with the rest of football.

Greenwood's sensibilities were occasionally offended by what he thought he saw in East London. Even though the area had always been poor, it had also been

an area of swaggerers...They would love somebody like Allison...They don't understand sincerity and intelligence. This community and this area doesn't understand or appreciate anything that this club stands for. Put this club in another area and the appreciation would be tremendous...People just don't have the same standards or respect...They just want to be the biggest and the best and to boast...Success at a club like this is frightening. It would attract a lot of the wrong people, the kind of people who will disappear as soon as you're not at the top any longer.

He was incorrect in his assessment of the relationship between Allison and the crowd. Despite his talents and role in remaking the club, Allison had never been popular precisely because of his swagger and intensity. Greenwood's harsh assessment of West Ham supporters runs counter to most other interpretations of them. He may have spoken with an outsider's objectivity, but on the other hand may have been unwilling or unable to deal with an alien, insular community that did not go out of its way to accept him. Despite Greenwood's scathing remarks about *some* West Ham followers, he readily admits that the aspects of the club he respects so much could not exist in a vacuum. The link between the club and its surroundings 'is there for all to see' and he admitted that 'the uniqueness of the club' was a product of its setting in its community.

Greenwood was hired for his talent as a football technician on the assumption that he had the kind of character that would fit in. When he got his name in the papers it was in response to questions about players and results. The board did not bring him in to 'win at all costs'. He was supposed to build on what the board felt was a solid foundation of young players and a tradition, albeit a recent one, of quality play on the field. There is no reason to think that the board ever asked Greenwood's opinion of the supporters; the issue was irrelevant. No one had any reason to ask him what he felt about West Ham's fans, and he certainly had no reason to volunteer his views on the subject. Public relations was not his job and public pronouncements were not part of the way he operated as manager.

When supporters think of managers it is usually in terms of the success of the club. There is little else upon which to judge them. West Ham had been different in this respect because its pre-Greenwood managers had been with the club for so long in some capacity that supporters could identify with them. The manager at West Ham was something much more than a transitory employee. Greenwood's employment changed all those perceptions. He was not 'an old boy', and he made no attempt to add affectations that would give the impression that he was part of West Ham tradition. For someone who tried to avoid publicity and keep his personality out of the way, however, Greenwood raised strong feelings from the moment he arrived. He was not only an outsider, but an Arsenal man. There were warm personal relations between Pratt and the Arsenal board and it was no surprise that he looked towards Highbury when choosing a manager. Pratt and his colleagues saw Arsenal as a well-run club with a sense of tradition and an unwillingness to cut corners. Many supporters viewed it as a domineering, aloof club that had bought its way to success and enjoyed lording it over its London rivals. The attitude of these supporters to Greenwood might be summed up as follows: 'We didn't think very much of him, and since he came from Arsenal he was off to a bad start already.'[20]

There was no reason for supporters to know anything about what Greenwood thought of them, or what he felt about anything other than football: the public view of the man was that he spent all his time thinking about the game. It was the only side of his personality he was willing to show to press or public. Concentrating on football and avoiding public display and controversy was as natural to him as courting publicity was to Ted Fenton. Greenwood's public face was a combination of an outsider's uncertainty, dedication to his job, and a sense of aloofness.

Greenwood was just as quiet in the years of triumph as he was in the early years when he was building the club that won the FA Cup in 1964. Allison and Greenwood, the men who brought a unique style to West Ham, both thought the spectators were irrelevant, especially those who came late to enjoy success. Trevor Smith summed it up: 'Ron Greenwood has never been the most popular man in the East End. He hasn't worked at it...Somehow he gives the impression that he's talking down to you.' The only contact between supporters and the manager, at least in the days before television analysts, was through the newspapers. The zeal with which Greenwood protected his privacy from the press reinforced the impression that he held the public in disdain, which in turn reinforced the public's view of him as an outsider.

West Ham supporters are like those at other clubs: their feelings about the manager are influenced by how well the club is performing. West Ham's past had been so mediocre that winning anything was still a novelty when Greenwood arrived. He might feel strongly that all the supporters cared about was winning, but they had developed some sense of pride in the way their club played. Greenwood took that part of their feelings for granted. By the end of his second season in 1963 many supporters had come to believe there was something special about the team and to expect, even demand, winning matches as well as good performances. The FA Cup victory in 1964 cast a new light on what supporters expected and what Greenwood thought about them. Success was not impossible for West Ham; why should the supporters be expected to settle for mediocrity?

The events of 1966 were a triumph for and a test of West Ham. Even though the club remained in the middle of the table it contributed three of the star players to the World-Cup-winning England side. The drama was greater because England's captain was West Ham's 'Golden Boy', Bobby Moore, and all the goals in the final match were scored by Hammers: Geoff Hurst and Martin Peters. West Ham's contribution towards winning the World Cup was a source of personal, patriotic and professional pleasure to Greenwood. The aftermath, however, reinforced his ideas about the shallow nature of many supporters and the dangerous trends that were taking place in football. His reaction to the exuberance that greeted his team was to draw back even further from the public and give the impression of total immersion in his world of training and tactics. His conduct violated the expectations that East Enders had of their manager. He was the leader of a club, *their* club, and they wanted him to show in public that they were together in something that was important to both of them.

Greenwood's approach both to the game and to the club changed little over his years with West Ham. This was no surprise to the men who employed him. Greenwood was what Reg Pratt and his fellow directors wanted, and they stayed with him because he was consistent. Pratt wanted somebody who would teach good football, bring victories and set standards. The manager had to be able to work within the structure at West Ham, to realize that money did not grow on trees and that the directors would not stand for being embarrassed.

The hiring of Greenwood was the most significant event of Reg Pratt's long tenure as chairman and represented his view of how the club operated and what standards it should represent. The event cannot be uncoupled from Ted Fenton's departure, and bringing in an outsider as manager was an open admission by the board that they had not carried out their stewardship as well as they might. They had been forced to go against the traditions of the club.

West Ham tried to ignore the modern tendency to concentrate on good public relations at a time when its first-division rivals, especially those in London, were courting publicity. The club's appointment of its first outside manager, especially one with an Arsenal and Oxford background, was a PR man's dream. But the club did absolutely nothing to capitalize on it. At many clubs, such an event would have given the chairman the chance to see his name in print as often as possible, but it was just the opposite at West Ham. Rather than replace the manager in the glare of publicity, Reg Pratt avoided the limelight. Greenwood was brought in to coach and manage the men. That was all. The arrangement suited Greenwood well. The public may have seen him as aloof, and some of the press might have preferred a manager who was better 'copy', but Greenwood was living up to both his own standards and the conduct that the board expected from 'the new boy at Upton Park'.

CHAPTER 9
The boys in the back room

The 'Bad Debt' is a defalcation by the late Secretary, Alan Searles.

Chairman speaking at the Annual General Meeting, 1940.

West Ham players get the glory on the field, managers get publicity for their decisions and directors get applause or brickbats for their stewardship over the club, but much of the work necessary to maintain the club on an even keel has been done by the staff – in Bernard Joy's phrase, 'the back room boys who have been there a long time'.

The 'back-room' activities have been carried out by the secretary, his assistants, the scouts, and the 'property manager'. It would be simple to draw up an organizational chart for West Ham, but it would not show how the club actually operates. It would ignore the blurring of distinctions between jobs and would not account for the way individual men have stamped their personalities on their jobs. West Ham has seldom looked for paper qualifications: specific men were hired to do specific jobs. Most of them grew up around the club and understood what they were supposed to do. Disputes between staff members were seldom a major issue.

The board took over the books after Syd King was suspended in 1931. New procedures were established to ensure that no club official could spend a significant amount of money without a counter-signature from the chairman or a designated member of the board.[1] The secretary's job had become more complicated as the club's stature had increased. The board used the dismissal of King as an opportunity to employ someone to do the administrative work and ensure that the chairman was not responsible for overseeing everyday activities. A full-time secretary also showed that West Ham was more than a minor London club.

The new secretary, Alan Searles, took control of the administration of the club, freeing Paynter to concentrate on the football. Searles had the confidence of the chairman; by 1934 he was supervising the ordinary expenditures of the club. Each year he got a bonus of £50, half of what Paynter received. Searles's ability to work without direct supervision made him useful to the chairman.

Searles's position with the board was very solid. In 1939 his wage was raised to £10 per week and his bonus went from £50 to £75, while

F. R. Pratt, director of West Ham
United from 1924 to 1941 and father
of R. H. (Reg) Pratt.

Paynter's remained £100.[2] Searles attended the AGM, and it became
part of the yearly ritual to express a vote of thanks to him. Besides that,
he received little attention; his job was handling details, not being a
public personality. In 1940, however, this changed. Searles was the most
important person at that year's AGM, even though he was not there. The
chairman's report on the balance sheet dealt with him:

> My first duty is an unpleasant one and that is to explain to you that the
> amount shown in the revenue account as a 'Bad Debt' is a defalcation by
> the late secretary. The directors have considered the 19 years honest service
> given by him prior to this occurring and decided not to prosecute, and ask
> for your confirmation of their action in this matter. There is also an amount
> of approximately £100 since the end of the period under review and your
> board proposes to treat this amount in this year's account in a similar
> manner.[3]

That was the last heard of Alan Searles at West Ham; there was no
mention of him after his dismissal. Both Searles and King had abused
the trust of the board, and in both cases financial peculations had been
involved, but Searles had been involved in criminal activities. In both
instances, the club handled the situation with as little publicity and
delay as possible.

Searles's part-time assistant was a teenager, Eddie Chapman.
Chapman played for Ilford boys and one prominent football
correspondent declared that he was positive that Chapman would some
day play for England. When West Ham offered him a contract
Chapman's father withheld his consent unless the club promised to allow
Eddie to work in the office rather than on the groundstaff. The elder
Chapman was afraid that even if his son had a successful career in
football he would not be prepared for work after it. On 17 August 1937,
'Strange and Chapman were engaged for the ground and office staff at a
wage of £1 5s 0d per week.'[4] Chapman was instructed by Searles in
normal office routine and came into the office before hours to learn

typing and bookkeeping. Despite, or perhaps because of, his forethought, Chapman never had a job away from West Ham. His tenure at West Ham spans almost 50 years.

When Searles left, the board tried to get an auditor/accountant to replace him. When their choice declined, the chairman appointed Paynter as secretary *pro tem* and Chapman as his assistant. The bank was informed that 'in the future cheques would be signed by two directors only'. This ensured that the financial dealings of the club did not burden the part-time administrators. Chapman's name appeared in the minutes on occasion, but not in connection with his duties as assistant secretary. In January 1942 he received special mention for scoring a goal in a first-team match and in September that year he was registered as a professional by the Football Association and League. He received a signing-on fee of £10 and continued to work with Paynter.[5] One of the women employed in the office, Edith Wilson, gave another meaning to the term 'family club'. She and Chapman were married in 1943, and she took over many of his duties when he joined the Forces.

During the war Paynter's duties were varied and unpredictable. He had to select a team and then get players to the match. He could count on assistance from Frank Cearns, an employee of W. J. Cearns Ltd. Frank, a book-keeper and company secretary, was well qualified to handle those aspects of his job that Paynter liked least. Cearns's other qualifications should be apparent from his name and his place of employment: he could be trusted to be honest and to have the interests of West Ham at heart. Paynter would not have accepted an outsider crashing into his domain. Paynter and Frank Cearns developed a good working partnership and the club benefited from an arrangement that cost it nothing.

'Paynter wasn't cut out to be a secretary,' as Chapman put it. He 'did it, but never liked it'. Unsurprisingly, Paynter stopped being secretary as soon as possible. In November 1946 the board stated that, 'in view of relieving Mr Paynter of secretary's duties so he could devote more time to players and team matters', the appointment of Frank Cearns was approved at a salary of £500 per annum. When Paynter had been appointed manager, some directors had been apprehensive about taking him away from his role as trainer; this time the board was unanimous in wanting him to devote all his time to the job that he did best.[6]

Two months after Frank Cearns became secretary, he got some experienced help. Eddie Chapman was demobbed and signed on as a player. He combined this job with the assistant secretaryship for a decade. It is easy to look at Chapman's career at West Ham and see it as an obvious progression: that he was in training to be secretary and would take over from Searles, Paynter or Cearns. It did not look like that to Chapman. When he returned in 1947 he was a player who happened to work in the office, not a 'back-room boy' who put in time on the pitch.

Eddie Chapman had a long and distinguished career with West Ham, serving the club for 49 years. Left: as a young player; right: as secretary and chief executive

Chapman was responsible for anything that the secretary wanted him to do. Cearns tried to make his relationship with his young assistant as informal as possible. 'Don't call me Mr Cearns,' he instructed, but it did not seem natural to Chapman to be on first-name terms with an older man who was the boss and a confidant of the directors.

There were difficult moments for Chapman, as he had ties with different parts of the organization. The relationship between Paynter and Cearns made Chapman's situation easier, but the office involved matters that affected players. Shortly after the start of the 1950 season Chapman approached the new chairman, Reg Pratt, with questions about his own prospects. He was upset with his wages as a player and unsure if he had much of a future with the club. There was no talk of a transfer. Normally, Pratt only talked to a player after the matter had been discussed with the manager, but in this case the manager stepped aside and Pratt handled the matter directly. The discussion between Chapman and Pratt involved unusual considerations – Chapman's multiple jobs with West Ham. After 'taking into consideration his position as a footballer and his work in the office, it was agreed to increase his salary by £1 to £10 per week, backdated to the start of the season'. The situation would be reviewed again at the end of the season.[7] Chapman was earning a wage equivalent to that of a veteran player who contributed regularly to the first team. He qualified as a veteran, but he was a reserve performer. He could still play a role, but is the first to admit that his best years as a player had been left behind during the war. His wage increase was not granted on the basis of his performance or potential as a player. It is a safe assumption that Pratt did not see Chapman's future 'position with the club' as being an inside forward.

Chapman continued as a player and collected another £300 benefit in 1955. He had sat in for Frank Cearns at board meetings when the secretary could not attend and no one seemed upset to have a player in the board-room. Chapman was given more responsibility for dealing with facilities and handling staff and wage arrangements. When Frank Cearns retired in 1956 there was no need to search for a successor: Chapman played his last match in May 1956 and on 1 August he was named secretary.[8] It was unusual for a club secretary to be an ex-player, unheard of for him to step out of the ranks into this important administrative post. For the first time since he had come to West Ham, Eddie Chapman was serving only one side of the club. He had learned the mechanics of the job along the way and had developed the ability to be discreet. There had been times when fellow players wanted to know what was happening 'upstairs', as well as instances when directors were curious about what was going on among the players.

Much of Chapman's work involved handling the everyday problems of a company. But this company was in the public eye and had unusual problems. Chapman was useful for journalists looking for 'human interest' stories about the club. How many other secretaries could they ask about what might be running through a player's mind? However, Chapman appeared in the press very seldom during his first few years as secretary, and when he did appear it was usually because another club official was reluctant to deal with the press or because something had taken place off the field that had to be explained to the public.

Ted Fenton was capable and willing to be the club's spokesman. Reg Pratt tried to keep out of the papers. This reflected his dislike of people, including directors or managers, who wanted to become celebrities by associating themselves with football. He was willing to discuss matters like the ground improvements and how the club intended to compete in the first division. He did not shrink from confrontation, especially when he felt West Ham was being singled out for unfair criticism. Pratt had a hot temper and did not want to display anger in public. He found it difficult not to reply to criticism of the club or its directors. Chapman as secretary took on part of the chairman's role in this area. When a bottle was thrown during a match against Leeds United, one newspaper called West Ham supporters the worst crowd in London. Chapman responded that West Ham should not be judged by the actions of one person in a crowd of 28,000. 'By and large, the Upton Park patrons are a pretty fair crowd. They appreciate football and are not slow to applaud football, whoever plays it'. He remembered that 'during those painful years before the promotion season' the crowds were usually more critical of the home team than they were of a visiting side.

Chapman had hoped to end the discussion of the bottle throwing as soon as possible, but two weeks later he was only too pleased to revive it. He released a letter to the press signed 'Miserable Ex-Hammer' from a 60-year-old man who had thrown the bottle. He had contacted the victim and asked if he needed financial help as a result of the injury. The offence had been caused 'by a split second of craziness' when the goalkeeper had kicked a West Ham player. He concluded the confession with a poignant note: 'Mr Chapman, this is the end of watching football for me at Upton Park, but I wish the club every success. I cannot sign my name. I am not a yellow belly, but I am still scared.'[9] Chapman wanted the letter to put the episode to rest. The throwing of the bottle was an outrage at the time, but it seems a tame and isolated incident compared to events that have become almost commonplace at football matches in the 1980s. Two months later, Chapman's 'broad smile' was described in the *Ilford Recorder* when the *News Chronicle* named the West Ham crowd 'at the top of the first division and on top of the country'.[10]

Promotion to the first division brought great changes to Chapman's duties as secretary. There was much more correspondence to handle and pressmen found their way to Upton Park. Attention was focused on the manager and players, but the secretary was responsible for helping the press to get their work done. Early in his job as secretary, Chapman understood that 'the press knows who to contact. We're employed by the board to run the club. We know how to answer the press and we're not about to say to a reporter "You'd better phone up the chairman".'

That is Chapman's attitude to his job. He is there to do what the board wants done, but he does not have to be told what that is in most instances. 'West Ham runs the way it does because the board wants to leave it to the secretary and the manager to be the spokesmen.' Chapman's freedom of action and ability to 'make commitments in the name of the board' arose from the trust lodged in him by Reg Pratt. Before Pratt talked to the press on any issue of substance he informed Chapman and the manager of what he intended to say. Pratt might ask for ideas or suggestions, but the final decision was his. The staff were unlikely to be caught by surprise and were able to cope with complex questions.

When Ron Greenwood took over as manager he had as little as possible to do with the press. Questions other than those dealing directly with performance were referred to Chapman. Since the secretary would not comment on players, journalists had to depend on their own insights and imagination to describe what was happening. This may have made for more exciting copy, but it did not give the club the chance to shape its public image. Greenwood was more cautious of the press than contemptuous; his team would do his talking for him. Transfers and possible moves always interest reporters, being one of the few areas of football journalism that might produce a 'scoop'. Greenwood would not talk about them.

The Greenwood-Chapman relationship in the early years consisted of the manager doing things his own way and the secretary pointing out to him how the system had worked previously at West Ham. Chapman could 'say how we have been doing things around here', but no more than that. It was up to Greenwood to decide how he wanted to tailor his actions to fit the club and how much he wanted to alter the traditional approach. During Greenwood's first two years as manager he did not handle transfer negotiations personally. After he had decided on a player that he wanted, Chapman would negotiate the price and the final details of the transaction. When Greenwood took over control of transfer arrangements there was no opposition from Chapman. Greenwood was doing what the chairman wanted, and anyway, West Ham had never formalized a division of responsibilities. For most of the club's history, the same men had handled the players and administration. The physical arrangement of the offices at West Ham encouraged co-operation between manager and secretary. Only a few feet separated their offices, and each knew who was going in and out. Greenwood and Chapman had assumed their positions within a couple of years of one another, and that made co-operation easier.

The secretary's job demanded attention to detail. He attended the board meetings, provided accurate minutes, and drew up the agenda. He supervised wages and the office staff. He put contracts out for tender and reported the offers to the board for action. Chapman had to establish personal links with other football club secretaries. The social dimension of football remains unnoticed by the vast majority of people who attend matches, but tickets for directors and their guests, for players' friends and other teams' representatives are a᷉ necessary part of the arrangements. The pre-match, half-time and post-match receptions maintain the old traditions of civility and sportsmanship between the clubs. Chapman took care of a myriad of small matters to do with the FA and the League, including requests for fixture dates, hospitality for and grading of referees, the purchase of tickets for international matches, and the dissemination of new regulations and proposals.

Promotion brought Chapman into the public eye. Until that time, the club had never been able to sell its quota of season tickets. Suddenly it was necessary to set up a waiting list. Hammers' supporters were affluent enough to pay for a guaranteed good seat for matches. Many of them had to travel so far that they didn't want to risk having to watch the match from an uncomfortable or awkward position. The traditions of walking to the match and being part of the terraces gave way to the new realities of prosperity and comfort. Getting to the top of the list 'might have been the proudest moment of my life...I never thought I would ever afford something like that when I was a lad,' said Johnny Speight, the creator of West Ham's most famous fictional supporter, Alf Garnett. Season tickets were coveted and the system made even a celebrity wait his turn.

Whenever the fairness of West Ham's policies was questioned, Chapman was the man to answer. The construction of the new stand eased the pressure for season tickets for a short time, but another waiting list was necessary in less than two years. The success at Wembley in 1964 and the 'World Cup trio' of Moore, Hurst and Peters brought new notice to the club and more ticket problems for Chapman. The number of season tickets sold had to be compiled with an eye to the public image of the club. Nothing could hurt that more than a feeling that West Ham did not have match-day tickets, or that people could jump the queue for season tickets.

Supporters could wait for season tickets, but Cup tickets were a very different matter. West Ham's dismal Cup record (it reached the final eight once between 1934 and 1962) did not prepare the secretary for the onslaught that took place in 1963 when the club got into the quarter-finals, and that was only a pale rehearsal for the following season when the club returned to Wembley for the first time since 1923. Chapman was caught up in the euphoria of the Cup run, but he had more serious matters to handle. West Ham could have sold enough tickets to fill the stadiums for both the semi-final and the final. Season-ticket holders were entitled to first chance at tickets, but provision had to be made for other supporters. On the Monday after the semi-final, Chapman's telephone never stopped ringing; hundreds of letters arrived. Chapman could have created a whole new past for himself just from the 'old friends' who suddenly appeared. There were supposed former players and their relatives, supporters who claimed to have seen every match for almost 70 years, as well as the dying and crippled who would be cured by the miracle of a pilgrimage to Wembley. The chairman insisted that West Ham should not be allowed to look mercenary or uncaring for its long-time, and long-suffering, supporters. Chapman organized a lottery based on the programme coupons for earlier matches. The club wanted some evidence of previous support to give such people the chance to be at Wembley. The system was not unique to West Ham, but Chapman operated it so that complaints were few. Even the local press commented on the fairness and efficiency with which he had handled the crush of success.

Chapman has tried not to make himself much of a public figure. An appearance by him often meant that something had gone wrong, but occasionally he was the public bearer of good news such as the plans to cover the north bank, or the availability of additional season tickets. He had a direct impact on many supporters through his ability to influence the chairman and the board. He oversaw or implemented ticket policies, ground remodelling, catering provisions, advertising and the relationship with supporter groups. In many cases the policies originated with him. Reg Pratt listened carefully to Chapman's suggestions and regarded him as much more than a glorified clerk. Chapman looked after the non-playing interests of the club on a daily basis and represented the stability and the past of West Ham. He was the quintessential clubman, the back-room equivalent of the long-serving player who grows up in the nursery of a club and then serves it throughout his playing days.

Chapman's background made it easy for him to deal with the other staff. He had shared the experiences of the trainers and coaches, and literally 'spoke the same language as they did'. It is difficult to think of an aspect of West Ham United with which Chapman has not been concerned personally. His knowledge of the sport and club combined with his close relationship with Reg Pratt turned the job of secretary into something closer to managing director. His long tenure is consistent with the stable image West Ham likes to project.

It sounds incongruous in an age of million-pound transfers, but many of the essential services at West Ham have been provided by volunteers. The practice had its roots in the Thames Ironworks Club and the relative poverty of West Ham United as a professional club. Stilemen, stewards, match-day office workers and pools operators have all been volunteers. It is easy to understand why the club would want to avoid paying people to do routine work if they were dependable, willing and trustworthy, but why should these people want to do something for the club without getting paid? One perceptive explanation comes from Jack Helliar, the third generation of his family to have an 'honorary job...which was a fancy way of saying you didn't get paid'. Neither his grandfather nor his father gave a second thought to doing a job without pay. It was 'recognized that you carried on and did jobs for the club...There was always somebody around doing it. There was never any sense that any of the work was demeaning...It meant that you weren't just a spectator.'

The Helliars were different from other 'honorary' workers because they also had a business relationship with the club. The Helliar firm was the club's printer from 1902 to 1983, but their sentiments were much the same as those of any supporter. Jack Helliar is convinced that it meant a great deal to his father to be a steward. 'He wasn't just Samuel Helliar, the printer for West Ham. He was part of the club.' Jack Helliar's grandfather had been a brass founder at the Thames Ironworks and was on the original committee of the club that became West Ham United. When he set up as a printer in 1902 one of his first accounts was West Ham United. He had recommended George Handley for membership on the board, but there was never any question of Helliar's joining that body. 'It's never been a question down there at Upton Park of standing for the board. It's always been by invitation.' He was a tradesman, a supplier to the club, definitely not board material. Besides his work as a printer, he became a kind of general factotum for the committee, doing odd jobs. Unlike most volunteers, Helliar received some publicity for his efforts when, on 24 April 1903, he paid a fine in court for having sold lottery tickets to raise money for West Ham United.

Jack Helliar has been a regular figure at West Ham United for his whole adult life – much more than just the printer who produced the programme and tickets for the club. In the late 1940s Ted Hufton, the former goalkeeper, looked after the press bar. The small room down the hall where reporters phoned in their match reports and picked up the material for their stories was extremely important to the club. It needed the publicity that it received *gratis* from the press. When Hufton felt he could no longer carry out his duties in the press room, Helliar was asked by the chairman, 'Would you like to look after the press room?' That informal approach is a trademark of operations at the club, but it should not be confused with sloppiness. Helliar had all the qualifications needed to do the job. He knew what was happening at West Ham United, he knew what interested the press, and he knew how to keep his mouth shut. Most of all, Helliar was a familiar figure and someone whom the board, manager and players could trust.

Over the years, the press has treated West Ham well, even if it has been critical of the club's inability to be successful in the first division. The stereotype of West Ham's lack of steel and its elegant, thoughtful, but not very successful football was reinforced by the willingness of one reporter to build on the generalizations of another. 'Pack journalism' operates in football as it does in politics, but West Ham was a club 'that was liked by the press…even respected for its integrity and unwillingness to cut corners'.[11] This made Helliar's job easier than it might otherwise have been, as West Ham continued to disappoint its supporters and fail to live up to its potential.

Jack Helliar's role as a member of the back room at West Ham was atypical, for he was never a regular employee of the club. Helliar was a presence; someone who seemed always to be around when things were happening. His size and demeanour made it easy to recognize and remember him. On match days there were occasional nuggets of information that he could pass on to journalists. He was a useful man to talk to on the way to see the manager, chairman or secretary. Symbolically, as well as literally, Helliar was charged with the care and nourishment (including liquid refreshment) of the press. He is another sign, like Chapman, St Pier and the former players who have become trainers and coaches, that West Ham takes care of its own. Helliar is also a walking repository of West Ham's history. He has seen many of the great and not so impressive moments in the club's history. Helliar wrote West Ham's match programmes for years. The programme notes set forth the club's views and the features helped to establish the club's identity. The chairman used the programme to explain what West Ham was doing for its supporters and to counter unfavourable publicity in the press. When collecting programmes became a major hobby throughout Britain, Helliar's version of West Ham United was read by scores of people who never attended West Ham matches. It is worth noting that

Helliar was always honest and astute enough not to gloss over problems when the club was doing badly.

Another 'honorary' employee was involved in many of the dramatic changes that shaped West Ham for years to come. Jack Turner, an almost shadowy figure during his time at West Ham, has become even more mysterious in retrospect. No two observers share either the same opinion or even the same memory of what he did or what difference he made to West Ham. Turner was involved in scouting and dealing with professional players during the period in which the club transformed itself from a perpetual second-division side into a respectable member of the first division. Turner's time at West Ham coincided with two of the most significant administrative changes since 1945 – the elevation of Reg Pratt to the chairmanship and Ron Greenwood's appointment as manager. These events determined Turner's status at the club.

Turner's arrival on the scene was like a boyhood dream come true. He was born in 1914, and West Ham 'was my club as a child...If you cut your finger and your blood is claret and blue, that's me.' He grew up kicking a ball around the streets seven days a week, the only entertainment for him and other children. Young Turner didn't 'know anything about football, except that I enjoyed it'. Football players were something special. Before he went to his first West Ham match in 1920, Turner was told by his father, 'Some of those men are more clever with their feet than we are with our hands.' But they were more than clever, they were giants and heroes. Because the players were locals, he knew where they lived and could see them on the streets. Like Reg Pratt, with whom Turner would work so closely almost 30 years later, Turner's special hero was Puddefoot: 'If he walked by me on the street, I would cross myself.'

Some of the pain of Puddefoot's departure was eased by West Ham's 1923 Cup Final. The week before the Cup was magic for Turner: 'If you can, imagine Jubilee, Coronation and Christmas all in one.' All the talk of a supporter boycott because of Puddefoot's sale disappeared when West Ham started winning. The lesson of that year remained with Turner when he became involved with the club. He knew, as only a disappointed young supporter could, how much winning meant to him and his friends. Turner left school at the age of 15, knowing that he was not good enough to earn his living as a professional footballer. He went into property and insurance, but never lost his enthusiasm for football or his passion for West Ham. In 1941 he refused Charlie Paynter's offer of an office job at the club: the chance of success was much better in the insurance business. Years later, Turner expressed regret over that decision because it might have led to something after the war and 'of all the jobs in football I would have liked, was that of secretary'.

Turner visited West Ham's offices occasionally to see Paynter and Ted Fenton. The latter invited him to help with some administrative tasks, and introduced him to Reg Pratt. The chairman thought Turner could be useful to West Ham. It was the best of both worlds for Turner: he could do something for 'his club' and not give up his business independence. There was no question of becoming a paid employee: it would be an 'honorary' position. Turner contends that when he came to West Ham he 'couldn't believe that the directors couldn't see that football was a business...that it was much more than a sport'. It was 'a club that had several good houses and few good players...a middling club with little money or ambition. It had people with no vision and a lot of power.' He thought that the board was standoffish towards its players: 'almost nineteenth-century in its boss-worker relationships.' This negative appraisal might be questioned in the light of Turner's break with the club in 1966, but his assessment fits in with comments made by players, press and supporters in the 1950s. Although Turner left the club at Reg Pratt's wish, he still singles out the former chairman for special praise. In Turner's view, the tradition that had to be overcome at West Ham was that of W. J. Cearns and his board, 'who ruled like iron and spent money like a man with no arms'.

Turner's original job was to deal with the club's houses. He had to tell players to vacate properties when their contracts with the club had ended. He took over some of the work that had been done by the chairman and the manager. Fenton had been trying to be the boss and one of the boys at the same time; now he could put more distance between himself and the players and not involve himself with their money problems. Turner stepped in between manager and players, a role that became the cause of ill feeling between Turner and Fenton's successor, Greenwood.

Reg Pratt, guided partly by a paternalistic desire to do what was best for the young men even if they did not realize it themselves, decided to expand Turner's role and sell club houses to players. The potential advantage to the club was that it would no longer be a landlord. The idea was not initially popular with many of the players. We tend to forget that at the time even established professionals were young men with very uncertain prospects for the future. They did not plan very far ahead; the nature of their profession and their background made them think in terms of what they could get then and there. Even if a player wanted to buy his club house, he probably did not have the money for a down payment, and would have difficulty getting a mortgage. That was where Turner came in. With the full support of the chairman, he set up a scheme to have money deducted from the players' weekly wage packets and invested in building societies. The *quid pro quo* was that the societies would make mortgage money available. Next, he approached insurance companies with a similar offer. Within a short time, West Ham's plan to sell houses was transformed into a type of annuity for the players.

Turner described his work as 'politely compelling players to save'.

The housing scheme at work. George Hayward signs the papers watched by (from left to right) West Ham players Andy Smillie, John Lyall and Bobby Moore, and property manager Jack Turner

Some players saw it as sinister, or at best irrelevant. Older players like Dick Walker already owned their own homes. They were not prepared to let someone from the club, an *insurance* man at that, tell them how they should dispose of their wages: 'Footballers were very wary about people like that.' Some players, like Ken Brown, went along with the scheme. Turner *'finally* talked me into saving money...[it] was the best thing I've ever done in my life'. Noel Cantwell had 'given no thought whatsoever to the future' before he was convinced into saving money with Turner. He put aside £2 per week, 'but usually got it back'. Cantwell's close friend Malcolm Allison wanted nothing to do with Turner and made that point forcefully to other players. Allison's feeling had less to do with the money than it did with Turner's role as a representative of Reg Pratt. Hard feelings were mutual; Allison thought of Turner as a outsider trying to get something for himself. Turner saw the opposition from Allison, 'which I took as a compliment', as just one more sign that Allison wanted to dominate as many people around the club as he possibly could.

Turner's other role at the club also reflected the problems of West

Ham's past and the changes that were taking place. He served as a scout, in a youth scheme set up by Reg Pratt. The youth scheme came into existence in the 1950s and was Reg Pratt's way of coping with an unpleasant reality. West Ham did not have the money to compete in the open market for players, and it had to do something drastic. Turner was part of the club's aggressive efforts to sign the best local players. The youth programme was the best way in which Pratt could make his mark on the future of the club. Scouts stressed that West Ham was the local club and reminded players that they stood a better chance of playing at West Ham than they did at Arsenal or Tottenham, '[where] they can always go out and buy whatever player they want, rather than use the young ones'.

If Jack Turner is known at all to the football public it is because of his association with Bobby Moore, a bond that lasted long after Turner left West Ham. Bobby Moore is the name always mentioned to balance against the boys who got away, like Venables and Greaves . Whether or not Moore was as good a club player as he might have been or whether there was a good enough side around him does not diminish his importance as a player and as a symbol of West Ham. For football fans throughout the world and thousands of West Ham supporters, Moore was visible proof that the Hammers were something more than an unfashionable small London club. His presence showed that the top East London players would play for West Ham. It was Turner who made the first report to the club about Moore; he was not very impressed with the boy. Fenton made Turner go back for another look and got other men from the club to evaluate him. The final decision to sign Moore was partially a reaction to the club's inability to acquire another young player who went to Arsenal.

After Moore became a star, he and Turner developed close ties. This began when Moore asked Turner to help cancel a contract with an advertising agency. This led to Turner taking care of other promotional activities. Turner refused to become an agent; he formed Bobby Moore Ltd. with himself as a director. Looking back on it, Turner contends that 'Moore should have got away from me and been handled by someone like Mark McCormack'. That would have been profitable for Moore, but it would have deprived him of a man he could trust, who knew him before he reached celebrity status, who could relate to the footballing and personal aspects of Moore's life as well as discuss investments and endorsements.

Turner's business dealings with players turned into a personal relationship with some of them. Brown and Cantwell, among others, approached Turner for advice on property and planning for the future. It proved easier for Turner to interest players in the savings plan when they came to the club as youth players. No player was compelled to deal with Turner, but it was clear that he had the support and encouragement of

Pratt and Fenton. Turner believed strongly that players needed help in coping with the money and status that they had suddenly acquired, and the informal nature of his work with the club helped him to deal with players more easily than if he had been one of the staff.

The changing titles that appeared on the door of Turner's office, such as 'Property Manager' and 'Personnel Manager', did not describe what he did. The combination of scouting, handling the properties and dealing with players' finances gave him access to players at different levels and at different times in their careers. Jeff Powell caught the essence of Turner's role: 'Turner could be responsible for nothing or everything at West Ham according to how the mood took them.'[12] Part of Turner's attraction for players was that he was connected to West Ham, but still seemed to be his own man. When players from other clubs asked Turner for help and wanted to set up arrangements with him, Turner always refused them, but he continued to act as an informal and unpaid advisor to some former West Ham players.[13]

Turner is a man of strong opinions, about himself, football and West Ham. He has no doubts whatsoever that he did 'something special' for the club while he was there. 'For West Ham to buy me a silver tea service is a sign of how much I was doing, especially since the only thing the club bought was a wreath when you died.' He feels that a lot of people did not know, or want to understand, what he was doing. But he did get notice and recognition, a 'good seat in the directors' box...Other people had to shift.' Not bad for the local boy who wanted to be a footballer but couldn't make it. Turner remembers fondly the relationship he had with Reg Pratt: 'We got very close...I would be at the ground three, four days a week...because I was a person he could talk to.' Given Jack Turner's admiration for Reg Pratt and the fact that it was Pratt who made it possible for Turner to develop the relationships with players, it is ironic that the end of Jack Turner's role at West Ham United was the result of Reg Pratt's most dramatic act as chairman.

When Ron Greenwood became manager he set out to establish his own approach to doing things, which extended beyond the field and football tactics. A strong-willed man like Greenwood could not be expected to sit back and operate business as usual at West Ham. One interpretation of his actions was that he needed to bring in a new approach to a not-very-successful club. Another view is that he did not understand the value of tradition at West Ham and set out to do things his way 'rather than try to join us'. The latter is certainly Jack Turner's view. He is convinced he had to leave West Ham because of Greenwood's desire to see him gone. 'We clashed immediately...Greenwood didn't want me there...I didn't blame him because he wanted to interfere with something he knew nothing about.' Football is a game of passions and personalities; in this case, the struggle took place in the back room rather than on the pitch and resembled a clash of men trying to stake out territory in a bureaucracy.

When Turner first came to West Ham, he was an extension of the board's traditional paternalism, but with an important difference. He dealt with the players as individuals and could not use the power of the club to push them. His success in establishing a personal relationship with many of the players vindicated what he and Pratt were trying to do, but sowed the seed for his clash with Greenwood. By 1961, Turner's close ties with individual players existed regardless of his role at the club. The closer he got to players, the more he might find himself in the position of being between his club and his friends. When contracts became a negotiable item, how should Turner advise his friends (and in some cases clients) to react to offers made by their manager?

Greenwood and Turner were never close, and their relationship rapidly worsened. They both had strong feelings about players and what was best for them, and there was no doubt where the responsibility and power resided. Greenwood was the boss and needed the complete confidence of the players in his judgment and vision of West Ham. His enthusiasm for coaching was more than a reflection of his philosophy about the game. He pushed reluctant players like Ken Brown into taking a step that might help them after their playing days were over. Turner's presence at West Ham represented many of the virtues that Greenwood praised: tradition, care of players and loyalty, but Turner stood in the way of change. Any antipathy between Greenwood and Turner put Reg Pratt in the middle, but there was little doubt about how the chairman would react. Turner went to Pratt and said that he did not see how he could continue to work with Greenwood, that the situation had become too personal because Greenwood was telling players not to deal with him. It did not matter whether Greenwood had said anything or not. Turner could only react to what he believed to be true. The chairman asked Turner to remain, but the situation did not improve. The new prosperity and success at West Ham seemed to exacerbate the problems. Greenwood was supposed to improve the club by rousing it from its traditional complacency with the backing of the board. When West Ham decided to try to compete with the big time of football it also made the implicit decision to scrap part of its approach to management. It was hard to see a place for Jack Turner at the new West Ham.

The final decision to have Turner leave was made by Reg Pratt. The chairman must have concluded that the club would be better off without his services or that the price of keeping him was too high. The parting was not easy, and Turner remained bitter for years about what he claimed were inaccurate comments about his work at West Ham. Club officials have had little or nothing to say over the years either about what Turner did or about why he left West Ham. The club was living up to its traditions: it would rather allow people to wonder, to impute wrong motives and policies, than make a public issue. The official explanation for Turner's departure was that he no longer fitted into West Ham United.

Turner was the chairman's agent, but he was not responsible to him for his dealings with players. What started as a simple scheme to deal with West Ham's properties was transformed into a wide-ranging effort to allow players to gain greater control over their futures. The possible complications of Turner's role were symptomatic of the complexities of running a football club. It was hard to exercise control over a volunteer and even harder to criticize his actions.

Scores of men have been West Ham's 'boys in the back room' over the years. Many of them, such as the stilemen, ushers and guards, have carried out the mundane tasks without which the organization could not have produced its weekly football matches. West Ham's identity has been preserved in the 'back room'.

Eddie Chapman's role at West Ham has encapsulated how the club has developed over the years. Like St Pier and the directors, he represents the stability that West Ham has always tried to foster. He has become so fully wrapped up in the image of West Ham that it is difficult to separate him from the *persona* of the club. His public visibility has depended on how much, or little, the chairman or the manager wanted to deal with the public. Chapman's role expanded as West Ham established more complicated links with its supporters and the public. When West Ham decided to deal with an organized supporters' club, Chapman was the liason. He served on the joint committee that dealt with the receipts that went into the Building Fund. The myriad of details that make up the secretary's job – of which tickets, arrangements with the police, travel arrangements and dealings with other clubs are only a few – go unnoticed by the public. Above all, Chapman's job is to run the club smoothly. There are no ground rules for secretaries and no bureaucratic chart to set the pattern for West Ham's operation. Much of Chapman's value to the club has been his ability to improvise combined with his knowledge and almost instinctive feel for 'how things are done at West Ham'. That is the key to how West Ham works. The jazz musician Fats Waller responded to the question, 'What is Jazz?' by saying, 'If you have to ask the question, you'll never know the answer.' West Ham operates with the same type of unspoken standards and practices.

Jack Turner's roots at West Ham went back as long as those of Eddie Chapman. For more than a decade the two men had offices a few feet away from one another at Upton Park. They were there when West Ham underwent the most significant changes in its history: the 'soccer academy' of articulate, outspoken players, promotion, the commitment to scout and sign local players, the influx of large amounts of money into the sport, the effort to get players to plan for their futures, the purchase of the ground, the creation of a supporters' club and the hiring of an outsider as the manager. Chapman and Turner paved the way for West Ham to adapt to these changes. It would probably never occur to people involved with West Ham to compare the two men: Chapman, the long-serving player and official who represents the club before the public, and Turner, a figure behind the scenes who left West Ham with no fanfare. However, their careers at West Ham coincided in more than time. Turner's skills and background showed how the club was responding to a new generation of players and financial circumstances. Chapman's personality, and his attention to the public side of his job, pointed to the new complexities of football. West Ham had to face the challenges of other forms of entertainment and adjust to the business of football. These changes were accomplished without destroying the framework that made West Ham different from other clubs. The changes in the back room were fostered by the elevation of Reg Pratt to the chairmanship. He moved against the strongest force operating in any organization, inertia. West Ham came up with its own innovation. It accomplished this through men with personalities as different as Eddie Chapman, Jack Turner and Reg Pratt. West Ham's corporate personality was changing; it was being transformed from a paternal organization led by the iron-fisted W. J. Cearns to a co-operative operation led by Reg Pratt.

Instead of trying to understand men like Turner, Chapman and Wally St Pier by applying a bureaucratic or business model, it is better to think of football as a product of passions, personalities and mythologies. A bloody struggle for power in the back room of West Ham United was improbable, but if it had occurred the floors would have been awash with 'claret and blue'. A sense of belonging to something special motivated the 'boys in the back room' more than a wage and much more than a feeling that they were just doing a job.

CHAPTER 10

Some players have been special

When I had a chance to get paid to play for West Ham, I told my employer, politely, what he could do with his work.

Ken Brown, West Ham player, 1952-66.

This history of West Ham United has made a special effort to look at the structure of the club and the role it has played in the local community. However, we should not forget that it is football that makes West Ham different from any other business or activity. Without the men on the field, nothing else about the club would be special. The traditions of the club have their roots in players or the stories about them. The glorious memories of the electric tram and the White Horse Cup Final of 1923 were reflections of the ability of the players to take West Ham to Wembley. The recent mythology of West Ham – its entertaining play, its failure to win championships, and its dependence on local talent – is a commentary on the players. It would be superficial to claim to understand the history of West Ham United as a litany of its players, but it would be impossible to describe the club without looking at the accomplishments and the distinctive personalities of individual players.

One of Syd King's first additions to the team in 1905 was George Kitchen, who lent a note of flamboyance to the club while he protected its goal. He was the lynchpin of the 1911 Cup run which established the club as something more than an average Southern League side. West Ham reached the fourth round for the first time in its history, defeating Nottingham Forest and Preston North End on the way to a memorable winning match against Manchester United.[1] While West Ham was savouring that victory, G. K. Webb was capped for England, the first West Ham player to gain that distinction. Webb's success was tinged with irony: he had retained his position in the first team the year before only because the chairman had cast the deciding vote in his favour at a selection meeting.[2]

Webb and Kitchen gave flair to West Ham, but its first player to achieve heroic proportions was Sid Puddefoot. He scored goals at an unparalleled rate and was surrounded by the best team in West Ham's history. The team included quality players like Ted Hufton and George

143

Kay, who would move with the Hammers to Wembley and the first division. Puddefoot signed for the 1920 season at top wages, £9 per week for the whole year, a status he shared with Hufton, Kay, Cope, and Tresadern.[3] The public had no reason to know that two months before Puddefoot signed his new contract he had asked to be put on the transfer list.[4] The board had 'deferred consideration' of the matter. Puddefoot took the hint and did not further his request. The same day as Puddefoot's request, the board noted the signing of V. Watson for a wage of £4 per week and a signing fee of £10.[5] At the start of the next season he was the lowest-paid full-time player. Two weeks into the season they raised the wage to £5 per week, bringing him up to the same wage as three other players.[6]

The careers of Puddefoot and Watson became linked dramatically over the next two years. When Puddefoot left for Scotland, Watson was ready to replace him. Besides gaining a £5,000 transfer fee, the club was also able to substitute a £6 per week player for one making the £9 maximum wage. There was more than money involved; Syd King saw something special in Watson. Puddefoot's departure and the resulting events validated two maxims of sport management: that it is better to sell a player too early, while his value is high, than too late, and that it is possible to add to the strength of a team by subtraction. Puddefoot was at the top of his form, but as long as he was there, Watson could not perform. Syd King gave Watson his chance and he became one of the all-time leading West Ham goal scorers. His total of 317 goals in peacetime League matches is topped by only five other men.

The team that went out on to the Wembley pitch in 1923 was anchored by veterans like Hufton, Tresadern and the captain, George Kay. But it was the relative newcomers, Watson and Jimmy Ruffell, who added something special. They both had long careers with the club. By 1924, Watson and Ruffell had joined four senior professionals at the top of the wage scale.[7] Ruffell made six appearances for England over a four-year stretch. He probably would have had more caps had he not refused the offer of a summer tour with the FA side because he had planned a holiday for his family. King tried to bring new players into the side to bolster its ability to compete in the first division. Jim Barrett joined the club in 1925 and played more than 400 matches for West Ham between then and 1939. Vivian Gibbons, a prominent amateur player, joined the club a few years later.

West Ham did not have enough capped players for the chairman to be blasé about Ruffell. West Ham's top players had chequered, sometimes short-lived careers playing for their country. Watson was a centre-forward, the same position as some of the great players in the game, and Hufton had the misfortune to be in goal in 1929 when England lost to Spain in its first defeat by a continental team. The cruellest blow came in 1928, when Jim Barrett left the field after eight minutes in his only

The softly-spoken, speedy Jimmy Ruffell had a long successful career at West Ham. He was capped for England and played an instrumental role in getting West Ham to Wembley in 1923

match for England.

The three Internationals, Ruffell, Watson and Hufton, also led the wage table for West Ham. In 1925, they had been part of a group of seven players including Kay, Moore, Bishop and Henderson who were on the maximum weekly wage of £8 and £6 in the close season. Three years later, Ruffell, Watson and Hufton were the only men on the maximum. Barrett continued to earn slightly less than his colleagues. After 1926, West Ham languished in the lower third of the table except in 1930 when the team finished seventh.

Gibbons's career did not live up to his expectations or those of the club. He left West Ham in the middle of the 1931-32 season, 'dissatisfied with playing different positions and being left out of the side a couple of times'. The local football columnist commented: 'It must be particularly annoying to him, to be left out when he was willing to play.'[8] But willing is not the same thing as able. The imposing figure of Vic Watson stood in Gibbons's path. A professional would have been forced to adapt to playing second-team football and waiting for the chance. Gibbons, the amateur, was not willing to do that.

Desperate attempts were made to avoid relegation in 1932. There was even the short-lived return of Puddefoot. He brought nostalgia and hero-worship back to the ground, but his talents were far from what they had been a decade earlier. Rather than softening the blow of relegation, Puddefoot's short appearance with West Ham added to the sense of pathos that he had not been part of the club during its successes.

West Ham barely survived in its first season in the second division. One of the heroes of the promotion side, Earle, was given a free transfer and Puddefoot was placed on the transfer list. Ruffell, seemingly over the peak of his great career, dropped back to the middle of the pack in wages earning only £5 per week, while Watson, Barrett and Collins were earning £7 and £6. Joining Ruffell at £5 was a recent local signing, Len Goulden.[9] This inside forward was one of Charlie Paynter's favourite acquisitions, and in a short time he had become the foundation for a revival of hope. He played well enough for a second-division side to be capped more than ten times between 1937 and 1939.

The club's resolution to offer Sheffield United as much as £500 for a player 'if he looked really outstanding [when observed]' was a sign of how far West Ham was willing, or not willing, to go in its efforts to get back into the first division.[10] The club finished seventh in the 1934 season. Goulden and Watson formed an effective combination and even Ruffell showed a return to form. If wages marked the importance of a player, Barrett and Morton were at the top of the list. A better indication of Morton's value occurred in the privacy of the board-room when the directors turned down an offer from Chelsea of £5,000 for him, replying that they 'had no intentions of parting with the player'.[11]

The transfer stream began to flow in the opposite diection. A couple of minor moves in 1934 preceded a blockbuster deal. James Marshall and David Mangall arrived in March 1935, a manoeuvre that, according to the press, could cost West Ham almost £4,000. Both players had a dramatic effect before either of them donned a West Ham shirt. It was impossible not to notice Marshall: how many players are qualified doctors and later leave the game to assume the position of medical officer? Mangall cost more than any player the club had purchased, and Marshall cost more than that. This was enough to merit a big story in the news rather than the sports section of the *Stratford Express*: 'Hammers Make History.

Thousands of Pounds for Two Players. Bold Bid for Promotion.' The correspondent reminded his readers that the directors' former policy had not been to spend money but to concentrate on developing local talent. Obviously, that had not been good enough to get the club back into the first division. This purchase showed how much the directors wanted promotion.[12] The reporter might have known that the arrangements that brought Marshall from Arsenal included an additional fee of £750 (the basic price was £2,000) if West Ham gained promotion during the 1935-36 season. Marshall and Mangall were joining a team that had barely missed promotion the year before. The old favourites, Ruffell and Watson, were going in different directions. Ruffell was signed on for 1935-36 at close to top wages, Watson was granted a free transfer. But it was the young blood that gave the promise of a return to the top.

Marshall made his first impact on the club months before the season started, but as Dr Marshall, not as a player. The club was on a European tour during the summer when F. R. Pratt was struck down by appendicitis. After a successful operation in Stockholm, he made it a point to thank club officials, including Dr Marshall, for assistance during his illness.[13] It must have been comforting to know that the club was carrying its own personal physician along with it. But West Ham had not paid £2,000 for Marshall to diagnose the ills of its directors. He was there to take the club back into the first division. The season turned out to be even more frustrating than the previous year's close miss. The club finished fourth, but it had promotion in its sights until it stumbled disastrously in a late-season home match against Charlton Athletic, the eventual second-place finisher. (It was after this match that Bert Davis made his monumental error of judgment and tact by comparing the merits of being in the second division with the expenses of going up to the first. It might have been even more embarrassing if the press had known the terms of Marshall's purchase. Then the *Evening News* could have given a precise figure to accentuate the shame of the hapless West Ham director: 'Fear of paying a £750 bonus to Arsenal' would have made a juicy headline.[14]

Mangall and Marshall came to West Ham in an atmosphere of almost euphoric optimism, but they did not remain very long with the club. Mangall's transfer at the end of his first season prompted questions from the normally quiet shareholders at the AGM. West Ham received £1,000 from Millwall for him, £780 less than he had cost a year earlier.[15] West Ham had an immediate use for the money: it went to Arsenal to pay for C. Walker, who was transferred on the same day.[16] West Ham began to resemble a revolving door for a few years.

The club's penurious reputation would have been shattered if Tweedie had not refused to leave Grimsby Town for West Ham. West Ham had pursued him for half a season. The club made a series of offers, each of which was refused by Grimsby until the figure reached £5,000. At the start of the 1936-37 season, West Ham got word that this enormous (by their standards) offer had been refused.[17] The club slipped down to sixth in 1937 and received another jolt when Marshall informed the club that he was taking a job as a medical officer. The board agreed to release him from his contract and accepted his offer to assist the club.[18]

The principals in the big deal of 1935 were both gone by September 1937. The club continued to slip down the table over the next couple of years, but it had the foundation of a solid team. Charlie Paynter and his staff were bringing along a group of young local players of whom Goulden was certainly the best. There were others who would have important effects on what happened at Upton Park for years after Goulden retired. Ernie Gregory joined the club as a young goalkeeper in 1936 and made some brilliant saves during the year that West Ham returned to the first division. Two years earlier a young boy from Dagenham, Dick Walker, had signed up as a professional.

The directors' dedication to a winning side was shown dramatically in the deal that they did not make. When Everton asked whether West Ham 'would be prepared to transfer Goulden and Morton, the board said definitely "NO"!'[19] At the same time, West Ham made another bold bid in the transfer market. This time, the club went to Scotland and bought Archie Macaulay for £3,500 from Rangers.[20]

The pieces were beginning to fall into place: West Ham had purchased quality players from major clubs like Arsenal and Rangers, made local signings like Herman Conway, Ted Fenton and Dick Walker, and had veterans like Goulden. These men were the foundation of the club that opened the 1939 season six days before war was declared against Germany with a 3-1 victory at Plymouth, and ended it with a victory at Wembley a few days after Dunkirk.

The War Cup victory against first-division Blackburn Rovers was accomplished by the side that Charlie Paynter regarded as the best of his career at West Ham. Goulden and Macaulay were the leaders, but Sam Small scored the winning goal in the Final. For many players it was their last chance for a major victory; for others it was an introduction to long careers at West Ham United. Ted Fenton and Dick Walker both made significant post-war contributions to the club. Other team members, who were not on the pitch at Wembley, included Eddie Chapman and Ernie Gregory.

It required a certain sleight of hand for the club to field a representative team during the war. Paynter and his assistants spent more time worrying about trains and the vagaries of the military than they did about the condition of the players. West Ham had done some pre-war planning, and when the international situation worsened after Munich, the chairman suggested that 'the first team join the reserve police and the second team get into the Territorials'. Arrangements could be modified. When Dick Walker left the police after three months,

WEST HAM UNITED FOOTBALL CO., LTD
Boleyn Ground, Green Street, Upton Park, E.I3
▼

WEST HAM UNITED v ARSENAL

FOOTBALL LEAGUE REGIONAL COMPETITION

Monday, 8th April, 1940   **Kick-off 6.0 p.m**

WEST HAM UNITED
Colours : Claret and Blue

RIGHT   1   LEFT
Cpl. H. Medhurst

2   3
Bicknell   **Walker, C**

4   5   6
L/Cpl. N. Corbett   **Walker, R**   **Sgt. M. Masson**

7   8   9   10   11
Foxall   **Sgt-ln. E. Fenton**   **Foreman**   **Goulden**   **Gore**
                         or Cpl. A. Macaulay

Referee : Mr. H. C. WILLIAMS
Linesmen : Messrs. J. J. SORRELL (Red Stripe Flag) and A. DEVINE (Blue Stripe Flag)

11   10   9   8   7
Bastin   **Jones, B.**   **Compton, L.**   **Lewis**   **Drake**

6   5   4
Jones, L.   **B. Joy**   **Pryde**

3   2
Hapgood   **Male**

1
Platt

LEFT   **ARSENAL**   RIGHT

OUR VISITORS

The heartiest of welcomes is extended to this evening's guests—the Gunners. We anticipate their second visit of the season with additional relish. The game has developed in keenness as this war-time competition has progressed, and we expect to be regaled with as keen and interesting football as if it were a peace time First Division local Derby.

Arsenal had a comparatively easy journey for the first of the Regional Competitions, but the second finds the Hammers well in the van.

LAST SATURDAY WEEK

Last Saturday week's game at Stamford Bridge provided soccer's greatest war-time shock. The Hammers provided a 'Blitzkrieg' of such intensity that the home defence was left no alternative but retreat before the onslaught of our attack. With the Pensioners must have been the shades of Wellington, for Sam Small certainly did pick up his musket—and used it—four times. George Foreman did the hat-trick and Ted Fenton with two and Stan Foxall one completed the ten.

LAST SATURDAY

At White Hart Lane on Saturday our lads were again in great fettle and the result fairly indicates their superiority. George Foreman eclipsed his hat-trick of the previous week by scoring four goals. Len Goulden and Charlie Bicknell shared the other two.

TO-MORROW

To-morrow, April 9th, kick-off at 3.30 p.m., a match will be played here in aid of the Duke of Gloucester's Appeal for the Red Cross Fund. The contestants will be " H " Div. Metropolitan Police and " K " Div. Metropolitan Police Several well known professional players will take part in the game. Admission 6d.

NEXT SATURDAY

Brentford provide the opposition here next Saturday and as they defeated us 4—3 on February 17th our lads will be all out to prevent the Bees repeating their win. Kick off at 3.30 p.m.

cont. overleaf

OFFICIAL PROGRAMME—Price 1d   No. 22   Hellier & Sons, Printers, 237 Barking Road, London, E.13

The program for 8 April 1940 reveals the presence of two sergeants, a corporal and a lance-corporal in the West Ham side

Many West Ham players joined the Territorials on the eve of the Second World War. Archie Macaulay is playing the accordian in this light-hearted scene photographed less than a week before war broke out

Charlie Paynter got him a job as a toolmaker: 'anything to keep footballers home.'[21] At the outbreak of war, almost all the players joined the Forces, and for the next couple of years part of East Anglia was defended against German aircraft and invasion by men who felt more at home on a football pitch. But Paynter was able to put together a team that was close to normal though even a cursory look at the programme would remind anyone that the country was at war. A team that included Sgt Medhurst, Cpl Atwell, C.S.M. Fenton and Sgt R. Walker was proof of that.[22]

War-time football brought back echoes of problems from the sport's pre-professional past in complaints about coaching and broken-time payments. There was a division between civilian and military players. The latter presented no problem since their wages, small as they were, were guaranteed and paid out each week. The football authorities assumed that civilian players were making a reasonable wage and that they deserved no payment for broken time. Broken-time payments were 'strictly forbidden and drastic action would be taken for any infringement of this rule'.[23] The need to remind clubs of the rule is a good indication that it was being broken. The authorities were trying to maintain some equity between players and, more importantly, to protect the clubs. There was a real danger that broken-time payments could be

West Ham players serving in the Forces board an aircraft in 1940. Harry Medhurst is on the steps, future captain Dick Walker is wearing a beret, and future manager Ted Fenton is on the far left

used by some of the richer clubs to recruit players who were either too young for the Forces or in a restricted civilian occupation. They could establish themselves as virtual free agents waiting to be asked to play football. Broken-time had the potential to evade the spirit of the maximum wage payment.

If the maximum wage was important to the League, sanctity of contract was its life's blood. The unsettled living arrangements of the players necessitated some changes in their contractual obligations. It made no sense to demand that a player perform for the club that held his contract if it was physically impossible for him to be there for matches. Players were allowed to join other clubs on an *ad hoc* basis, which necessitated negotiations between the clubs involved. Throughout the war, there was a mass of correspondence concerning such arrangements. The arrangements for a 'guest player' were handled by the club that wanted him and the one that held his registration; the former had to initiate the process. Clubs tried to be accommodating – if a club refused to release a player, it would endanger his skills and put itself in a bad public light. The best reason for going along with requests was to maintain the system of reciprocity that was necessary to keep the game

Chairman W. J. Cearns and manager Charlie Paynter surrounded by West Ham players in uniform, 1940

alive during the war. Every club, including West Ham, needed 'guest players'.

The war-time system worked because an understanding existed between the men who ran the clubs. It ensured that the players did not gain control of either their wages or their playing situation, but the necessities of the war created something closer to freedom of contract than players had ever had before. West Ham's experiences in 1940 showed how the system worked. Liverpool gave West Ham permission to approach players stationed in Suffolk. West Ham gave permission for Mansfield Town to play Hubbard, 'except when his services were desired by us'.[24] This reaffirmed West Ham's rights over its players. It was when Paynter learned that the train connections would be very chancy for Hubbard that he was allowed to play for Mansfield.[25] On the other hand, Reading's request for Ted Fenton's services was greeted with a flat rejection. Sgt-Major Fenton was stationed at Colchester and West Ham assumed that he would be able and should be willing to play for his club.[26]

When the war ended, Charlie Paynter started to reassemble his team. The first step taken by the board was to sign two new scouts to assist Ives and St Pier. It then turned its attention to the professionals whose registrations reverted to their pre-war clubs. By August 1945 it began to look like business as usual for West Ham, but the cast was very different from that of 1940. Some players had lost their skills due to inactivity, age, or lack of top-quality competition; some, like Foxall, had suffered injuries that meant they 'would never be fit to play professional football again'.[27] Players were scattered throughout the world; some, like Ernie Gregory and Eric Parsons, were stationed in Germany and could expect to come home soon, but others, like Norman Corbett, faced the uncertain future of knowing he was 'on his way to somewhere in Europe'.[28] West Ham was trying to collect its players. Letters were sent to Macaulay, who was stationed in Scotland, and to the Falkirk FC, reminding both that his permission to play with that club 'ceases automatically with his release from the forces'.[29] The board was willing to extend his loan for three additional weeks until the end of the year.[30] Macaulay returned to London with little enthusiasm to continue at West Ham. He asked to be placed on the transfer list, but the club turned down his request. He had a meeting with the board, a very unusual occurrence, and 'following kindly further advice from the board', appeared more contented.[31] The 'contentment' lasted less than half of the next season. In November 1946 Macaulay again requested to be placed on the transfer list and this time the board went along with his wishes.[32]

Macaulay was a sought-after commodity. He met representatives of Sheffield Wednesday and Arsenal before agreeing to sign with Brentford. The price was £7,500 plus Brentford's promise to purchase the West Ham property that had been rented to Macaulay 'if they did not find him suitable accommodation within three months'.[33] Macaulay had brought West Ham more than they had paid for him before the war, as well as getting a series of favourable conditions for himself. Everyone was satisfied, with the possible exception of Sheffield Wednesday and Arsenal, but later Arsenal finally purchased Macaulay from Brentford. Macaulay was not the first prominent player to move. Len Goulden had gone to Germany as part of the Chelsea touring party in August 1945, and was transferred to Chelsea later that month for £4,500 plus whatever he had coming in his accrued share of benefit.[34] George Foreman left for Tottenham Hotspurs for a £1,250 fee.[35] At the end of the 1946 season, Charlie Walker became secretary-manager at Margate with the consent of the board and the proviso that he could play for Margate as long as his League rights were retained by West Ham.[36]

Ted Fenton was given permission the same day to accept a similar appointment at Colchester. Earlier that year, when the Colchester chairman had asked W.J. Cearns for permission to talk personally to Fenton about coming to Colchester, the request had been denied. West Ham declared that it had no desire to release Fenton, but a month later the club relented.[37] West Ham was getting rid of most of its established players, many of whom had grown up with the club.

None of the players who remained at West Ham after the post-war shake-up was more representative of the character of the club than Dick

Walker. He joined West Ham just after it slipped from the first division. By the time he seized a place in the League side from 'Big' Jim Barrett, the club had settled into the mediocrity that marked its time in the second division. Walker had a tough first few years; there were many fans who still called for the return of his popular predecessor. More than a decade later, Malcolm Allison would face the same kind of reaction when he took over from Walker. No one would ever have described Walker as a skilful player, least of all Walker himself: 'I couldn't play, but I could stop those that would. West Ham was a hard club.' Walker's assessment does not square with the post-1958 opinion that West Ham has always tried to play skilful and elegant, if not winning, football, but it seems closer to reality. He was a great favourite with the West Ham crowd for years. For many of them, including members of the football press, he typified what made West Ham a different club, and the Boleyn Ground a unique place to play. Walker's effort for his team was total, and supporters responded to that. They had a special place in their affections for the sometimes self-deprecating humour that Walker demonstrated when he exchanged jokes with the crowd leaning over the 'chicken run'. No one ever mistook his humour for not caring about the game: any opposing players who did would have been brought down to earth abruptly. Walker personified the East Londoner's need to work hard for anything he wanted and the humour that acted as a buffer against the harshness of everyday life. He combined that with a kind of swagger that made people realize that playing football for West Ham was something special.

Walker's arrival at West Ham was different from that of many of his team-mates. When he signed for West Ham in 1934, he thought of it as his big chance to get paid to play. There was nothing special about who paid; he would have played for anybody. He had never seen a West Ham match and knew nothing about the club. His older brother, who had left home long before Walker became a footballer, was a Tottenham fan, so Dick thought Spurs was special. 'The first [professional] football match I ever saw, I was in.' Walker was brought up in the huge new council estate in Dagenham, a big lonely place. There were few football supporters, but there were people playing the game all the time. When he was chosen to play for the district boys at the age of 13, the biggest problem was buying boots. His first pair cost 3s and he wore them as ordinary shoes by taking out the studs. The family was not on the dole because his sisters were working. Not being hungry meant 'scrounging a bit', and keeping warm meant being able to 'nick a bit of wood from a construction site to use in the fire'. Sunday football was his chance to be good at something and to play against better competition. He was noticed by West Ham. The telegram telling him to come for an 'A' team match against Arsenal was delivered to him at the labour exchange.

After his first match in West Ham's colours, Walker was introduced to the more devious aspects of professional football. He was told to come to a shop in Shepherd's Bush whose owner ran an amateur football team, Park Royal. In order to qualify as an amateur but still get paid, Dick had a job as an electrician's mate, although 'I didn't know how to change a light bulb.' There was plenty of time to play football. He and his mates 'trained like professionals', which was appropriate enough since they were getting paid like professionals. The Park Royal team played well enough to win everything in London and gave Walker the chance to be picked for a team that went to Paris. He got 'terrific money – £4 or £5 a week in 1933 made me the richest man on our street'. The next year, he was old enough to sign as a professional and he joined West Ham. After his year at Park Royal as an 'electrician' it was a big jump up to a professional side. Midway through the year, the 21-year-old was dropped from the team, which meant a cut in wages from £5 to £4. Even that did not look bad when he saw the alternatives as going on the dole or becoming a barman again.

Walker knew he wanted to stay in football for more than the money: 'I loved playing football…and there were other things. I moved back with my mother. I might not have been very well known yet for my football, but we were famous because we were paying the rent.' Within a couple of years, when he was in the first team, the advantages of football became clearer. People in his street started to point him out and he 'knew what fame was when bus conductors wouldn't take a fare and people would start to talk to me in pubs. 'It was like having people put out flags on the street when I walked down. I always wanted to stop and talk to them.' Football gave him the chance to move out to Chadwell Heath when he got married. He lived in a place 'a little posher. It had curtains on the windows.'[38]

Walker was part of the Depression generation, men who came to West Ham for a job in a world where jobs were rare. He became even more than the captain of West Ham and one of its most popular players: Walker was a transitional figure in the club's history. He stayed long enough to see the arrival of players who brought promotion and a new style of football to the club. Ironically, it was one of Walker's contemporaries, a man with a background very much like his, Ted Fenton, who laid the foundation for the change at West Ham and ensured that Walker left the club.

The new players came from a variety of sources. Malcolm Allison was transferred from Charlton for £7,000 and brought to West Ham his tremendous drive for success, his understanding of the game and his willingness to push and bully people. He seemed the antithesis of the traditional West Ham player. He was impatient with the club, the other players and the crowd. Smiling at mistakes was not Allison's style; giving orders was more in character. He raised the ability of the men around him and was unconcerned with the reaction that he got from the home crowd. Supporters regarded him with a combination of admiration for what was happening and distaste for how it was taking place. Even when they revelled in being an extension of the 'West Ham academy of football', they never showed much regard for Allison.

After he left West Ham, Allison's career made him a media personality. His flamboyant personal life and fights with officials have created the image of a strong-willed nonconformist who goes out of his way to look for trouble. He displayed many of these characteristics at West Ham. It was a yearly ritual for him to object to the wages offered him by the club. He challenged supporters, tried to ignore the manager, and regarded the directors as an annoyance. His influence could be seen in players like Frank O'Farrell, John Bond, Noel Cantwell and Dave Sexton. Many of them were superior players to Allison and they were strong assertive personalities in their own right who went on to have very successful careers after they left West Ham. Even Ron Greenwood, no great admirer of Allison, recognized the existence of 'the older school of Malcolm Allison, Noel Cantwell, and company'.[39]

West Ham had finished a very unimpressive sixteenth in 1956 despite a solid group of senior players who were developing their style. The season had one high point that in retrospect was an indication of a brighter future. The club put on a brilliant display in the March Cup-tie against Tottenham Hotspurs. They went out to a 3-1 lead only to be equalized later in the match and then lost 2-1 in a desultory replay. The team that almost upset Spurs in March 1956 included players who made great contributions two seasons later when West Ham was finally promoted: Ernie Gregory, John Bond, Noel Cantwell, Andy Malcolm and John Dick. The board turned down two requests that would have changed the character of the club. In May 1956 Allison asked to become a part-time player. The board refused because there was a greater need for him on the field than working with the young prospects. Cantwell asked for a transfer shortly afterwards, a request that was curtly and firmly denied.[40]

Before the 1957-58 season was far advanced, the most noticeable omission from the team that had gathered around Malcolm Allison was Allison himself. He went to the doctor shortly after the seventh match, a 3-2 winner at Swansea. The diagnosis was tuberculosis, and after surgery and a lengthy recovery he returned in March as a spectator to see West Ham score eight goals against Rotherham. His influence was still felt throughout the season, through the tactics that had evolved at the Cassatarri Cafe and the personal impact he had on other players.

In its drive to promotion, West Ham gained the reputation for attacking and innovative football, but much of the character and personality of the team lay at the back with Ernie Gregory, John Bond and Noel Cantwell. Gregory was the link with West Ham's past: to him, Charlie Paynter had been a manager, not a legend. He was 36 years old midway through the season, nearing the end of a long career that had seen him win an England 'B' cap against France in 1952. He gave the impression of solid imperturability, although anyone standing close enough to the West Ham goal might have heard some rather colourful language. Some of his choicest remarks were directed at Cantwell and Bond. They were putting into practice what they had talked about so often: playing the ball in their penalty area. Gregory might have appreciated their skill and intentions in the abstract, but in practice he wanted them to boot the ball away and keep him out of trouble.[41]

If there was anyone who could pound a ball for distance, it was John Bond, 'Muffin the Mule'. He looked like the solid old-style full back but did not play like one. Cantwell appreciated Bond's ability with the ball, as well as noting that 'he couldn't tackle a fish supper'. By 1958 Bond was regarded as the most improved player on the team, and there was much talk that he should have been included in the England World Cup party. He had come a long way from the player of uncertain talent at another position who had come to West Ham in 1950.

Cantwell was the antithesis of his partner, Bond. The Irishman was a natural athlete who moved with grace and sure instincts. He had played a series of positions and gained schoolboy honours in Eire, and went from the 'A' team to the League side in his first year at West Ham. Cantwell's quick rise did not make him complacent. He applied himself to the game mentally as well as physically. November 1957 brought a new responsibility for him: it was Cantwell who had persuaded his good friend Allison to see the doctor. The surgery and convalescence that probably saved Allison's life thrust Cantwell into the role of captain. His style of leadership was very different from that of his predecessor. The players had been together long enough to know what they could do and to respect the ability of their team-mates. It was probably no longer necessary to bully players, even if that had been Cantwell's way. One of the players who responded to the new situation and made a surprising contribution to promotion was Ken Brown.

The promotion season was Brown's first as a regular player. He had been brought up in the style of play developed over the past few years at the 'academy of soccer', but in other ways Brown was a throwback to older West Ham traditions. He was a favourite of the crowd from the beginning; his smile and ability to accept a mistake were welcomed. In that respect, he was like a second Dick Walker, although Brown's talents on the field outstripped those of the former captain. Brown was born and raised in Dagenham, started playing football at 12 and was chosen for the Dagenham Boys at 15. His progress off the field was just as rapid. Before he was 18 he had completed an apprenticeship as a machinist and he had a good job with a solid future, when his boss told him that he would have to cut back on time away from work. He was playing in a London midweek league where West Ham was paying him for broken time. The

Ken Brown typified the home-grown East End player. A great crowd favourite, he was part of the 'Academy of Soccer' and the promotion side of 1958, and went on to become a successful manager at Norwich City

17-year-old had to make a choice and 'politely told him [the boss] what he could do with his work'. Brown took a cut in wages from £12 to £9 a week for the chance to play football. That was what mattered to him, not necessarily playing for West Ham. Growing up in Dagenham, he had not paid much attention to any professional club. He had no favourite, and knew as little about West Ham as about any other club.

Brown's real education in the game came from Dick Walker. Walker was an important senior player, 'everybody knew him', and a young player like Brown 'wouldn't dare to speak to him...He was smart, somebody to look up to.' There were not many technical skills that Walker could pass on to Brown, but he did teach him 'never to let anybody down, to work and play hard'. There were lessons about football that had nothing to do with the game. Brown and Walker walked to and from the bus together on their way to training. Walker suggested that he and Brown share the fares – one paying one week, the other paying the following week. It was a convenient and equitable way to handle the trip, and it took a while for Brown to realize that bus conductors would not let Dick Walker pay. Walker did not ask for favours, he simply received them. We have noted already that an unwritten standard operated at the highest level of the club – directors, bank managers, politicians and others did not have to discuss the code of conduct that determined their

Ernie Gregory, shown here coaching Peter Shearing in 1960, followed his long career as a goal-keeper for West Ham by becoming its long-serving coach

relationship. It was understood in the same way as bonds between certain players and the local community were understood.

Brown went into the army to do his national service a year after joining West Ham. When he returned in 1954, much had changed. His future as a player was uncertain, for a new group of quality performers had joined the club. Most of his time was spent in the 'A' side. He did not worry: 'In those days you knew where you stood...every player had his place...I knew when my time would come, I would make that spot mine...I had to be more patient than most people since Malcolm Allison was more or less running things.' Brown's experience in 1957-58 typifies the ironies and coincidences in football. His personality and ties with Walker were a part of the old tradition at West Ham, but his chance to succeed came because of the new atmosphere based on the Allison generation. In 1958, the year that Allison missed through illness, Brown played the position vacated by Walker. It was the year that West Ham gained its promotion to the first division.

The team that was promoted was one of those rare successful combinations of men at different stages in their lives. Winning a championship was the high point of Ernie Gregory's long career, a fitting tribute to years of solid performances. Cantwell was of the new generation and the success was the start of more and greater triumphs for him. John Bond showed that players should not be judged on first impressions, as well as proving Ted Fenton's ability to judge talent and show patience. But the promotion season is often associated with a player who almost did not come to West Ham – Vic Keeble.

West Ham scored 102 goals in the season. Right back John Bond netted 10 and inside left John Dick led the club with 26, but it was Keeble whose name would always be connected with goals and victory. Soon after Keeble arrived, John Bond told a reporter, 'It's made all the difference in the world to us',[42] and at the end of the season Fenton admitted, 'I didn't seriously begin to think in terms of promotion until after I signed Vic Keeble. Then I thought it would be possible.'[43] It was not the first time Fenton had signed Keeble, nor was it the first time West Ham had attempted to bring him to London. Keeble had joined Colchester in 1950 for a £10 signing-on fee from the then manager, Ted Fenton. Shortly afterwards, Fenton went to West Ham and convinced the club that it should obtain Keeble. The offer was to exchange Derek Jackman for him; Jackman was uncertain about his future, however, and Colchester rejected the offer. Instead of going to London, Keeble joined Newcastle where he scored more than 50 goals during his six years with the 'Magpies'. At various times during Keeble's career at Newcastle, Fenton enquired about his availability. He renewed negotiations at the start of the 1957 season.[44] West Ham had money, including the £25,000 it had received for Harry Hooper, but it attempted to make an exchange part of the deal for Keeble. The club had replaced Hooper with Mike Grice, a £10,000 purchase from Colchester who asked for a transfer after a relatively unsuccessful first year. This time, Fenton made sure that he got the man he needed, and Keeble was finally reunited with his first manager.[45]

It is hard to overestimate the contribution made by Keeble. The sentiments expressed by Fenton and Bond were echoed by other players, none of whom wanted to play down his own role. Keeble's arrival made

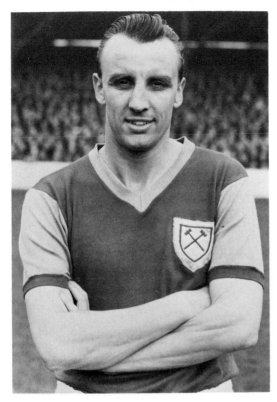

Vic Keeble scored the goals and created the opportunities that brought West Ham promotion in 1958 after its record stay in the second division

West Ham supporters feel that the club was willing to spend money and competent enough to bring in the right player. Keeble helped exorcise the Bert Davis legend and erase the memory of the sale of Harry Hooper Jr. Within a few months, Keeble and his team-mates had achieved promotion to the first division.

Keeble had a short career at West Ham. He played his last first-team match in the 1958-59 season and injuries forced him out of football the next year. The board took the rare step of trying to arrange a testimonial match for a player who had played only 76 matches for the club. It was more than the 45 goals he scored during that time that gave him a special place in the hearts of the board, as well as the supporters. Keeble symbolized the year when everything finally went right for the Hammers.

Football management might try to establish long-range plans but the comings and goings of players often appear to be coincidences and acts of fate. Early in the 1958 season, Manchester United visited the club. West Ham's no. 6 shirt was worn that night by the 17-year-old Bobby Moore. West Ham was near the top of the table but Billy Landsdowne and Andy Nelson were both injured for this important match. There were two obvious choices for a replacement, Moore and Malcolm Allison. The man

Phil Woosnam, the 'scholarly Welshman', brought cool talent and intelligence to West Ham when he joined the club in 1958

who had stamped his personality on West Ham never had the chance to play with the club in the first division. It was a hard decision for the manager and the captain, Noel Cantwell, and there was additional

Ron Greenwood, who succeeded Ted Fenton as manager in 1961, brought a string of honours to the club before he left to manage England in 1977

drama as Allison had been in charge of coaching the young players including Moore. Years later, it had become easy to romanticize that evening as the beginning of the Moore era; at the time it was definitely the end of the Allison dream.[46]

Moore was dropped after a few matches and and returned to the status one expects of a 17-year-old. His road to the first team was blocked by John Smith, who appeared to have a secure place for years to come at West Ham. When Smith requested a transfer in March 1960, Fenton and the board looked for the best possible deal. The key was Vic Keeble. West Ham needed someone to replace the ailing centre forward and Tottenham Hotspur's David Dunmore appeared to be the man for the job. An even swap of Dunmore and Smith took place on 28 March 1960. Dunmore was ready to step into the first team and Moore was there to take Smith's place.[47]

Reputations in football often have less to do with a player's performance than circumstances beyond his control. John Smith was certainly one such player. It seems unfair to someone who played more than 350 League matches and appeared for his country at the under-23 and youth level that his claim to fame should be that he was the man whose departure left a place open for Bobby Moore. Smith's inability to establish himself with Tottenham should not blind people to the fact

Johnny Byrne, the most expensive purchase West Ham had ever made, came to the club for £65,000 in 1962, a sure sign of the board's confidence in its new manager, Ron Greenwood

that he was a bright prospect at West Ham. Bobby Moore commented years later: 'If John hadn't gone to Spurs I might have been a reserve footballer who threw in the towel.'[48]

Journalists and supporters love to attach labels to players, something that makes them different and often has little to do with football. Once such labels become common currency they develop a life of their own. Phil Woosnam exemplifies the impact of labelling. His price-tag was the first thing supporters noticed about him. He represented a commitment by the directors to the club supporters, but Woosnam found his price a burden. He was supposed never to have a bad match. He brought precise skills with him and was supposed to be the man to ensure that John Dick and Vic Keeble could score goals in the first division. The Welshman was 'a thoughtful intelligent inside forward...he looked as much the academic as he did the athlete'.[49] Would Tony Pawson have used the same terms had Woosnam left school at 15 to play football? Woosnam was a rare creature in football, a 'graduate'. His approach to the game made it easy for commentators to make references to his background. Ron Greenwood saw in Woosnam 'a creative inside forward...always first to spot and exploit opposition weakness'. But Woosnam was never free just to play the game. There were his price tag, his education, and what Greenwood described as 'giving so much of himself...to help out other players...he robbed them of their individuality'.[50]

Woosnam also became the club's skipper. During the gap between Fenton's departure and Greenwood's arrival, he took on many of the functions of manager. Greenwood believed that Woosnam thought he might succeed Fenton as part of a general overhaul of the administrative side of the club. If the Welshman had harboured such hopes they were never pushed and Greenwood took control with no difficulty.[51] Woosnam was part of another new trend at West Ham: an increasing number of internationals in its playing side. By the time Greenwood arrived it had seven, and West Ham's youth policy and willingness to buy players was beginning to pay dividends. But Greenwood was looking for a player with special skills who could fit into his plans for the club. He found that man in Johnny Byrne of Crystal Palace.

'Budgie' Byrne came to West Ham with a record price tag. His skills and approach to the game made him more readily appreciated than the cool, detached Woosnam. He had a temperament (Greenwood described him a being 'like a real East Londoner') that stood him in good stead during his first few months with the club.[52] However, Byrne tried too hard to justify his purchase and played himself into a string of bad luck. For most of his first season nothing seemed to go right, and the West Ham crowd finally became impatient with him. Their discontent was tempered because the club had a good season, and everyone looked forward to the opening of the 1962-63 season with confidence that Byrne would live up to his promise. During the close season, there were rumblings of discontent among some of the club's top talent. Moore, Brown, Woosnam, Dick and Peters all refused the offer of the same terms as the previous year; instead they signed monthly contracts that gave them £15 per week.[53] The club made a point of assuring the public that none of these players were transfer listed and that West Ham would not part with any of them.[54] In November, however, Woosnam went to Aston Villa; the next month, Malcolm Musgrove went to Leyton Orient. Woosnam's departure showed that Greenwood had faith in the young players that were coming through the development system. It was also a sign of the club's maturity and self-confidence. It could sell a high-priced acquisition without fearing that supporters would accuse it of not recognizing talent or getting rid of Woosnam just for the money. At the start of 1963, only two members of the promotion side remained, Ken Brown and John Bond. Only Bond was a regular first-team performer.

It was Ron Greenwood's 'Hammers' that were the future of the club and gave it the best moments in its history. The club won two major championships and became famous because of the World Cup trio of Hurst, Peters and Moore. All of them joined the club within a three-year period, Peters being the last when he signed in November 1960. Moore and Hurst were established players by the time Peters played his first League match at Easter in 1962. Ironically, Peters's opening came when Greenwood put him in Hurst's place for the match. Despite the presence of the future 'World Cup trio', West Ham never finished higher than eighth between 1960 and 1967. All three players went through periods of uncertainty where or how they would fit into the team. When Hurst was finally given a chance to play at the front he began to assert himself. After a while, a very special partnership developed between Byrne and Hurst: one that resulted in more than 40 goals a year between them in their first two full seasons together.[55]

Peters was endowed with great natural talent. Greenwood was one of many people in football who thought Peters could have excelled at any position on the field. The danger existed that his versatility might work against his career, that he might remain what he described as 'a general dogsbody'.[56] Greenwood assessed Peters as 'a connoisseur's dream, the answer to a manager's prayer, although the fans did not always appreciate him...He was not a typical English player and the terraces didn't relate to him.'[57]

That was not the case with Bobby Moore. Very few players have ever struck the imagination of West Ham supporters in the same way as 'Moro', the 'golden boy'. His enormous popularity defied efforts to compare him with earlier West Ham heroes. He was not a goal scorer like Puddefoot or Vic Watson; he did not have the infectious friendliness or good humour of a Dick Walker or Ken Brown; and he lacked the underdog-made-good quality of a John Bond. Moore had the easiest quality to recognize and the hardest to define: presence. He looked like something special, off the pitch as well as on it. He moved with a sense of purpose and inspired confidence.

Everyone agrees on one essential feature of Moore's personality: he was always in control of himself. He exuded the sense that he knew what to do and would find a way to get it done. Greenwood's assessment that Moore's 'timing was impeccable in everything'[58] sums up the opinion of most observers.

Moore became a national hero after the 1966 Wembley World Cup victory, but it was his leadership at Wembley in 1964 and 1965 that ensured his place in the hearts of the West Ham faithful. By 1966, some of them could remark with a wry grin that 'If Bobby gets any more Cups at Wembley, he'll go down with metal fatigue.' Trevor Smith, a sports journalist who covered Moore's career at West Ham, is convinced that Moore's background 'was just an additional source of pride to the supporters...He would have been just as popular if he had not been a local.' His presence and the success that came in his wake created a special bond between him and the supporters. There was no one like Moore, but then there had never been successes for West Ham like those of 1964 and 1965.

When West Ham went to Wembley in 1964 the roles were reversed from 1923. West Ham was the favoured side playing against a second-division club. The final was almost an anticlimax for the Hammers. The semi-final against a favoured Manchester United team played in the mud at Hillsborough had brought out the best in Hurst and Moore, as well as two goals from Ronnie Boyce. Moore was the first to admit that his club did not play well in the final, but all criticism was lost in the euphoria of victory.[59] A year later, Moore led West Ham out onto the Wembley pitch for the final of the Cup Winners' Cup against TSV Munich. No one at West Ham could have complained about either the result or the quality of the football.

The following season was the crowning glory of Moore's career, but a series of disappointments for West Ham. The club finished in the middle of the first division, a position that had become its usual home, and went out in the fourth round of the FA Cup. A chance of glory lay in the defence of the Cup Winners' Cup. A superb performance by Borussia Dortmund's Lothar Emmerich in the semi-final leg ended the Hammers' quest. It might have been revenge for Hurst, Peters and Moore to know that Emmerich was part of the West German side they defeated at Wembley a few months later, but that did not lessen the disappointment of West Ham supporters. Two Cup victories in as many years had brought a sense of expectation to West Ham. For the first time, West Ham supporters felt they belonged in the highest echelons of football. England's victory in the World Cup on 30 July 1966 gave a huge if artificial boost to those expectations. West Ham partisans saw the World Cup victory as theirs; Moore was the captain and the goals in the final were scored by Hurst and Peters.

In fact, the World Cup was a mixed blessing for West Ham and, in some respects, for Moore, Hurst and Peters. Supporters expected them to lead the club to victories and had trouble coping with the normal West Ham results. Their team-mates were put in a difficult position. When West Ham won, the press often chalked it up as another victory for Moore, Hurst and Peters, but when the club lost, it was often put down to the inability of the supporting cast to play their parts properly.

Between April 1964 and April 1967, West Ham players gave supporters the FA Cup, a European title, the World Cup and a series of League disappointments. Some traditions were continued, some links with the past were broken and the basis for the next two decades was laid. Football is a team game, but it is also a collection of individual stories. We shall now step back and look at five other players and their West Ham careers: the player who could not be, the one who never was, the one who left, the one who came and the one who became the new legend.

John Lyall, the articulate son of a policeman, turned down the opportunity to continue at grammar school in order to sign with West Ham a year before Bobby Moore. It was his decision, but friends, teachers, and his parents made sure he knew the problems facing him. A bright future was predicted for him, for he had skill, intelligence and determination. He played a few matches between 1959 and 1962 and turned down a chance to move to Brighton. It was a twice-broken leg, not lack of skill or dedication, that ended his career. When Bobby Moore led West Ham out of the tunnel at Wembley in 1964, John Lyall was already working in the office and thinking about coaching. His career as a player ended a few months after his twenty-fourth birthday.

Lyall had wanted to be a part of West Ham ever since he was a child. Gordon Banks probably never thought much about West Ham until after he had secured a place as goalkeeper in England's World Cup side. The traditions of West Ham stopped him from coming to the club. West Ham made some preliminary enquiries about Banks's availability a year before the World Cup. Leicester City had no plans to release him then, but the situation had changed a year later. Peter Shilton was on the scene to replace Banks, and the latter's market value was at an all-time high. West Ham was committed to replacing its goalkeeper and the situation seemed perfect for Banks to join up with his 'international skipper Bobby Moore next season'. The *Ilford Recorder* made the case for 'Why the Hammers must switch to Banks'. He would be 'ideal for West Ham and he might be available for £50,000'.[60] Banks was 28; Bobby Ferguson, the goalkeeper West Ham was considering, was 20. Banks had experience, skill, and drawing power, Ferguson had only youth and potential. 'Too often in the past, West Ham have damaged themselves by their less than ruthless attitudes in a world where the quality of mercy is very much strained. Whatever agreements have been reached with Kilmarnock must be put aside. Banks of England is the man.'[61] He might have been the man for the *Recorder*, but not for Reg Pratt and Ron Greenwood. The argument against Banks was simple – Greenwood and Pratt had made a commitment to Kilmarnock and that was too important to set aside. Personal honour was involved; West Ham's word had to be good if the club were to be trusted in future negotiations.[62] In the past, West Ham officials had been contemptuous of other clubs that went back on their word. In the future Greenwood would be furious when West Ham lost a player he felt was committed to the club while his club touted him

Billy Bonds arrived at West Ham in 1967 and went on to hold the record for the highest number of matches played for the club. He was appointed club captain in 1973

around for a slightly higher price. The club refused to participate in a football version of 'gazumping' and turned down the opportunity to bring in the best goalkeeper in the world. A week after the *Recorder* had appealed for Banks, it headlined the purchase of Bobby Ferguson for £60,000 – a world record fee for a goalkeeper. Woosnam, Byrne and

Ferguson had ended the legend that West Ham would not spend, but another set of standards remained firmly in place, and Banks became a West Ham player that never was.[63]

At the end of the 1967 season, a headline in the *Recorder* showed the ever-changing nature of football: 'Hello Billy at £50,000, Goodbye Kenny at £4,000.'[64] Ken Brown, the only remaining member of the promotion team of 1958, had played his last first-team match months earlier. His testimonial match was a fitting farewell. Billy Bonds signed that week from Charlton for £50,000.[65] The price was higher than West Ham wanted because Dennis Burnett and Trevor Dawkins had refused to go as part of an exchange. Over the next 15 years, Bonds combined roles that had been played by Brown and Moore. Bonds became a crowd favourite and the quintessential clubman, and after a few years it was impossible for supporters to think of him as anything other than a lifelong Hammer. He became captain when Moore left and provided a sense of drive and leadership that took the club to two FA Cup victories. Within a few months, the end of the Fenton tradition left with Ken Brown and the basis of the post-Moore tradition began with Bonds and Trevor Brooking.

In April 1967, a small notice in a local newspaper noted the 'Reserve debut by Trevor Brooking...former England Boys' wing half, making his reserve team debut at right half, had a good game and showed great promise'.[66] Two seasons later, Brooking made his League debut in a match at Turf Moor. Like Lyall, he was a local man, a policeman's son who had attended a grammar school. Brooking brought intelligence and intensity to the game as well as a set of remarkably refined skills. He was West Ham's most important international performer after Moore left, and became the new legend at West Ham.

We have looked at only a few of the players who stamped their personality on West Ham United and became part of its folk memory. Some, like Brooking, started with the club; others, like Bonds, were transfers. Some were long-serving like Ken Brown; others passed through quickly like Vic Keeble. Some were noticeable for their intensity, like Allison; others were carefree, like Dick Walker. Some had natural talent, like Peters; others, like Bond, were 'like a blinking mule'. Some, like Woosnam, were marked for qualities that had nothing to do with their play; others, like Hurst, were judged strictly on their accomplishments. Some, like 'Budgie' Byrne, were important because they came to the club; others, like Sid Puddefoot, were immortalized because they left. Some, like Vic Watson, had brilliant careers at West Ham, but never received wider fame; others, like Moore, performed on a world stage. It is important to recognize the diversity of their backgrounds, their styles and their contributions. Football has so many elements and changes so rapidly that it is impossible to generalize about the character of the players and qualities that made them an important part of the mythology of West Ham.

CHAPTER 11
Professionals play for pay

When it came to the manager and the board, I'd learned how to take care of myself.

Frank O'Farrell, West Ham player, 1950-56.

Whether football is regarded primarily as a sport, a business, or even an art form, the players are essential. They provide the contest and the distinctive character of the game. Their skill raises football above the level of what the spectators can do. Even so, it is salutary to remember what happened in the United States in 1982: the professional football players' union went on strike with the slogan 'We are the game'. Logical, perhaps, but foolish. The phrase convinced fans that the players were selfish and unrealistic: the former because they wanted too much money, the latter because the 'game' was bigger than the total of its parts, human or otherwise.

Many analyses of the relationship between a football club and its players have emphasized the employer-employee situation. The similarities between footballers and workers were obvious. The sport developed in the context of an industrialized, urban society with players drawn mainly from working-class backgrounds, who mostly returned to labouring jobs after their time as footballers. Directors were natural employers, drawn from the business and professional classes. This helps to explain the relative power of the two groups but ignores much of what makes football different from any other traditional business. The 'product' of its workers and administrators is ephemeral. In many ways football is closer to the entertainment industries, but there is one crucial difference: an opponent is an essential ingredient of football.

From its very beginnings, West Ham United assumed the dual roles of employer and parent towards its players. The men who had created organized football 30 years earlier had endowed it with unique moral and spiritual characteristics, and it was felt that the players could not be counted on to protect these attributes if left to their own devices. (This was one of the issues involved in the lengthy and acrimonious debate that took place on professionalism, which led men like Arnold F. Hills to abandon the sport (see Chapter 1).) Footballers were not thought to have the strength to resist temptation. The board was vigilant in protecting the moral character of the players and the club's resources.

Footballers differed from most other workers in that they had a skill that was in demand and in short supply. A so-called free market would have given them greater control over their wages and conditions of work than other employees, but exactly the opposite occurred: management created contractual restraints to maintain competition between clubs on the field by restricting economic competition between them for players. This gave footballers a special status, that of semi-indentured workers. In most industries, the ultimate sanction held over workers was the threat of dismissal. In football, this weapon lost much of its impact; the better the player, the less his club wanted to lose him. The power of a club to retain a player gave it the ability to exercise control over his actions.

The discussion of how West Ham United acted towards its players (at least until the mid-1960s) must be viewed against the backdrop of the retain and transfer provisions of the contract and the maximum wage. One example of the club's ability to reward and punish occurred in the first few months of 1914, when the board dealt with two first-team players: Lonsdale and Tresadern. The former, reported by the manager for 'being absent without leave', was fined and directed to play in the reserve match the following week.[1] The fine was his weekly wage, since he had not participated in 'production' that week. Demotion was an object lesson that he should not take his career and lucrative income for granted. It told other clubs that something was amiss with Lonsdale; this might have diminished his transfer value, but it was worth it to the board. West Ham reminded Lonsdale and the other players of their responsibilities and discouraged them from thinking of transfer as a reward. In the case of Tresadern, the board showed that it could help as well as discipline: it agreed to loan Tresadern £5 (his weekly wage) for business purposes. The loan was to be paid back at a weekly rate of 10s with no interest.[2]

Each April a list was presented to the board by the chairman and manager which named those players to be retained for the following year and the terms to be offered. It was often accompanied by a list of players the club was willing to transfer and the fee it hoped to obtain. The players were not consulted before the wage list was compiled, nor did they have any direct influence on it. At face value, the offer was a take-it-or-leave-it arrangement for the player, but it was more complicated than that. The club obviously wanted the player or why would they offer him a contract? The maximum wage made it difficult to establish large differentials for players, forcing the manager to make minute distinctions. The general pattern that emerged throughout the 1920s and early 1930s was that three or four players were paid the maximum; everyone else fell into a spread beneath them. In 1920 Cope, Kay, Huston, Tresadern and Puddefoot were all granted the maximum of £9 both in and out of the season. 24 other players were offered terms at the same time, ranging from £7 per week all year round, to the low of £4 10s in the season and £3 10s in summer offered to Vic Watson.[3] The club that won promotion and a place in the FA Cup Final in 1923 included only three players on the maximum wage, Hufton, Kay and Tresadern. Watson and Jimmy Ruffell, men who went on to establish international reputations for themselves, were paid respectively £7 (£6 in the summer), and £5 all year round.[4] West Ham rewarded a combination of long service and quality of play.

The players knew what their team-mates were paid. It is as difficult to ignore the possibility of jealousy and envy entering their minds as it is to prove it. In theory, each player was an independent worker paid according to the board's perception of his contribution to the club. Because of the team nature of the sport, players were dependent on one another to perform well enough to give each of them a chance to make more money. In 1927 two players asked for their wages to be increased in September, four months after signing their contracts. Their request was refused.[5] The timing of this unusual action might have had something to do with the signing a week earlier of Henderson, who was brought into the side at the high wage of £7 year round. He was assured that this would be increased if he 'played in the first team fairly regularly until the end of the season'.[6] Until 1932 there were no recorded instances of a player refusing terms or directly questioning them when they were offered. Players complained about issues other than wages, such as the size of a transfer fee: if it was too high, a player would not be able to move.

West Ham's fall into the second division in 1932 did not drastically alter wages in the first season. Players of proven ability like Watson and Ruffell continued to receive the maximum. In the 1932-33 season, West Ham's performance slipped badly. The club fought off Chesterfield and Charlton to avoid the embarrassment of sliding into the third division, but the disappointment of the board was reflected in the terms offered to the players in April 1933. Three of them, Watson, Barrett and Collins, continued at the maximum, but the rest of the playing staff was grouped at the lower levels of the wage scale. Four players received free transfers and five were listed as eligible for transfer at fees ranging from £100 to £400.[7] The board was unhappy and so were some of the key players. Four of them refused to accept the terms, including Barrett and Collins. They could not ask for more money on a weekly basis, but they insisted on having benefits paid to them at the end of the season.[8] West Ham had previously granted benefits consistently to five-year players, but the terms differed from player to player. The benefits granted to Barrett and Collins (£500 and £300 respectively) initially contained a condition that was new for West Ham: they would take effect only 'if we remain in the second division'.[9] This stipulation was unique, since it was an individual reward based on team success. The veteran players would get the money that they assumed was theirs by right only if the team won. This may have been the board's response to the threat of diminished revenue in the third division. They might have been using the benefit to show players that they couldn't count on anything if the team disappointed the board. In the event Collins and Barrett accepted their benefits on slightly different terms. The latter was offered £500 with no mention of any conditions, but the offer made to Collins was complicated and gave him a choice. He could have £350 (the same as the original offer), 'which could be increased at our discretion if his play and our financial and league position warrant such action – or a definite £400'.[10] The board retained the idea of an 'incentive bonus' but backed away from forcing the player into accepting a deal whereby his personal finances were dependent on the play of his team-mates.

Thus in 1933 there was some bargaining between individual players and the board. Players raised their objections and hoped that the board would back away from its plans. There was more than money involved for the players: they feared that the rules of their relationship with the board were being changed. The directors had been affected deeply by the sad performance of the club during the past season; they might have been acting from pique, or perhaps they saw their proposal as a way to inspire the players. In either case, the board backed away quickly from the severest parts of its offer, although the provisions for Collins still showed its dissatisfaction.

The board wanted to keep wages as low as possible but at the same time reward individual players. When an important player refused to accept terms it could have harmful consequences for the atmosphere necessary to create winning football. The board could maintain the original offer, raise it or decide to transfer a player, and each option had built-in drawbacks. Remaining firm would show the directors' faith in their original judgment but could cause resentment and hurt performance. Raising the wage would satisfy the player, but could undermine the authority of the manager and be a bad example to other players. Transferring a player was the worst option, for it could weaken the club by the loss of his skills. If the board transferred a player it gave him the chance to negotiate a better wage and collect a signing-on bonus. Thus a potential transfer became a reward, not a punishment, for a player who showed an unwelcome sense of independence.

When football resumed in 1945 after the war the contract situation was little changed. Players were concerned with getting back into the game with West Ham or finding a club that would give them employment. For a few years, the size of the wage was almost a secondary consideration. The pre-war players had been conditioned to accept wage terms, but if West Ham's experience was any indication, the new generation was not going to be as easy for the board to deal with. Starting in 1950, there was a steady pattern of players not accepting the first set of wage terms offered to them. Each year, between four and seven players chose not to sign when the terms were first offered to them, and on about half those occasions the terms were increased, usually in the range of 10s per week. The players who wanted adjustments were usually first-team members. The yearly battle over the small difference in wages became a ritual for a few tough-minded players making the only gesture they could about their wage. Then it was up to the club to make a decision. The players who had come to West Ham from the Republic of Ireland, Danny McGowan, Tommy Moroney and Frank O'Farrell refused each year to accept the original terms offered to them. McGowan and O'Farrell were sometimes successful at getting their offers increased but neither of them acquired the reputation of a troublemaker because the disputes were kept within the club.

There was no sense among the players that they were making a general statement by not accepting terms. It was a personal matter: they thought that they deserved more. One exception to this was Malcolm Allison. It is no surprise that he objected almost every year to his wage offer; it was part of his general policy of challenging the management of the club on virtually every front. It is hard to separate how much Allison objected to authority in general, or how much was reaction to what he thought was wrong or stupid about West Ham's management.

The payment system that operated throughout the 1950s was based on the club's evaluation of the player's past contribution as well as what he might do for West Ham in the coming season. The wage spread shows that the club's priority was to reward past service. The system promised every player that his wage could reach the top level as long as he continued to keep his position. It was supposed to minimize envy since younger players could count on getting top wages in the future. The system included a wage plus bonuses for winning. Appearance money was reintroduced before the 1953 season as an effort by the club to 'reply to the recent discussion on players' wages, between the Players Union and the Industrial Dispute Tribunal'.[11] The restoration of the £1 bonus to some of the players each week seemed like a small enough concession to end the possibility of work disruption. The decision was an indication of the weakness of the union more than of the generosity of the clubs.

The most significant effort to change the certainty and simplicity of West Ham contracts was made by Allison in 1958. He was attempting to return to football after his bout of tuberculosis. The club offered him £17 per week for the following year, the maximum being £20. Rather than refuse the terms or ask for more, Allison made a counter-proposal: he wanted £20 in the playing season if he gained a first-team place, backdated to the start of the season. The board rejected the last provision and decided to offer him £20 after he had made ten first-team appearances. The board felt so strongly about this that the chairman was instructed to tell Allison that if he did not 'accept the terms, we are prepared to grant his request for a free transfer'.[12]

There was more at stake here than the money involved in Allison's wages. It was a clash of personalities, philosophies and perceptions about a player's status. West Ham's first reaction was one of willingness to part with Allison before it would accept his terms. Allison was saying that he was capable of playing again; the club wanted proof. As we have seen there was little love lost between Ted Fenton and Allison, and Reg Pratt did not take kindly to having any player write a unique set of provisions for himself. A week after the board's abrupt reply to Allison, the issue was reconsidered and a decision was made to rescind the previous minutes and grant him the maximum wage, if he played in ten first-team matches, and backdate it to 1 August. Until then, his wage would be the £17 per week that had been originally offered to him. Allison had negotiated new terms with the board, the only case in which a player had acted virtually as a free agent and obtained what he wanted for his services.

The 'Golden Handshake' testimonial match Allison received should not obscure the novelty or the importance of his last contractual struggle with West Ham United. Allison had made a tradition of not accepting terms, but this time he challenged how the board set terms, rather than just the amount. His situation was unique and had no effect either on the board or on his fellow players. Subsequently, West Ham continued to set terms for players as it had since 1900. The number of players who refused the terms remained constant, most of them accepting the offers unchanged within a few weeks. The board made occasional adjustments, always in the case of an established player who was approaching the maximum wage. There was no instance of a player getting the maximum after rejecting terms for less. If that had happened, the directors would have been admitting that they and the manager could not see when a player had reached the pinnacle of his skills.

The men who rejected terms usually repeated the practice over a period of years. One of them was Frank O'Farrell, an introspective, well-read man, who discusses many things in terms of principles. However, he did not view the almost annual rejection of his wage terms in that light. He felt he deserved more money. He was making a statement to the manager and chairman about his own worth and indicating that they should not take him for granted. West Ham players of the 1950s, the same men who demonstrated such great independence from management in their attitude towards football did not feel they were being abused by the wage system under which they worked. When they considered it at all it was in terms of how much or little they were getting, not why. The system had been there for longer than they had and there was little reason to speculate about its disappearance.

Before we decide that the West Ham players were unusual in their lack

Before we decide that the West Ham players were unusual in their lack of concern over an issue that should have been absolutely vital to their self-interest, it is worth noting that George Eastham and the Professional Footballers' Association raised their case only after Eastham had refused to accept a transfer. The decision in the Eastham case had a dramatic impact on the wage structure in football and provided later commentators with a useful view of broader issues. James Walvin's trenchant remark that the decision 'was eloquent testimony to the squalid nature of football's industrial relations for so long' brings the issue into sharp focus.[13] It extends the discussion beyond the issue of wages and terms of employment to the realization that in this area football was a unique industry. Its past and the realities of the law finally caught up with management-player relations in football and forced significant changes to be made, the long-term impact of which neither side understood.

The impact of the Eastham case was its cumulative effect on the policies of individual clubs towards specific players. Changes took place in the real world of football, not in the abstract realm of judges' chambers or solicitors' rooms. Bearing in mind how West Ham set the wages for its players and the exceptional response of Allison, O'Farrell and a few team-mates, a comparison with later events shows the real changes caused by George Eastham. On 25 May 1965 the West Ham board ratified bonuses that were to be paid to players for having won the Cup Winners' Cup. The amounts involved were very high by previous standards, ranging from £400 to £100 per man. On the same day, the board handled another player-related issue: it revised the terms for certain players. They were offered two-year contracts with a further two-year option period.[14] The amounts of money and the new terms were proof that something had happened to push the board into a new sense of generosity, or at least enlightened self-interest.

The most important change took place weeks before the offers were actually made. On 20 April the board discussed players' terms for 1965-66. The recommended increases were approved, as well as a 'new form of incentive bonus scheme'. Two weeks later, the chairman reported back to the board that a number of players had taken up their option on terms for a further year. Several were still to discuss the matter.[15] The chairman's use of the word 'discuss' reveals the reality of the new relationship. A discussion could take place only when the two sides met on relatively equal terms, and this began to happen throughout Football League clubs. Management was forced to realize that henceforth its employees would be paid not what they *should* (in management's judgment) earn, but what they *could* earn by retaining the right to take their unique talent elsewhere.

CHAPTER 12

More than a wage

We didn't think a lot about money...but we were doing a lot better than most of the people we knew.

Dick Walker, West Ham player from the late 1930s to 1952.

The relationship between West Ham and its players went far beyond wages and transfers. The wage offers showed the philosophy of the board and the status of any particular player, but there were other rewards, including benefits, that could be offered to a player and not violate FA or League regulations. The board also exercised disciplinary control on the off-field activities of the players. Training sessions did not give the manager enough opportunity to supervise his players or make up for ways in which they might abuse their bodies. The board and the manager instituted measures to ensure that the players had no excuse for not doing their best at every match.

The board was particularly concerned with the inability of players to withstand the temptation of drink. A system of fines for drinking and other misconduct was introduced with the founding of the club. A pattern was set in 1901 whereby players were placed on probation if they had drinking problems. Serious action was also taken against players who missed training or a match due to what the board considered was their own fault. Unauthorized absence was the most common offence requiring disciplinary action.[1] The board only dealt directly with offences by first-team players; players of lower status would be dismissed or dealt with by the manager. An example was the Simmons case in 1921. Simmons requested a transfer which the board granted, as long as they received a sum 'no less than we paid for him'. A month after the start of the West Ham season he was 'absent without leave'. The club responded by suspending him *sine die* and reported him to both the FA and the Football League.[2] This ensured that no other club could approach him, and publicized him as a troublemaker. This made it very difficult for him to obtain a transfer and for West Ham to get a fee for him, but the club could not afford to allow a player to break the rules with impunity.

The board avoided potential troublemakers by not employing them. At the end of the 1914 season, West Ham had agreed on a price with Exeter City to purchase a player named Fort. Syd King was sure that Fort could step into the West Ham first team immediately, but two weeks later the board wrote to Exeter: 'We do not require Fort as we hear accounts of his misconduct.' This misconduct had nothing to do with his play on the field.[3]

When players did have problems, they reached the board via the manager. King set standards for training and conduct and decided when players had overstepped the bounds. It was in his interest to make sure that players lived up to their obligations. The board tried not to interfere when cases were not referred to it. A noteworthy exception to this 'hands off' approach happened in July 1928 and concerned the training activities of a star player, Stanley Earle. The club had come together for training in mid-July and at the end of that month it was reported to the board that Earle had not turned up. The report about Earle did not come from King. An inquiry 'discovered that an extension of the close season leave had been granted by the secretary [King]'. No mention was made of why the inquiry had been undertaken, but clearly more was involved than a player missing a few days' early training. 'The board expressed dissatisfaction that any one player should be given a privilege over his fellow club mates and remarked that the secretary's absence at this time of year was not desirable.' Charlie Paynter, the trainer, was told to get in touch with Earle immediately. Earle was not held directly responsible for his absence. He had, after all, asked for and received permission from King. The board's reaction showed concern for the impact that the circumstances might have on the team as a whole.[4] It was essential to create a sense of harmony and team spirit, and exceptions to this could cause hard feelings. The target of the board's displeasure was Syd King, who was also absent: the directors wanted to ensure that other players did not ask for exceptions and that King would not repeat his error. The board decided to crack down on what seemed lax practices on the part of a star player and the manager.

The board had a major impact on the players' lives. The club's concern about living accommodation was one example of this. Young local players presented no difficulty: they could continue to live at home until they got married, or go into lodgings near the ground. The players trained four or five days a week, plus the match, and the manager was adamant that they should be available for each session and live close enough to commute to the ground easily.

The club often made lodging arrangements for players, which worked to the benefit of all concerned. The landlady had a lodger with a regular income whom the club would ensure was not disruptive. The player did not have the trouble of finding lodgings and knew that he had a landlady who wanted to keep in the club's good graces. West Ham was doing everything possible to keep its players away from bad influences. Such lodging arrangements were one more example of the paternalism the club had exercised from its beginnings.

The policy on living arrangements changed after 1945. German bombing had been particularly harsh in East London, and thousands of homes and rooming houses had been destroyed. What might have been considered an intrusion by the club before the war became a perk after it. The directors had the connections and funds to help their players.

Charlie Paynter was given responsibility for housing. There were pre-war players, most of them older and married, as well as younger players just starting out. West Ham had increased its scouting and looked further afield. Young players now came from the Republic of Ireland, and lodgings had to be found for them. They had to be properly supervised; the club was, in effect, looking for surrogate parents. Frank O'Farrell arrived in England for the first time in 1948 when he came to play for West Ham. He thought he was in a country that spoke another language, and realized that most of the people he met had as much trouble understanding his strong Irish accent. He needed 'digs' where the landlady could 'understand strange Catholic customs – fasting and fish on Fridays'. He was 20 at the time, but seemed younger. His team mate, Noel Cantwell, was only 17 when he arrived in London in 1952. His loneliness was relieved only by a landlady who 'treated me like a son', enjoyed football, and did not make much money out of the arrangement. The friendliness at his lodgings made up for there 'not being much of an Irish community in that part of the East End'. People were friendly not because they were football players but because the landlady made them a part of the street and community. There was also a positive side to being Irish: rationing was still in force in England and O'Farrell came back each summer with things for his landlady and her friends that they could not buy in London.

Religion was more important to some of the Irish players than their nationality. They met other Catholics at social functions as well as at church. O'Farrell joined the Catholic Action Group and assisted in making its census of the local Catholic population. During one interview he realized how closely some people paid attention to West Ham United. One woman told him that she would start coming to Mass if he made the first team. 'She kept her promise and even started bringing her husband who wasn't even Catholic.' The family atmosphere that some players like O'Farrell and Cantwell found in their lodgings was exactly what the club wanted. It kept the players happy and out of trouble and made it easier to recruit new Irish players.

Before 1939 the board had generally turned down requests for players to live any significant distance from the ground. In 1946 the question was not whether the club wanted players to live near the ground, but whether they could find anywhere to live at all. The club not only stopped trying to enforce residence regulations but on the eve of the 1946-47 season it passed a resolution 'to compensate players who are forced to travel because of the inability to find accommodation'. The compensation was tied to the wage level of the players: those earning more than £8 per week would get £8 extra per quarter. The others would be dealt with on an individual basis.[5] The board was thus subsidizing an arrangement that it had previously prohibited. It did not apply for Football League permission to pay for transport – a sure sign that the compensation was not regarded as a bonus.

Travel compensation was an unsatisfactory stop-gap measure. It was costly and a step towards institutionalizing a policy disruptive to the orderly management of the team. In order to meet the 'pressing need for accommodation for players' the board decided to purchase a house in Barking and instructed the secretary to look at other suitable rental property in the area.[6] Within two months, the club purchased three more properties and was making plans to renovate them. It was so involved in residential property that it hired an estate agent 'to manage our newly purchased properties'.[7] For 15 years, starting in October 1945, discussion about club properties was a regular feature of the board's weekly deliberations. There was never any question of using properties to generate income, but in a very short time, instead of just fulfilling a need, they became a reward for players. The properties were not 'company homes', since no compulsion was placed on players to live in them. The club had assumed a new role as landlord to the players, which meant that housing could be the cause of occasional ill-feeling between players and the club.

In the first year, the board purchased ten houses; it owned 18 separate properties by 1950.[8] Some of these were turned into flats suitable for unmarried players. There was no lack of interest in the accommodation on the part of the players: as soon as a player vacated a flat or house, there were requests to move into it. In the first few years of the housing scheme, rent was kept below £2 per week – in most cases it was less than £1 10s. The houses cost between £500 and £1,600, and individual players negotiated with the club over rent and terms. P. Peters got permission to buy the furniture in the furnished flat he was renting from the club for £150 less a credit of £1 per week for the time he had lived there. In exchange, his weekly rent was lowered from £2 to £1.[9] Ironically, three months later Peters asked permission to live in Reading. The request was turned down by the secretary, and Peters remained in his flat as long as he was with West Ham.[10] Charlie Bicknell approached the board with a business proposition concerning his house: he wanted the board to 'meet him half-way' towards the cost of papering and distempering his house. He also had problems with the plumbing, and although he had told the estate agent nothing had been done before the tank overflowed. He did the necessary repairs himself and wanted the club, his landlord, to help pay for them.[11]

The club houses helped to recruit staff. When the club offered the position of assistant trainer to Hooper from Sunderland he was also offered a 'house to let at an economic rent' as soon as the club could buy one to suit him. He took both the position and the house.[12]

The frequency with which property matters appeared before the board showed the small, almost personalized, business approach that operated at West Ham. The board, its estate agent, and Ted Fenton, then assistant manager, were all involved with the houses. The board could not leave the matter to the estate agent, who would treat it as another business matter and try to get the best possible terms. That was not why West Ham had bought the houses and was not what the board wanted from them. The properties were supposed to be a way of strengthening relations with the players, a way of showing that the board and its employees were part of a club in fact, as well as in name. It seemed, however, to be a waste of Fenton's time to deal with property matters, especially as he began to take over more of Paynter's duties. This was clear to Reg Pratt, then vice-chairman, who supervised the property dealings for the board. When Pratt became chairman in 1950 one of his first moves was to bring someone into the club on a part-time unpaid basis to act as property manager to the club. The introduction of Jack Turner was a step that had consequences more far-reaching than Pratt had in mind when he brought him in.

Whatever Reg Pratt's reasons – an effort to get the players to plan for themselves, another way of showing them that the club knew best, ridding West Ham of the burdens involved in managing the properties – the new scheme was a significant break with the past. Whenever West Ham sold a house to a player, it lost some control over that player and forfeited a potential perk for an incoming player. The house-purchase scheme extended after a few years. Turner turned to insurance companies as another way of raising money; they were 'willing to talk to me because I had backers'. The primary backers were the players, but the obvious support of the chairman gave Turner's efforts added credibility. West Ham's involvement with local property, which had begun to meet a housing shortage for its players, had been transformed into a fringe benefit that fostered the family image of the club. It changed again when a club official (albeit unpaid) became involved with individual players in making decisions that had nothing to do directly with their relationship to West Ham. It was a far cry from the traditional paternalism, and caused rifts within the governing structure of the club – a problem that has already been discussed (see pp.139-40).

A successful career with West Ham meant that a player's wage could be supplemented by appearance bonuses and the extra payments that were permitted by the League for wins, draws and cup-ties. Best of all was the benefit for which players qualified after five years' service with the club. There was more than just money involved when a player qualified for a benefit: it was proof that he was a success. The benefit payment was large enough to give a player something to look forward to, and another reason for him to identify with the club. The benefit encouraged top performance and long service. Although the board never bragged about the size of the wages it paid, it treated benefits quite differently. It pointed to them with pride as a sign of the club's regard for its players, proof that West Ham retained the loyalty and services of its top players. The list of players who received benefits was one way in which the chairman could quietly refute accusations that the club was only interested in selling players and reinforce the idea that the board was creating a solid organization. In 1929, for example, the chairman gave special notice to the fact that Hufton had qualified for a benefit that year, since it 'was his second, the *only* player to thus qualify'.[13]

Before 1914 benefits were an uncommon occurrence at West Ham. There had been a rapid turnover in the playing staff while the club tried to determine how much it was willing to spend and at what level it wanted to compete. Two players, Whiteman and Woodards, had the misfortune to achieve their benefits during the 1915 season. They, and the board, had to bow to the disruption of the season, but the board passed the resolution that 'in lieu of the benefit this season…they be granted another when football recommences, each to be guaranteed £125'.[14]

After West Ham moved into the Football League the club began to retain its top players for longer than it had earlier. An increasing number of players bacame eligible for benefits. Each player assumed that his benefit was his right, but the amount of the benefit was not automatic. For example, in 1930 five players became eligible for bonuses; the board granted two of them £500 each, Earle and Hufton £550 each, and discussed Watson's request for £650.[15] The board's discussion took place three weeks after it had passed a formal resolution congratulating Watson on his recent achievement in an international match.[16] Watson's timing was good, but not good enough to persuade the board to grant him the amount he wanted. He had not served longer than Hufton or Earle, and even though he was the best-known West Ham player and at the top of his form, the benefit was not granted as a recognition of individual skill. It was symbolic of the length of time over which a certain level of performance had been maintained.

A week after Watson's request was denied, he signed his contract for the next year, including provision for a benefit of £500.[17] The board and the player had gone through the necessary ritual: Watson asked for an amount that would demonstrate his status and the board reaffirmed the purpose of the benefit. The board ended discussion by asserting its power. There was no sign of rancour and the matter was settled quickly. The issue did not arise again. Equity was maintained within the playing ranks and no one blamed Watson for trying to get as much as he could.

The Football League had strong prohibitions on the payment of money to players beyond their contractual terms. Unless it limited the offer of gifts, benefits and other types of incentive, the wealthier clubs could make a mockery of the maximum wage and compete for the best players. The restrictions placed on the clubs enabled clubs to remain economically viable by protecting them from their own fiscal ineptitude and from opposing clubs who were richer, or more efficient, or both. The financial restrictions enforced by the League were a determined attempt to make sure that the weakest or most inefficient would remain alive in order to provide competition for the other clubs. This sort of approach has been refined to its highest point in the very profitable (£11 million per year per club just from television revenue) National Football League in the United States. The 28 clubs divide incoming players among themselves each year, and one club has exclusive rights to sign each player to a contract. The clubs share equally in all television revenue and profits from championship matches, and divide gate money on a 60%-40% basis (home team and visitor) for regular season matches. This adds up to a combination of survival of the weakest and socialism for the wealthy.

The benefit was a legitimate financial device, according to the standards of the men who ran football. It was given openly and had to be approved by the League. It tied in with the belief that it was unethical to pay workers large sums for doing what they were already getting a salary for. The sums involved were large enough to motivate players to perform at top level, but the system was not easy to abuse. It was totally unlike the much discussed, but never documented 'fiver in the boot' – money that mysteriously appeared in a player's kit. Other gifts were monitored by the League, ranging from one-offs like wedding presents to expenses for a transferred player who remained in his former home.

West Ham's experience showed that the benefit was not necessarily associated with future performance. Two years after Hufton and Earle received sizeable benefits, the chairman reported to the shareholders that 'such old favourites as Eddie Hufton and Stanley Earle have left the club'.[18] They departed in the shake-up that followed the disastrous 1931-32 season. Vic Watson, who had received his benefit in the same year as Earle and Hufton, remained with West Ham for three more years, but he was granted a free transfer at the end of the 1935 season. At the same time he was given a benefit 'to be determined after ascertaining the number of first- and second-team appearances since his last benefit'.[19] The following year, West Ham granted £500 to Jimmy Ruffell, the third benefit he had received from the club.[20] Ruffell was finally approaching the end of his career; he had already confounded Paynter and his staff by returning to the first team at an advanced age after he had lost his place. The high point of the benefits was reached in May 1939 when the board authorized payments of £500 each at the end of the coming season to Barrett, Conway, Foxall and Dick Walker. £200 was authorized for Ruffell immediately, his share of a benefit that marked the end of his association with the club.[21]

Players were not the only employees to get bonuses. In 1939 an annual bonus of £100 was paid to the manager, £75 to the secretary and sums ranging from £50 to the trainer to £10 to Wally St Pier, the newly appointed assistant coach and scout.[22] These payments did not have to meet with approval by the League and were granted at the discretion of the board. The staff had no presumptive right to a bonus, but the club granted them each year at the AGM. Even in 1939, when the chairman informed the shareholders that 'gates were down badly, no doubt due to the international crisis and the great amount of bad weather', the staff received their bonuses and the players received the benefits that were promised a year before.

In 1944 the vice-chairman announced to the shareholders that he wanted 'to draw attention to an item which has not appeared in the account for some years and with which I feel every shareholder will be in hearty agreement, payment of players' benefits in the amount of £690'. This amount was equal to the combined profit of the previous three years. There were no dissenting comments raised by the seven shareholders and two directors at the meeting. West Ham could have avoided the benefit payments, but the vice-chairman's announcement shows that the club was proud to make them. It was an effort to show that players and shareholders were part of a joint enterprise which even the war was not able to shatter.

When football resumed full time in 1946, West Ham had many pre-war players. One noticeable result of this was that a large number of benefits had to be paid over the next few years. In 1950 the board asked the League to sanction the payment of benefits to ten players. They included pre-war first-team players like Dick Walker, and established players like Ernie Gregory and Eddie Chapman. The League was diligent in its scrutiny of benefits. It refused to allow payment to Hall 'unless he completed five years' service, was transferred, or ceased to play football'.[23]

Occasionally a player took it upon himself to remind the board that his benefit was due. In 1952 Frank O'Farrell enquired about his benefit, due the following month. There was a notation to pay him £750 (he was the first player to be granted a benefit at the increased rate), but this was countermanded by Reg Pratt, vice-chairman and head of the finance committee.[24]

O'Farrell did not receive the benefit he requested, but he used his accrued share as a bargaining tool when the club wanted to transfer him. In 1956 he was offered to Preston and told Ted Fenton that he would accept the transfer only if he was given a £600 tax-free benefit. This was more than the club felt he deserved. Ironically, he attributed his determination to stand up to the club to the vestiges of his 'discussion with Paynter' over first-team status, as a result of which 'I'd learned how to take care of myself'. O'Farrell got £575, and West Ham went through the standard procedure of obtaining permission from the League to grant the benefit.[25]

Many ex-players have vivid memories of the importance of the benefit as a sign of the bond between them and the club. Their attitudes are sometimes surprising. O'Farrell thought the club was a good one to play for, but the handling of the benefit was one of the few signs of a mean spirit. Allison, who had little good to say about anyone at West Ham, claims that his benefit and a later testimonial were the best things that happened to him there. Dick Walker's feelings about the good treatment he received at West Ham were summed up by his comment: 'After all, they even gave me three benefits.'

Up to 1956 only a few isolated incidents had occurred of former West Ham employees asking the club for financial assistance when they had fallen on hard times. The requests were usually from undistinguished players who wanted immediate help. The board avoided handing out cash, but occasionally allowed players to sell items such as programs or chocolates at the ground. The only instance in which the board granted an extended *ex gratia* payment involved the widow of Syd King.

The week after King's suicide, the board made a grant of £40 to Mrs King to purchase a grave for her husband and altered its previous resolution of £3 per week *ex gratia* payment to King in favour of his widow.[26] Three months later, the board decided to extend payment 'until 31 December 1933 when it would definitely cease'. Mrs King appealed to the board to understand her plight and change its decision. West Ham responded by granting her a payment of £2 per week for the following year (1934) and 'this allowance will be final'.[27] No further correspondence was exchanged until a week before Mrs King's allowance was due to expire. In December 1934 she sent a long letter in which she thanked the club for the allowance 'which enabled me to provide for the necessities and minor comforts of life', and then appealed for help. Her expenses had recently been increased because she was suffering from diabetes and required a special diet and medical help.

> The cause of this complaint is, I understand, due to the series of tragic and horrible shocks which I suffered two years ago. I am sure that my late husband's friends on the Board would not like to know that it is difficult for me to obtain these new necessities, and I am making an appeal for a continuance of the payment...My worry about diabetes would be removed if I knew I would receive the payment for my remaining years.
>
> I am positive that the Board will be pleased to offer me an opportunity of a happier New Year, making 1935 a better year for me just as it will, I hope, be a very successful one for the Club and all connected with it.[28]

Mrs King based her appeal on all the best causes – King's long tenure with the club, the West Ham sense of family, and the wish for a Happy New Year. The board looked at other considerations. Syd King had been dismissed by the club as a result of his insubordination and shady dealings, and only his death had prevented the dismissal becoming an open scandal. Some directors had felt that they were acting irresponsibly when they granted him the *ex gratia* payment. The grant to Mrs King went beyond anything that would have been given to her husband. There had been no thought of putting him on a lifetime retainer, which was what his widow was requesting. Her appeal was poignant, but was opposed to the board's concept of its responsibility. It might have set a precedent for the treatment of other long-serving members of the organization. Mrs King's letter gave the impression that West Ham should take some responsibility for the death of her husband and the resulting impact on her. The board gave no credence to that interpretation. Its reply was a short, over-polite note which sympathized with her plight, but reminded her that the decision to limit the payment had been made by directors who had been close friends of her late husband. She could not expect the board to change its position at this late date.[29]

Three months later, Mrs King made one final attempt to get the board to reconsider its treatment of her, 'but the Board regretted they could not alter this previous decision'. An exercise in charity towards a former employee could not become a model for future policy. The decision confirmed that West Ham did not have a responsibility towards employees who operated outside the standards of the club.

More than twenty years later, the board had to face a more ambivalent set of considerations when some of its former players needed help.

Jim Barrett had been one of the most popular West Ham players of the 1930s and his son, also Jim, followed in his footsteps. The elder Barrett had been ill and unemployed for many months when his situation became known to friends and ex-supporters. One of them wrote to West Ham in January 1956 asking the club to have a collection before a match to raise funds for Barrett.[30] For years West Ham had allowed charitable organizations to raise money at specific matches, but that had ended in 1951, when the club was limited to contributions to the charity fund from pre-season practice matches. The board's reply to the request reminded the writer of the club's policy about collections and added that 'We had helped Barrett on many occasions and were still trying to help him'.[31] The admission that it had been helping Barrett was unusual for the club, for it was generally reluctant to broadcast its charity and thus embarrass the recipient; moreover it did not wish to encourage other former players to approach the club for assistance. West Ham continued to help Barrett with clothing and efforts to raise money from other sources.

While efforts were being made to assist Barrett, the board was considering the plight of two young players, Brian Moore and Geoff Hallas. Their careers had been cut short by injuries after only a little first-team service. West Ham's insurance company offered £250 to compensate Hallas for his injuries, but the club had already given him much more than that in *ex gratia* payments.[32] When Moore returned from Ireland and informed West Ham that he was retiring on the advice of his doctor and parents, the club immediately applied to the insurance company for relief.[33] When the squad gathered for pre-season training in 1956 the board decided to do something special for Hallas and Moore: a testimonial match to raise money.[34] This was an unusual step for West Ham. The only other event like it since the war had been the 1951 testimonial match for Charlie Paynter: a special tribute to the 'grand old man' of the club.

Fenton immediately set about lining up an opponent for the Hallas/Moore testimonial, but he was turned down first by Manchester City and then by Newcastle and Wolves. He finally lined up a group of 'all-stars' whom the board had to insure for up to £20,000 per man.[35] Contributions came in as soon as the match was announced: Jack Helliar donated two guineas and the Leyton Silver Band donated their match fee of eight guineas.[36] The real pay-off to Hallas and Moore would be the gate receipts. The club tried to make sure that the players would receive as much as possible and got assurances from its accountant that there would be no tax due on the money.[37] However, two weeks after the match Customs and Excise requested payment of entertainment tax on the admissions. It would decide if, and how, to refund that amount to the players.[38]

When the finances from the testimonial match were calculated the board drew equal cheques for Hallas and Moore, based on the gross gate less the tax. Each man was to be sent a cheque for £991 11s 3d and separate cheques for £15 0s 3d from the donations. After authorizing the payment the board moved unanimously that 'these figures should be made known to the public'.[39] Everyone involved would thus know that the players had done well. While the figures were being calculated, the payment to Moore ran into a major snag: West Ham discovered that he was a registered player with Cambridge United and had played for them. West Ham had no claim, or interest, in his services as a player, but there were other considerations. The secretary immediately wrote to Cambridge to inform them of the serious nature of the injury to Moore's eye. He was instructed by the board not to send the cheque to Moore until Cambridge replied.[40] A week later, a cheque was sent to Hallas and Moore's share was moved to another account while Reg Pratt went to see Sir Stanley Rous of the FA to find out what to do.[41]

Cambridge United replied that it knew about Moore's circumstances and that everything his new club had done was within the regulations of the FA and in the best interests of the player. Moore was being given an opportunity to learn a good job, 'one that would fit him for a future life independent of football'.[42] The reply gave the impression that Cambridge felt it was showing a real interest in Moore's future, while West Ham had contented itself with paying him and forgetting him. West Ham's response was pointed; it withheld the money from Moore's benefit match, granted him an *ex gratia* payment of £500 and put the rest into a separate account.[43] West Ham was making a firm distinction between money from a benefit for an injured ex-player and a grant made at the discretion of the club. A month later, Moore's reply showed that he understood what West Ham were trying to do. He merely acknowledged receipt of the cheque for £500 and stated that he would accept it as part payment from the testimonial account and not as *ex gratia*.[44] If Moore had been an active player, this type of dispute and exchange would have been unthinkable. The disagreement went to the heart of what was involved in the testimonial and what restrictions the club could put on the grant of the money that had come from it.

The dispute with Moore went no further and West Ham won its point. The money was put into a fund for former players, and much of it eventually went to Jim Barrett. While the disposition of the Hallas/Moore testimonial was taking much of the board's time, another player-related issue was developing, which caused West Ham to adopt special practices for players whose careers had ended. Dick Walker's career was closing after 23 years at West Ham. During his time with the club he had done as well financially as any player. He had been on the maximum wage from 1938, received his first benefit in 1939 and two more benefits after the war. Walker thought of himself as typical of his generation of players: 'We didn't think a lot about about money, after all there wasn't much of it around. But we were doing a lot better than most of the people we knew.' Just as typical was the absence of any thought about his future after football. The club 'put pressure on players after the war to save money and buy houses, but it had little effect...other players didn't think or talk about the future'.

The future descended quickly on Dick Walker in 1957. He had already lost his place in the first team to Ken Brown, 'a lovely lad who I tried to treat differently than I had been by the senior players when I was young', and had slid down into the 'A' team. He was still making good money – £16 and £14 per week (the maximum for first-team players was only £20) – but he knew that his time at West Ham was coming to an end. He did not get on with the new manager, Ted Fenton; they managed to co-exist for over five years, but neither man much liked the other. Walker's recollection of the 1957 decision to leave was that Fenton 'had made it unpleasant for me long enough. It was finally time to go.'

Press reports about Walker's decision to retire prompted West Ham to do something about his future through the normal administrative channels. Fenton was told to mention to Walker the possibility of staging a testimonial match and to contact the Dagenham Club, which was rumoured to have an interest in employing Walker.[45] A month later West Ham ended Walker's career with the club by not offering him a contract for the following season. Dagenham had nothing definite to offer him in the way of employment, so the West Ham board instructed Fenton to have further talks with Walker.[46] Finally, at the end of the summer, 'following Fenton's interview with Walker, it was agreed that a benefit match would be arranged for Walker during the season and a further interview arranged to discuss Walker's future'.[47] Walker now had no job prospects and no training. When his summer wages with West Ham ran out, the club offered him a job at £4 per week 'to attend to the players' boots until a benefit match was played for him or until he commences training as a licensed victualler'.[48] As the 1957 season started, West Ham's former captain was doing the job he had done almost 25 years before as a groundsboy.

It was important to set up Walker's testimonial match as quickly as possible: he had become a sort of spectre at West Ham, a reminder of a past that Fenton wanted to expunge and with which most of the new players could not identify. Arrangements were made with Sparta of Rotterdam to come over to London to play in Walker's testimonial. After the Dutch club received its £700 guarantee and expenses were deducted, a cheque was presented to Walker for the remainder of the receipts. He also received the programme receipts and all the money collected at the ground. Within a few days, Dick Walker left West Ham's employ. Shortly afterwards he found a job as a scout with Tottenham Hotspurs. This move to West Ham's North London rival was made with the help of Reg Pratt.

West Ham regarded testimonial matches as something reserved for extraordinary circumstances. Moore and Hallas had promising careers which ended very early due to crippling injuries, while Walker was almost a local monument. Less than a year after Walker's testimonial, the board was making plans for a similar match to benefit Malcolm Allison. In many ways, Walker and Allison were opposites – in their personalities, their approach to the game and their relationship with the club. Walker was a long-serving player who had come up through the West Ham ranks and had no competing loyalties. He reached the pinnacle of his ambition when he became captain. He accepted the terms offered to him each year and was grateful for whatever the club did for him. Allison, on the other hand, regarded the board and the manager as people to be avoided. Their function was to set the stage and then leave him to act on it as he wished.

Why did West Ham produce the rare benefit of a testimonial for two men who were so fundamentally different? They in fact shared one obvious quality: their playing days were over. Walker had been hanging on at the fringes for a few years battling against age and the new generation of players. Allison's decline had been swift and tragic. His recovery from tuberculosis could not obscure the fact that his days as a top-quality player were over. Walker and Allison could not stay at West Ham, but the club could not ignore their departure. The testimonials proved that they were held in high regard. They were gracious gestures that helped the players and cost the club very little.

The Allison testimonial brought an all-star team to play against West Ham. The arrangement gave the club a chance to show its supporters that it was a first-class operation. Glamorous names like Charlton, Matthews and Haynes were to appear on 17 November, but West Ham supporters were even more excited by the presence of Phil Woosnam. New players and first-division success were more important than saying goodbye to a former star. Woosnam was supposed to ensure that West Ham's successful entry into the first division would be something more than a two-month wonder. His personality and his fee made him special, and it was appropriate for him to start at West Ham when the club was honouring Allison's departure.

In May 1960 Vic Keeble had to face the end of his career at West Ham due to injuries. The chairman discussed Keeble's future with him and recommended to the board that they consider staging a testimonial match for him during the following season.[49] The board applied for permission to grant him £450 as an accrued share of benefit. While decisions were being made about Keeble, the board organized a testimonial match against a visiting club from Costa Rica to honour Ernie Gregory 'for loyal and meritorious service to the club over the past 21 years'. The match netted £2,100 for Gregory, and West Ham negotiated with the Inland Revenue to ensure that Gregory received all the money due to him.[50] The club was not as successful in organizing a testimonial for Vic Keeble; the decision was made late in the year and scheduling was a real problem. Instead, West Ham decided 'to grant him £750 *ex gratia* in order to honour its obligation'.[51] In Keeble's case, West Ham was taking the payment out of its normal revenue. The obligation to which the board referred was a self-imposed one. The club had already paid the benefit due to Keeble; he had not been with West Ham very long, but he had made a special contribution to a great accomplishment. The board was careful to point out that the payment was *ex gratia*, thus negating any claim that the club was responsible for future payments to Keeble. Two years after Keeble's career came to its premature end, West Ham officials tried again to help him by presenting testimony to the Ministry of Pensions and National Insurance. The board made a strong statement 'that his ability and character were such that he could have continued for approximately a further six years and he would have had the opportunity to have earned considerably more due to the abolition of the regulations concerning the maximum wage'. Not only did the board testify to Keeble's ability and character, it also took significant note of the monumental change that had taken place in football between the time of Keeble's injury and the disposition of his application for support.[52]

Even after the abolition of the maximum wage, players continued to

Ron Greenwood, towards the end of his tenure as manager, watching a match with team manager John Lyall

'accrue' amounts towards a benefit. West Ham used the testimonial match to meet extraordinary circumstances. The most interesting testimonial case occurred in 1964. John Lyall arrived at West Ham in 1955 as a 15-year-old, the kind of player the club pointed to with pride. Lyall was almost the epitome of the scouting system that Pratt and Fenton liked to brag about when they said that West Ham was going to challenge the 'big clubs'. When he signed professional forms with West Ham in 1957, one reason was that the club treated him 'like something more than a kid'. The manager allowed him to work in the office rather than on the groundstaff, an arrangement that fitted in with his academic skills and gave Eddie Chapman, the secretary, a good, free assistant. Lyall had every reason to look forward to several years of good football with the club, which had just gained promotion, but unhappily his career as a player was dogged by injury.

Almost every time that Lyall's name appeared in the club minutes it was in the context of the injuries that brought his career to an end. He missed most of two seasons and had a serious knee operation early in his first-team career. In his first match after the operation on 8 January 1964, he damaged the leg again.[53] Two weeks later, specialists confirmed that there was no way Lyall could expect to play in the future.[54] The board immediately applied for permission to pay him an accrued share of benefit of £250, then changed its request and asked for £400. Lyall had no immediate plans for the future nor any source of income; the board took it upon itself to help, and he was aided by the totally unexpected run West Ham made in the FA Cup.

Lyall was offered the job of secretary to the players' FA Cup pool. His office skills qualified him for the job but there is little doubt that he was chosen because he was still part of the extended team. The job ended shortly after the FA Cup and Lyall still had to plan for the future. West Ham decided to apply to the FA for permission to stage a testimonial match 'in view of his enforced termination of employment with us due to an injury'.[55] The decision was unusual because Lyall was not a veteran like Walker and had made no great contribution to the club like Keeble. A parallel can be drawn between between Lyall and Hallas, but Lyall's benefit took place in the post-Eastham world of football.

The Lyall testimonial was a great success, enabling the club to set up a special fund for him that included £3,590 14s from the gate and £207 5s from the sale of programmes.[56] It was also an artistic success – a game that pitted West Ham against a team of London all-stars. The football was entertaining, much more than a mere friendly match. The most striking feature of the match was that it was played on schedule. It took place on the Monday after the conclusion of West Ham's regular season, the Monday *before* the Cup Final, which fielded West Ham against Preston North End. It had been 41 years since West Ham had appeared in an FA Cup Final, yet five days before that all-important match the club staged a testimonial. What of the possibility that a key player might be injured? Was it fair to the players to go through with the testimonial? Was fair to the supporters who had waited so long for the club to achieve success? None of these considerations deterred the board or the manager. Greenwood saw the match as a good work-out, a chance to give the players some practice against top-quality opponents in a setting where 'no one would be trying to hurt anybody'. Reg Pratt's explanation was even simpler: 'After all, we had promised the match to John and he deserved it.' Lyall saw the match as 'typical of what West Ham will do for you'. These comments about the Lyall testimonial may be coloured by the knowledge that everything worked out well in the event, both at Upton Park and at Wembley. We must also remember that Greenwood, Pratt and Lyall had a strong sense of loyalty to West Ham and wanted to see the best in its actions. But however we interpret their reactions, we must return to the fact that the club staged a match for a player whose contribution to the club had not been very important on the eve of the Cup Final. West Ham officials refer to the match with satisfaction, but try to avoid portraying it as something unusual. They like to think the action represented the 'West Ham style', something that made the club different from other organizations.

CHAPTER 13

Something besides football matches

> It's hard to explain what the club is, but I do know that it's *my* club. I've
> been brought up with it all my life. One thing is sure; it's something that
> has always been there. You can't explain it...People that don't understand
> think that you're bloody stupid, that you're crackers getting so involved.
> It's hard to understand yourself, especially when your ulcer starts acting
> up...but you can't tell yourself not to get involved.

This comment by Colin Green, a 45-year-old local printer who has been
going to matches for 35 years, shows how the club affects some
supporters. West Ham United's existence matters to thousands of men,
women and children, many of whom have never seen a professional
football match. Uncounted numbers of people could recount stories
about someone like '80-year-old Aunt Nell who can tell you more about
West Ham than anybody else and she's never been to the bloody ground.
But it's her whole life.'

West Ham was rooted in the various communities and subcultures
that made up the extended East End. Its role as the leading professional
football club in the area ensured that thousands of football fans would
worry about the club and many times that number would recognize it as
part of their lives. In its spectacular 1923 season, the club was impossible
to ignore: there were endless parades, rallies, flags and decorations
marking the run up to the Cup. The post-Wembley celebration has
become part of local mythology, the electric tram emblazoned forever in
the memories of thousands.

What has the club done apart from providing a football side, and
should it be expected to do anything more for its patrons than any other
local business enterprise? Over the years there have been complaints
that the club has not tried to make people feel that they were part of it.
Efforts to create a supporters' organization were rebuffed by the club for
decades as the directors saw no need for it: they thought that West Ham
and its players were already part of the local landscape. Shortly after the
move to Upton Park, West Ham increased its collections for local
charities. A football match was a good place at which to raise money, but
West Ham had to ensure than an afternoon of football was not overrun by

charity collectors. At the same time, the club did not want to be accused of being oblivious to the needs of the poor and infirm; West Ham allowed collections and made donations as a company. The minutes of the club are full of requests for both; at least one a week was brought to the board's attention. More than half of these were granted, and the big problem was the date to assign to each collection. Every charity worked on the sensible idea that it would collect more money at matches played against fashionable clubs when the weather was tolerable. Many spectators had the impression that 'there always seemed to be somebody or other collecting at Upton Park'.[1] There were emergencies that required attention such as when disaster struck the Welsh colliers in 1913; a nationwide collection was instigated, which raised £2 16s 3d at a West Ham match. The club brought the amount up to £5. When the Dock Labourers Union asked for collection rights the same month, the club responded by recommending that they collect 'outside, as collections inside are poor'.[2]

Until 1914 almost all requests for collections were from local organizations and charities. The war changed that; the club co-ordinated contributions for its players to the War Fund and publicized this as much as possible. Syd King reminded the press that the club was going to add £60 from a practice match to the players' donation.[3] By November, the club asked for more donations and apologized for its small contribution of a guinea, regretting that 'gates are much smaller, principally owing to adverse press agitation against football'.[4] The FA favoured a drastic change in the game in response to the new wave of patriotism. League officials and players wanted a more gradual approach. The latter group were no less patriotic or concerned about the war, but football was not just a game or a diversion to them; the cancellation of the season or the Cup meant the end of the players' employment. Every season they were away from the game subtracted from their already all-too-short career expectations. Club officials could not blithely disregard the economic realities of the game. They had bills to meet, rates to pay and repairs to make. West Ham directors knew this, but they also understood the need to appease the public. Their response to the attacks on football showed their displeasure that the professional game was being singled out for abuse. The board chose not to deal with a request from a newspaper for the 'particulars of players who had enlisted'.[5] This attempt to demean football and the patriotism of professional footballers was especially irritating since the source of the question was *The Times*. Over the years that newspaper had ignored professional football as far as it could, preferring to cover matches involving amateur, university and old boys' clubs. The Cup was an exception; even *The Times* could not refuse to cover a sporting event that was the showpiece of the nation sponsored by an organization with impeccable establishment credentials.

The curtailment of football in 1915 did not prevent West Ham from

playing its pre-season practice matches. These had become the club's major effort to raise money for charity and gave the club a chance to combine training with good works and public relations. At least £100 was raised each year after 1910. The club's two favourite charities, the West Ham Hospital and St Mary's Hospital, received significant contributions from every practice match from 1908 to 1940, except during the First World War.[6] Hospitals were visible, permanent elements in the community just as West Ham was. They provided a public service and were dependent on unpaid directors and volunteers and a cadre of highly skilled professionals. The directors of West Ham United often also served on the boards of local charities.

West Ham's rise into the first division and appearance at the Cup Final coincided with a new level of local economic hardship. The club had more money available from practice matches, but it was besieged by new requests. The charitable situation became so complicated that the board decided that a formal policy was necessary for the allocation of practice match funds. It declared that in the future, '75 per cent will be given to local hospitals'. The other 25 per cent would be left to the nomination of the directors and the secretary in equal parts of one-tenth.[7] The plan conformed to the existing policies of the club and was flexible enough to cope with new demands. The intent of the board was clear: local charities must realize that there was little money available for groups other than hospitals. The rules ensured that there would be little competition in the board-room to gain advantages for someone's favourite charity.

The Docklands Settlement was a large, long-established facility that provided for the needs of the homeless and destitute. It harked back to West Ham's roots and the club had periodically assisted it with contributions and collections. In 1923 the Settlement came to West Ham with a much more ambitious proposal: it asked for a match to be played solely for its benefit. The board worked to organize an event that would also show West Ham's new status among football's elite. The opponent would be Tottenham Hotspurs and the board requested that the Duke and Duchess of York honour the match with their presence.[8] The match was played on 17 March and the Duke attended.[9] The 'Duke of York' match became part of the folklore of the club, a fitting addition to the 'White Horse' and the 'Electric Tram' of the previous April. The warden of the Settlement thanked everyone for making the match possible and promised that the proceeds would be used to provide sports facilities 'for every lad that wants to use them'.[10]

When the West Ham children's hospital asked for a collection in March 1935, the board felt it should explain its refusal: 'It was resolved that, as we have had so many letters complaining about the number of collections on this ground, we regretted that we could not grant permission.'[11] For the rest of the 1930s, the board rejected most requests for collections. The club assisted causes in ways other than granting funds or allowing collections: it gave space in the programme for groups to describe their activities and solicit support. Regular donations of spare gear were made to various organizations, ranging from schools to shelters for the homeless and the West Ham unemployed. Local schools used the ground for special events. The annual match between West Ham and East Ham boys was the centrepiece of the local season. The club gave the 'Chairman's Trophy' to the winning side each year.

The charity collection system operated like everything else at West Ham: through an ill-defined but well-understood set of standards. In September 1938, the board demanded assurances from an organization that 'nothing political or controversial would be said in the appeal which was to be made on our radio'. If the board was worried, why had it granted the organization's request in the first place? The answer was that it had come from the Football Association to give assistance in 'ARP propaganda'.[12] Less than a year before war broke out, there was no consensus about the goals of the ARP (Air Raid Precautions). Other requests to West Ham showed that though the nation was drifting towards war, the attitudes of the football community changed slowly. The club could not obtain approval from the Football League for the National Fitness Council to mount a 'fitness display' during half-time at a League match. This had nothing to do with politics: the reason was mundune albeit compelling; the fitness display would not fit into the normal half-time interval.[13]

In September 1939, the government reversed the First World War policy of stopping football and decided that the sport would help morale on the home front. Football was given a special status and the clubs had to show that they and their players deserved it. New organizations appealed to West Ham for assistance and many of them received it: matches were arranged and collections were taken to provide cigarettes for prisoners, Christmas collections for soldiers' families and aid for bomb victims.[14] West Ham's charitable activities were sometimes of an unusual nature. In late 1941, the club received a circular from the FA asking for collections for 'Mrs Churchill's Fund'. St Dunstan's had been promised a collection for that date but changes had to be made. The date set was that of a Cup-tie and the board decided to turn it into a major event. The East Ham mayor and aldermen were present and the AFS band provided pre-match entertainment. The collection raised £57, and the board augmented the sum to £75. This was more than any club in the country had collected and the board made sure to tell 'our patrons through the medium of the programme' at the next match.[15] Two weeks later, the directors were delighted to receive a 'personal letter from Mrs Churchill' thanking them and concerned to gain their help in raising money for 'her Aid to Russia Fund'.[16] This prompted more requests to West Ham than any other war-time charity. When the mayor of East Ham asked for assistance less than two months after the FA collection, the board reminded him of the large amount it had raised, but the club agreed to a collection as long as it was taken at any time other than the

Arsenal match. That was promised to St Dunstan's, which would finally get a prime date. West Ham staged collections for many other nations including China, Poland and Romania. Servicemen and foreign fighting forces were given special passes and rates to attend matches. The board offered the ground to the US army for 'anything suitable to them', but the army had to refuse since 'our ground was not large enough for baseball'.[17]

After 1945, organizations applied for collections and benefit matches to rebuild facilities that had been damaged during the war and to make up for years in which they had not been able to raise funds. The board received more requests from deserving organizations than it could possibly handle. One of its first refusals for a charity match went to the Docklands Settlement.[18] Non-football related circumstances helped shape club policy. One tradition of West Ham United remained intact even after the founding of the welfare state – the August practice matches. The beneficiaries of the proceeds were changed but West Ham did not ignore the bodies with which its board members and their families had been identified for decades. The Attlee government brought a new sense of social responsibility to the government and voluntary services augmented government-financed institutions. The National Health Service was one notable example. The charitable funding given to hospitals dropped, but West Ham's contribution helped National Health Service hospitals to provide for the comfort of the men and women who were part of the extended West Ham community.

Scenes of East London during the blitz and stories of how the community was brought closer together by sharing the nightly dangers and uncertainties have achieved mythic proportions. 'They can't bomb us into submission' reinforced the 'us versus them' attitude that had always been a part of East London culture. Some of the damage inflicted by German bombs made its impact only after 1945. The war had reinforced local pride, but its aftermath did much to destroy the community. The need to demolish substandard dwellings and provide housing quickly for thousands of people led to social engineering as well as rapid construction. Huge tower blocks transformed the community for ever.

The Boleyn Ground was damaged severely at the end of the war by a flying bomb. Play could be resumed, but the ground was not good enough to live up to the needs of a top-class club. The board went through all the proper channels to acquire the building materials to start repairs, but its enquiries fell on deaf ears. No permits were forthcoming. At the end of 1947 matters were still the same. The directors had hitherto protected the privacy of their operation jealously but they were now so frustrated that they took the unprecedented step of making a public appeal for suggestions as to how to solve their problems.[19] An article in the programme described the situation briefly and assured supporters that the poor conditions for watching football were not the fault of the board. The board was prepared to spend the money if it could get permission to do so.

The danger in asking for suggestions from the public was that people took it seriously. Within a week, letters had arrived and the board felt compelled to answer one of them in some detail. The secretary was instructed to inform Mr Johnson that the board was still negotiating with the Ministy of Works 'and that anything in the way of a mass protest by your supporters at present would not be advisable'.[20] A 'mass protest' at football 40 years ago should not conjure up modern images of gang warfare, but it did mean interference from supporters, something the directors had always wanted to avoid. A week later, the board received a letter detailing plans that were potentially disruptive to the orderly operation of the club that the board prized so highly. An organization had been formed under the title of 'Hammers Supporters' Club'. It informed the board of its existence and that the Supporters' Club would 'like to co-operate with us in the true sporting spirit'. The board's reply was distinctly unsporting; a few seasons ago it 'decided against having anything to do with a supporters' club and after due consideration they see no reason why they should still not adhere to that decision'.[21] The board's actions were less harsh than its rhetoric. It agreed to announce the Supporters' Club coach tour to a Cup-tie at Blackburn.

When West Ham had been in the first division there had been occasional correspondence from local residents wanting to know if they could become formally affiliated with their club. The club answered such requests curtly, if it chose to answer at all. The directors were not interested in the idea and as long as there was no compelling reason for a supporters' club the directors regarded an organized group of supporters as unnecessary.

When the West Ham Supporters' Club was formed in 1947 it had no real agenda or plans. Six months later, West Ham received another unsigned letter from the Supporters' Club asking for an appointment to 'clear up any misunderstandings that may exist between the Supporters' Club and our Club'.[22] West Ham's reply, 'We were unaware of any misunderstanding and referred them to our letter of the 17th December 1947', was a realistic appraisal of the situation from the board's position. There were no misunderstandings because there was no relationship; the Supporters' Club had no special status and deserved no special treatment. The meeting did not take place, the newly elected secretary of the Supporters' Club had to be satisfied with a copy of the letter that had been sent to his predecessor six months earlier. The Supporters' Club was a grass-roots organization. The members developed some sense of being part of a club. It was one way to recreate the community that had been lost over the previous ten years.

The relationship between West Ham United and the Supporters' Club

was distant at best, hostile at worst. The directors preferred to act as if
the Supporters' Club did not exist. Less than a month after West Ham's
curt reply to the Supporters' Club, the board received an unsigned letter
that the Supporters' Club 'deplored our actions of first come first served
for our replayed Cup-tie'. Why the Supporters' Club had a right to
deplore anything was a mystery to the board. The same letter also asked
the directors to agree to the title of the Supporters' Club 'being either
West Ham United Supporters' Club or West Ham United Football
Supporters' Club'. The reply was even more dismissive than the earlier
correspondence: 'We [West Ham United FC] were not interested in what
title they gave themselves.'[23] The Supporters' Club found it difficult to
gain any recognition. When it complained to the FA about the treatment
of some of its members at Luton, the FA informed West Ham that it
intended to take no action unless the club filed a formal complaint. West
Ham responded by stating that it had 'nothing to do whatever with this
or any Supporters' Club', but would try to do something about the
allegedly bad treatment that its supporters had received at Luton. The
Luton episode had given the Supporters' Club a chance to speak out for
its members and to attach itself to the football club. It succeeded partly
in the former but failed completely in the latter. The football club took
another opportunity to distance itself from the Supporters' Club, thanks
to a complaint made by a season ticket holder, Mr Segal. He had been
rebuffed when he tried to join a coach party to Luton. West Ham reacted
by refusing to make future announcements on behalf of the Supporters'
Club.[24]

The venue for the second annual dinner of the Supporters' Club, the
Robin Hood Hotel, might have been symbolic of how the organization
felt about its situation, but any group that can attract 120 people for its
dinner is not exactly moribund. A local newspaper described the 'high
hopes of the football club supporters' and the secretary of the Supporters'
Club talked about increasing membership from 400 to 1000. It was
affiliated with the National Federation of Supporters' Clubs, whose
motto was 'to help and not to hinder parent clubs'. Just in case the West
Ham board was not convinced by the motto, the president of the
Supporters' Club declared, 'There was no suggestion of interfering in the
slightest degree with the football club'.[25]

There was more than ego and propriety involved in the board's refusal
to recognize the Supporters' Club. It extends to a deeper issue in English
football: what is a 'club'? Generally we understand it to mean a shared
enterprise, something to which its members belong and over which they
have control. When directors talk about 'our club' they mean something
more than the emotional ties that bind them to West Ham United. They
are responsible for the continued existence and possible success of the
enterprise. When an individual supporter talks about 'my club' he knows
that although he may have little control over it, he has a long-term

interest in its future and policies. He could stop buying tickets, and if enough people did so, the directors might have to make changes. The danger is that the club would not have the money to buy the players or improve facilities, and the situation would worsen. Any effort to pressurize a football club runs into emotions that are the bedrock of football. The decision to watch and follow a team is not made in a rational or calculated fashion. Incompetent play on the field or the suspicion of even greater incompetence in the board-room is usually not enough to transform someone into an ex-supporter. Paradoxically, only deeply committed supporters care enough to do something about forcing changes on a club. The casual supporter goes on to another club or another activity.

By the early 1950s the football club and the Supporters' Club had arrived at an accommodation. The board was probably sincere when it informed the Bury FC directors that the overall relationship 'that exists between parent and supporters' club is cordial'.[26] The new atmosphere owed much to the personalities of Reg Pratt and Tom Jenkinson (who became chairman of the Supporters' Club in 1951). A Labour councillor and last mayor of West Ham, Jenkinson's roots were very different from Pratt's. For most West Ham fans, 1923 triggers memories of Wembley, promotion and the electric tram. For Jenkinson, it was the year that 'Dad and Mum moved into the Poplar Workhouse...a place that was more like a warehouse than anything else...where kids like me used to wait for crusts of bread and scraps'. He started work in 1926 as a delivery boy and claims that his introduction to politics came during the General Strike when he was part of a group of youths who tried to overturn a lorry. Jenkinson did not become a West Ham fan until he moved near Upton Park after the war. He saw the Supporters' Club as 'a social club of people who shared the same ideas and the same interest'. Pratt was receptive to Jenkinson's approach to develop some informal links between the two organizations. Representatives of the Hammers came to give talks at meetings of the Supporters' Club, although 'members were always disappointed when people asked for fees...A lot of them came *gratis* including Fenton and Pratt'. There was no chance of Jenkinson using West Ham for political purposes: he was well aware that West Ham kept its distance from local politics: 'The Directors have tried to keep out of civic affairs. They're watertight...[and] don't let the club mix with anything else.'

Promotion affected everything at Upton Park, including the Supporters' Club. It had a dramatic rise in membership and in the number of people who wanted to go to away matches. The directors saw the value of London voices singing and cheering on 'The Irons' in distant grounds. 'In appreciation of the wonderful support given by away travel for our first few away League matches in our initial season in the first division, it was decided to reimburse the [West Ham Supporters' Club] with a cheque for £392, being the cost of their away travel up to and including October 18th.'[27] This was only the beginning; two years later, the groups held a formal meeting to set up a joint fund-raising campaign. Finally there was something that the Supporters' Club could do for West Ham – bricks, mortar and improvements to the ground were needed. Previous suggestions to raise money for the club had been rejected because directors were angered by the hint that they needed help and disturbed that supporters might suggest how the money should be spent. Money raised to buy players could quickly turn into demands to buy and sell particular players. The new arrangement between the chairman and Supporters' Club officials resulted in a 'Jackpot' competition. The idea had been proposed by the Supporters' Club, but it had taken a long time to interest the directors. Each group had been running a small scheme of its own; the new operation dwarfed the previous ones. Purchase of the ground had given West Ham great new responsibilities and the board was trying to bring it up to top-class standards. The Supporters' Club looked more attractive to the directors since it would be raising money for a property owned by the board.

The Supporters' Club took over the operation of the jackpot competition, even spending £250 to purchase a caravan to assist in sales. The first cheque from the competition was paid over to the club in April 1961 when the 'West Ham United Football Club Ltd Building Fund' account was opened. Two signatures would be honoured – Reg Pratt's and W. J. Johnson's, the latter being the honorary treasurer of the Supporters' Club – a dramatic sign of co-operation.[28] Eddie Chapman held regular meetings with representatives of the Supporters' Club to discuss how to raise money, but not how it would be spent. The football club sent out letters to season ticket holders asking for support, and tried to recruit agents for the competition. Chapman appealed in the press for support for West Ham's various competitions 'which are run for them by the Supporters' Club'. He was afraid that people thought the money was being raised *for* the Supporters' Club and wanted to take the opportunity to assure them that 'Every penny we get from this source is used to improve the ground and the spectators' comfort.'[29]

The building fund was transformed into a development fund, which provided the club with money to assist in the grand scheme to rebuild and modernize the ground. The 1964 dinner of the Supporters' Club was billed as a celebration and lived up to it. Pratt was the main speaker, but the FA Cup was the main feature of the top table. In the midst of the euphoria Pratt reminded the audience, 'We will need every penny.' He announced that the new stand would be ready for opening the following season and that such important changes would not have been possible without the co-operation of the Supporters' Club.[30] Pratt used the 1964 AGM to deliver a lecture about the complicated nature of football finances. 'Much had been written in the press about the need for clubs to provide more comfort for their patrons...The only way therefore for clubs to meet costs is out of taxed income and from the donations from Supporters' Clubs schemes.' There were plans for future improvements which the club was contemplating, 'given the right kind of support'.[31] Five years earlier that support would have meant gate money, the sale of players and guarantees by the directors.

The harsh realities of football economics brought the club and the Supporters' Club into a working arrangement with benefits for both. By 1964, Pratt was no longer reluctant to recognize the important role the Supporters' Club played in the progress of the club and the role that it might play in the future. The board's disdain for a supporters' club was replaced by praise for this Supporters' Club's ability to raise money. The meddling that the directors had feared had not taken place, nor did the Supporters' Club embarrass the board.

The existence of a club like West Ham had political overtones although not necessarily in electoral terms. It commanded the loyalties of thousands and was a highly visible part of the local landscape. Each fortnight it attracted an audience that outstripped any other attraction in the region. When West Ham had major triumphs, civic leaders were more than willing to be associated with the club.

The most frequent connection between the board and local authorities concerned the rates. 'The club was always complaining about the rates', according to Councillor Jenkinson, but the board saw it as nothing more than an appeal for simple justice. After 1920 the club appealed against its rates at least once every five years. Negotiations between the club and the local authority extended over months, sometimes years, becoming less than cordial during the Second World War and the years immediately following it, when the board was granted a significant decrease in its rates. But the Inland Revenue was not as benevolent: in the aftermath of the damage caused by a flying bomb the club asked for tax relief. The authorities refused, but West Ham's position was upheld, though only after months of talks and angry letters.[32]

West Ham appealed to local politicians for assistance on rare occasions; the most significant were the efforts to prevail on the national government to end the entertainment tax on football admissions, and to push the Ministry of Works into allowing West Ham to buy the material that was needed to complete some of the post-war reconstruction of the ground.[33] In the former case, West Ham joined other clubs, the League and FA officials as part of a nation-wide lobbying effort. In the latter instance, the club approached its local members of Parliament.[34] In both cases the directors were fighting for something that would have a direct impact on the supporters. The club could seem to be acting as the steward and advocate for its patrons.

Earlier, we used a comparison between the Brooklyn Dodgers and West Ham United to give a broader context to the norms of English football. The political climate surrounding football is another area where this type of comparison is helpful. Comments by political scientists about the relationship between the electoral fortunes of Harold Wilson and England's success at Wembley in 1966 and failure in Mexico City in 1970 cannot be dismissed lightly. American politicians have seen the usefulness of identifying with sports teams, especially successful ones, for almost a century. Many baseball teams were founded by local political organizations and presented to the supporters as a 'gift' of the party. Candidates for office have long courted the public support of prominent athletes, so why shouldn't they go for a whole team and its supporters? A regular feature of important sporting events in America has been the appearance of an officeholder. Television coverage of the World Series or the Super Bowl does not seem complete until the President has made his phone call to congratulate the winners and to remind the viewers that the game represents all the most noble attributes of American life. Richard Nixon's dedication to football became an important feature of his public personality, being one way this withdrawn, suspicious man felt that he could relate to the 'common people'. When thousands of college students came to Washington to protest against the invasion of Cambodia, Nixon went out to speak to them and discussed the football records of their universities. A flamboyant (though by no means unusual) example of the blending of sport and electoral politics was carried out by John V. Lindsay, the Mayor of New York. In October 1969, this model of a patrician politician, elegantly dressed as ever, was thrown into a shower and had champagne poured over his head. Far from being embarrassed by this, Lindsay enjoyed every minute as the television and news cameras photographed him with the New York Mets celebrating their World Series victory. As much as some English politicians might want to use football for publicity, does the picture of Reg Prentice, long-time local MP, or his colleague and self-proclaimed Hammer supporter George Brown, cavorting in the bath with victorious West Ham players seem possible?

The West Ham chairmen have had few requests for favours from local politicians and those that have been made have always been made quietly. Politicians wanted small things, usually tickets. The club accommodated them when it was convenient, but almost never in the directors' box. Politicians made little effort to become allied with the club. The bizarre exception was when Pratt was 'approached once by a Tory MP for Ilford who wanted to be made a director...Since he was so conceited anyway, the effort must have been more personal than political.' Pratt regarded the incident as the kind of comedy relief that lightened the pressures of being a chairman. He tried to ignore it and then pointed out to the MP that his appointment would not do any good for him since everyone would see it as an all too obvious effort at self-aggrandizement.[35] The club would always reject advances from local political figures who thought they could use the Hammers to promote their own careers. The popularity of the football club was not transferable.

The club's lack of involvement in the political scene was further indication of the unique role it maintained within the local community. West Ham fulfilled a public need and was dependent upon public support. The club was involved in a continuous exercise in public relations, which meant more than selling tickets. The unique role of West Ham in the life of its community was based on the folk mythology that surrounded it: directors held the club and its traditions in stewardship. That determined the policies of the club and acted as a restraint on everyone who dealt with it. The club has touched the lives of tens of thousands of people in ways that have nothing to do with what happens on the field. The Hammers have been part of something much larger than the club, the League, or even the game of football.

CHAPTER 14

A lot of things made the Hammers special

West Ham was like Christmas tree ornaments – it came down after the New Year.

Local saying.

Match results, the number of goals scored by Watson or Goulden, the matches played by Bonds, the caps won by Moore – these are all an important part of what makes West Ham United special. Some supporters who were lucky enough to see Ronnie Boyce's goal – the one that brought the Cup to West Ham for the first time in 1923 – still remember it exactly. Many remember more than what actually happened. Events expand over the years: the difficult save becomes impossible, the winning goal comes from an incredible angle, and the injured player becomes almost fatally injured as he carries on to the end of the match.

The impact of memories goes far beyond people interested in football: the seven-year-old girl who witnessed the electric tram in 1923 never forgot that it was something to be proud of and that it was connected with West Ham United. The roar coming from the ground affected even the most casual of Green Street shoppers. The worker at Dagenham who had to listen to his mates recount match post-mortems on Mondays could not escape knowing something about the club. People who had no interest in West Ham United had to live with its fortunes on a weekly basis in the 1970s: that was the price they had to pay for their enjoyment of the long-running TV series 'Till Death Us Do Part', whose author, Johnny Speight, has had a life-long relationship with the Hammers.

Any attempt to perform an analytical breakdown of the West Ham tradition faces two big problems – it is much more than the sum total of its component parts, and many of its elements seem irrational to an outsider. Also, few supporters care about the reality behind the club's traditions, many of which stem from its infrequent success. The importance of Wembley in 1923 went far beyond the glory of a Cup Final and the welcome cash it brought. Readers of the local papers could not avoid football by ignoring the sports pages, for stories about Wembley, West Ham and civic plans to honour the team were everywhere. The match was billed as a struggle between north and south, a contest between a modest second-division team and one with a history of victories. The match itself was almost an anti-climax; the pride and celebration were simply because West Ham had got so far.

West Ham's crowds were singing long before it became fashionable. They sang 'I'm forever blowing bubbles', a very incongruous song for a football crowd, one that talks about bubbles rising in the air, fortune hiding everywhere and dying dreams. It is strange that the song should echo in the part of London that has always been associated with tough men and women and even tougher times: the heart of the General Strike, the scene of the most grinding poverty of the Depression, the favourite target of the Luftwaffe, the site of so much disruptive post-war social engineering, and the haunt of fabled criminals. However, until West Ham was promoted, 'Bubbles' might have seemed appropriate for a club that could never quite fulfil the dreams of its supporters. And later the song seemed to fit a West Ham style that was supposedly frothy and light.

What difference does it make to supporters that a long-forgotten, young local player had a head of blond curls that brought him the nickname 'Bubbles' at the same time as 'I'm forever blowing bubbles' became a world-wide hit? No one persuaded the Upton Park faithful to sing the song in the first place, let alone retain it after the player had gone and the song had run its course. The history of 'Bubbles' gives some insights into the character of the people who have continued to make West Ham a unique club. East London has been the place for dreamers, even if few dreams come true. One way of coping with life was to develop a sense of humour tinged with a dose of irony. That was the way to change reality, without withdrawing from it. Players and journalists who came to West Ham from outside remembered the humour of the crowd as its most distinctive feature. Even at the worst times, maybe especially then, someone would see the humour or absurdity of what was happening. 'Bubbles' was just one more example of that approach to life.

Frank O'Farrell is typical of many players in his view of West Ham's special properties: 'It was a close intimate ground...and was more like a family than anything else.' East Londoners have maintained a strong sense of extended family, which is one reason why the club was and is so important to people. West Ham United shows that the community is different and important. This is clear when West Ham supporters talk about other clubs: Charlton and Millwall, which might appear most like West Ham, are different because they are 'across the river'. The Orient is close, but decidedly small beer. Chelsea and Fulham are in completely foreign territory – West London.

To Bernard Joy, the sports journalist, West Ham seemed like 'a small provincial club like Bolton, Blackpool or Huddersfield until 1958...One where all the support was local and it meant so much to the people who lived around it.' But the club and its supporters knew that there were only two clubs that mattered for comparison – Arsenal and Tottenham Hotspurs.

Arsenal was the epitome of success on the pitch, respectability in the board-room and class in the backroom. It was difficult for anyone from West Ham to complain about the Arsenal operation, especially since they were trying to emulate it, albeit at a reduced level. The West Ham players who moved into the first division in 1958 felt special playing against Arsenal. They were certainly not awed; if anything the match gave them the opportunity to show that the club belonged. When West Ham went to Highbury for the first time Fenton surprised his players with a new strip. Whether its purpose was to take their minds off the importance of the match or to reassure them that they were as good as Arsenal, the tactic seemed to work. West Ham had an important victory that justified the pride of its supporters. Fenton admired Arsenal and, ironically, when West Ham replaced him, the club looked to Arsenal for his successor.

West Ham supporters revelled in any defeat of Arsenal because of the glorious record of the Gunners. There was something deeper about the rivalry with Tottenham. One feature of this is something that few people in the game care to discuss at any length. West Ham supporters identify Spurs as the Jewish club or, in much less polite terms, 'the Tottenham Yids'. Many of the Jewish families that lived in the East End headed north or north west once they had made enough money to leave. In the eyes of their former neighbours it was bad enough of the Jews to move, but they compounded their desertion by supporting another football club. This judgment makes for good folk mythology, but it distorts the realities of religious and social mobility. For instance, it ignores the fact that the largest single synagogue congregation in Europe is situated in Redbridge, in the heart of the extended West Ham territory. However, Jewish supporters of Tottenham have fitted into the stereotype that others have created for them: graduates of the rag trade who wanted to be associated with an institution like the Spurs because it was successful and had a certain flair. It does not matter if the Jewish element among Tottenham supporters is real or imagined. It is another example of Jews filling the role they have had in non-Jewish communities for centuries – that of providing a 'them' to point at.

West Ham United is, in the words of one long-time supporter, 'not just a limited company or eleven men kicking a ball about...it's what this area is all about'. A friend of his who has been going to matches for over 50 years wanted to give an unsentimental view of the club and its traditions, but he realized quickly that 'you have to take a romantic approach towards something like this club. Even if our feelings and memories about it are not exactly true, why have the press and so many people adopted them? If enough people believe something about West Ham United, and it means enough to them, well, then it becomes true, doesn't it?'

West Ham lived off the thrills of 1923 for nearly two decades, a time when joy was hard to come by in the local community. The area was characterized by its 'uniform drabness', living testimony to the crisis in British society that condemned thousands of people to lives of misery and desolation. Images of the Depression impressed themselves for ever on people's memories. The Relieving Officer could break families up; 'council children' were dependent on local charity for their survival and the 'dreadful brown jerseys' that they were forced to wear to school made their condition clear to everyone. The overall impression of outsiders who moved into that part of London was of its deprivation. Ken Astin, the internationally known referee, spent a lifetime teaching in a primary school in Redbridge, a relatively affluent area, but some of the children under his care came from homes where food was scarce and clothes were rags.

In such an atmosphere, street football was the only amusement for many children. The boots that they wore to play in were bought (and sold, and re-bought) in the 'in and out shops' that were as much a feature of the neighbourhood as the looming presence of the Boleyn Ground. Football at all levels was an antidote to the realities of daily life. The club, however, was not a charity: it needed gate money to survive. Children ran errands, collected scrap, or became involved in the minor illegalities of gambling in order to find the money to go to matches. The directors formally rejected a scheme to allow the unemployed to come to matches without charge, but gate officials allowed an unemployed man to enter free each time someone with money paid to go in.

During hard times, the East London community took on adversity with a kind of perverse humour. This attribute was a feature of Upton Park, especially the 'chicken run', which did not come down until it had shaped the football-going habits of three generations. It was 'pneumonia end, a drab, wet place to watch a match'. No one there would dream of carrying an umbrella, even less of complaining. It was where the wits seemed loudest and crudest, where emotions ran highest, and where the ability of the East Ender to survive in his own style was on display. East Enders cannot bear to be patronised. Outsiders cannot make the same criticism as one of their own can. For decades, it troubled the men who ran West Ham United to hear the club described as 'unfashionable'. It was a hard charge to answer since the word had no precise meaning. The phrase 'unfashionable West Ham' gained even greater currency in 1966 with Bobby Moore and the World Cup trio. The national sporting press described them as playing out their careers on a nondescript ground in a modest part of London. But to call West Ham 'unfashionable' was to accuse it of not achieving something that it had never sought. Supporters

The famous 'chicken run', which was torn down in 1968 to make room for the new stand. Despite its lack of comfort, it was the sentimental home of the old supporters, the place where 'the roars were loudest and the humour always there'

and club officials asserted that the club suffered from nothing more than a lack of the pretentiousness and dishonesty that marked many successful organizations.

Supporters could see the wry side of the club's history. They used the old joke that 'West Ham was like Christmas tree ornaments, it always came down after the New Year' to soften the blow of repeated disappointments. One of the men who made Tottenham Hotspurs so successful, Danny Blanchflower, understood the bond between West Ham and its supporters: 'West Ham gets 26,000 Cockneys turning up every week and they all sing "Bubbles" on good days and bad and they don't believe any other club exists.'

One seldom challenged article of faith is that West Ham has been built on a foundation of local talent and that the club has pursued that policy in a conscious manner. The idea makes good sense since East London has always been 'football mad'. It seemed natural for those boys to want to play at Upton Park and for the club to mine this rich vein of talent. Some local boys did indeed go to West Ham and become top quality players, but the statistics do not bear out the impression that West Ham was overwhelmingly local. From the beginning, the club has brought in more than its share of what Arnold F. Hills called 'the leavening factor' to raise the quality of local performers. West Ham United was more than 50 years old before it made any systematic effort to encourage top local players to come to Upton Park.

Supporters did not make a big issue out of the presumed local nature of the club until after it had achieved some success. No one on the terraces ever asked for a birth certificate to validate a goal scored by a Hammer or demanded that saving tackles only be made by men with the proper East London accent. When an outsider put on a claret and blue shirt, he became 'one of us'. The exceptions to this have been players who failed or appeared unconcerned. When West Ham finally moved back into the first division the supporters and the press had to find something unique about it besides its location, and it was then that pride in the local background of the club was transformed into supposed reality.

When West Ham players began to change the game in the 1950s, they brought the supporters in their wake. Few spectators knew exactly what was happening on the field, but they knew something was. It felt good to see players living out the 'us versus them' attitudes and doing things with a flair. But when the implausible crowned their efforts, when the bubbles did not fade and die, when West Ham were champions, then the supporters had to do something more than just admire what their heroes were doing on the field. The crowd adopted the idea that the 'Academy of Soccer' existed and revelled in being part of it. In the wake of success and the new style, the supporters and the club joined together to consolidate the myth that substituted for its history. Past failures were a prelude to the present success. The picture of a cheese-paring, unambitious club with little to show for its years since Wembley was replaced by an organization that was dedicated to playing entertaining football with a noble history of keeping high standards on and off of the pitch and trying to build itself on a foundation of local players and local values.

For most of its history, West Ham was reported regularly only in the local press. The *East Ham Echo* was the area's most important paper until it folded during the Second World War. It began to give West Ham featured coverage in its sporting section immediately after the club's move to the Boleyn Ground in 1904. When West Ham moved into the League, local papers increased the space they devoted to the club. The *Echo* took the lead by carrying more than match reports: interviews with the manager and players became common features. The *Echo* featured articles by the 'Rambler', the 'Old Timer' and other pseudonymous writers, which made football the staple of the sports page. The longest-running column, 'The Football Field', was a commentary on the state of the sport throughout England and included articles about tactics, personnel, and the future of the game. References were made to West Ham United, but the column was noteworthy for its absence of parochialism. However, when a major story took place at West Ham,

'The Football Field' was replaced by a story written by the local correspondent. Two generations after the *Echo* disappeared it is still recalled fondly by men who remember little about its news coverage or its editorial position.

The success of the *Echo* in using West Ham to promote itself was not lost on future journalists and their employers. After the Second World War, other papers expanded their coverage to fill the gap left by the *Echo*. Two of them, the *Stratford Express* and the *Ilford* (later *Newham*) *Recorder*, devoted a lot of space to the Hammers. They had the services of two talented writers and observers of the game, Peter Lorenzo and Trevor Smith. Lorenzo was a local boy who made good by getting paid for watching football. He was born a few hundred yards from the ground and went to his first match in 1935 when he was nine years old. When he went to work as a teenage reporter, Charlie Paynter took him under his wing, a gesture that was important to Lorenzo. It also introduced him to the symbiotic relationship between the club and the press. Lorenzo learned that men in football thought a reporter, even a young one, could be useful. Why else would someone like Alec Stock at the Orient ask a 19-year-old's opinion about football? Lorenzo was bright enough to realize that Stock wanted publicity and accordingly gave more space than usual to the Orient. Although West Ham was the big football attraction in the area, it was reluctant to share its newspaper space with anyone, and this point was made forcefully to Lorenzo when he was 'chewed out by Ted Fenton'. When Lorenzo became sports editor of the *Stratford Express* in 1956 he used West Ham to boost circulation by writing about the club throughout the year. He preferred the aloof nature of Ron Greenwood and Reg Pratt to the publicity-conscious Fenton because they gave him more freedom to write his own stories.

Trevor Smith's background was similar to Lorenzo's, though football was not so much a part of his youth. His relationship with West Ham began during the early 1950s. When he started reporting on the club, he would leave his bicycle at the little cottage on Priory Road 'where old girls used to charge tuppence to look after it'. Smith probably knows more than any man how West Ham's relationship with the press has changed and how much the club could mean to the press. West Ham's status led Smith to suggest the creation of the Hammers' page in a newspaper whose readership was concentrated in the areas east of the ground. The new section made Smith and his paper a force to be reckoned with at West Ham. He has generally had a comfortable relationship with the club, although there have been problems. Smith reported that a local player, John Sissons, had 'been tracked for two years by Wally St Pier and his gang', even though clubs were not allowed to approach schoolboys. After Smith's article appeared, a national daily paper, which was feuding with West Ham, jumped on the story. Smith had given it a way to dent the reputation West Ham so jealously guarded.

Greenwood was angry and wanted a retraction of the original story. Smith refused, but the whole episode blew over after a few weeks. The link between the major local newspaper and the club was too important for either side to allow a momentary annoyance to cause problems.

There are different opinions about the role of the club in the local community, but there can be no doubt that it has literally dominated the landscape ever since it moved to the Boleyn Ground. When West Ham first moved there it was a modest site, and this mirrored the ambitions of the men who ran the club. The events of 1923 made it possible to think in bigger terms: the new west stand was the directors' way of showing that the club belonged with the best.

There is a tendency to bemoan many of the changes that have taken place at football grounds. This criticism usually takes one of two forms – supporters' nostalgia for the irrecoverable past or outsiders' complaint that the essential working-class nature of the crowd has been challenged by the advent of creature comforts at the site of the local Saturday ritual. All too often, the latter is a form of condescension that rests on the belief that thousands of working-class men and boys revelled in hardship and would have resisted any efforts to introduce creature comforts at the ground. Of course no one went to West Ham to be uncomfortable, but very few thought about it: they simply went to watch football. When the ground was renovated after 1945, supporters had fond memories of what they had endured to watch the Hammers. Men and boys on the north and south banks tried to arrive at the same time for each match to meet their friends. Each had a section, even though the idea of reserving space was never considered. There was a special place for children on the south bank where they were often passed down to the front.

The most visible special section at the ground was the directors' box. The board maintained tight control over who it allowed to sit there. Regular seats were allotted to the Directors, their families, opposing clubs, the manager and secretary and a select group of people who performed special services for the club. These usually included the club's banker and medical officer, and ranking police officers. Some seats were not allocated so they could be offered to special guests at a given match.

Changes at the ground meant that it lost some of its distinctive qualities. But the most famous sacrifice to 'progress' is commemorated in the official club badge of crossed hammers and a castle. The latter represents the Boleyn Castle, after which the ground was named. This building had first appeared in 1544, going through many transformations until it was demolished by the club in 1955. It was never a castle in any true sense, but by the time West Ham leased the property from the Archdiocese of Westminster the house had become a local landmark. West Ham spent more than 50 years trying to cope with a building that served no useful purpose to the club, although it had sentimental value to local residents, supporters and non-supporters alike.[1] When war broke

The Boleyn Castle, seen here from Green Street, may have had some sentimental value for local residents, but it was more of an annoyance than anything else to West Ham United

out in 1914, the Castle was the home of the Boleyn Club, a social club that had no association with West Ham United. The Castle made it harder to plan changes that would improve access to the ground. From the club's point of view, the best thing would have been to destroy it, but the social club controlled the property. Throughout the 1930s the social club attempted to get help from West Ham's directors, but the board would have none of it. The directors wanted the social club to disappear so that the building could be put to some better use.

In March 1941 the building suffered bomb damage, but this was not serious enough to make it structurally unsound. The damage seemed to have a mellowing effect on the directors, almost as if the near miss had made them appreciate why some people felt strongly about the Castle, and the board helped to pay for immediate repairs. For the first time in years, the relationship between West Ham and the social club seemed friendly, but that changed the following year. The social club had no money to continue its operation and its directors decided to close the building. Some of its members appealed to West Ham for assistance, but in vain.[2]

In July 1947 the social club informed West Ham that it was winding up its affairs but retaining occupancy. The building's future was complicated by other organizations wanting to use rather than destroy it. In April 1948 the British Legion asked to lease it as a local headquarters; six months later the Knights of Columbus made a similar request.[3] In 1949 West Ham's landlord sent an angry letter to W. J. Cearns complaining about West Ham's cavalier attitude to a building that had both sentimental and financial value to the Archdiocese. West Ham's position was that the war had been over for almost four years, the club was trying to improve the ground, and there was still a dishevelled building – the Castle – sitting right in front of its main entrance. The Castle had to go, but West Ham had no control over it. Events took a new turn in 1951 when the club suggested that it might seek financial help from the Ancient Monuments Commission.[4] However, one by one every potential occupant of the Castle backed away from the expense of restoring and maintaining the building. The only custodian left for this venerable reminder of the borough's past was West Ham, which had no use for the Castle and no sympathy for the memories it contained. The decision was made easier for the club when part of the building collapsed in July 1954. The following spring it was declared a dangerous structure and the club obtained the necessary permission to demolish what remained of it.[5]

The club handled the public relations issue very skilfully after the Castle was demolished. Part of the ground reverted to the landlord, becoming the site of a school, but the main relic of the Castle is the West Ham crest, which bears a much idealized version of it.

Much has been said about the strong sense of propriety that West Ham's directors possessed and their unwillingness to cut corners in their operation of the club. However, there were times when the board had to decide between continuing along a path that was leading nowhere or taking action that might cause offence. The move to the Boleyn Ground accompanied by curt notices to Hills is one instance, another is the move into the Football League. At the end of 1918, West Ham led a move among London-based clubs to 'support a proposal for Southern League clubs, as a body, to apply to enter the Football League'.[6] West Ham also decided to vote against the resumption of what remained of the 1918-19 Southern League season. The Hammers did not carry the day, and the club decided to go its own way.[7] Two months later, its board voted 'without dissent' to apply for admission to the Football League. The board recognized the importance of this decision; it was one of the few times that the minutes recorded the tally of a vote taken on a resolution. A draft letter was approved for the signature of the chairman and plans were made to contact the League at once. The directors did not intend to let their cause speak for itself. They fanned out over England to win friends and votes: Davis to Birmingham, Taylorson to Grimsby, Hull and Lincoln, Cearns to Coventry and Syd King to Nottingham. Their efforts proved successful: the club was elected to the League on a second ballott and a meeting held in Manchester on 8 March. It was a red-letter day in the history of the club: some day it might even be able to compete for a first-division championship. The directors had counted on success and realized that their club would be playing against the best draws in football, and they made plans to capitalize on this even before the League meeting. Talks were held with the borough surveyor and Cearns Construction about important changes to the north and south banks and the possible addition of new stands, but West Ham's new alliance with the League could not be completed until it had left the Southern League, which did not take kindly to being brushed aside after a relationship of almost a quarter of a century.

At the same time as the West Ham board was receiving congratulations from other League clubs it was threatened by the Southern League with the loss of its playing staff. The Southern League protested to the Football Association and notified West Ham that it had been fined £500 and that the Southern League claimed rights to all the players presently registered on West Ham's books.[8] The board protested against the fine and appealed to the FA for action that would limit any further steps taken by the Southern League.[9] The summer before West Ham's entry into the Football League was anything but the carefree time it should have been. But West Ham seemed more concerned with getting its ground into shape than with threats from the Southern League. After all, it had the support of the League and the top clubs. The FA would not challenge the club and its decision. This might have been conceivable 40 years earlier, but too much had changed in the relationship between the League and the FA. League clubs were capable of going their own way if their autonomy was challenged. FA officials had miscalculated badly in 1914 and 1915 when they had attempted to use the outbreak of hostilities to revive the social divisions between professionals and amateurs, trying to assert some kind of moral superiority for the amateurs.[10] West Ham was not a major force in football, but now it had powerful friends. Its move into the League was another sign of how the balance had shifted in the overall governance of the game.

West Ham's exit from the Southern League was resolved in the kind of compromise so dear to the hearts of the businessmen who ran the club and the leagues. The club agreed to pay a fee to the Southern League and to make small contributions to the other local leagues to which it belonged. West Ham never admitted any kind of liability; the payment was a form of indemnity for forcing the Southern League to rearrange its schedule. Everyone agreed to keep their arrangements private and refrain from any public displays of displeasure.[11]

Now that West Ham was out of the Southern League, it could move ahead with plans to improve its ground and upgrade the playing staff. The men who ran West Ham had a strong sense of loyalty and tradition, but they were also businessmen and custodians of a quasi-public institution. When the chance came to take a leap forward, they could not pass it up. Old ties to the Southern League had to go the same way that connections with the Thames Ironworks and the Memorial Ground had been broken 15 years earlier.

The overall pattern at West Ham has been cautious and conservative. The board has husbanded its resources, tried to operate a stable enterprise and avoided either flamboyant gestures or publicity. Its members have had a strong sense of traditional moral values, no-nonsense patriotism, a belief in their ability to persevere, and an almost instinctive distrust of the supposedly insincere values associated with other parts of London. The community might admire the 'flashman' as a novelty who brought some relief from the drabness of everyday life, but such a man did not set standards for the community. The football club operated in the same way. The directors ran it cautiously, but they were prepared to take an occasional flamboyant risk. The move to the Boleyn Ground and into the League, the fanfare surrounding the construction of the stand in the 1920s and the record fees paid out when Greenwood arrived were all the more noteworthy because they contrasted with the pattern that had been set for years.

Another feature of the community was the strong sense that people had to *try*. Failure was a reality of life, but not making an effort was inexcusable. This typified attitudes about the Hammers. Individual players, no matter how brilliant, were not welcome if they did not put dedication into their play. Lesser players often found long-term careers and support by showing that the game and the club really meant something to them. Supporters applied the same standard to their judgment of the actions of the board. The directors' inability to bring victory was excusable as long as they gave the impression that they were trying as hard as they could.

Success made it possible to build up a retrospective legend about what West Ham meant to the supporters and to football. There was no conscious effort to create an idea of what made the club special – supporters knew what made it special to them – but after 1958 it made good sense to adopt many of the views articulated by the press, as well as by the management and the players. The belief that West Ham had always been dedicated to playing attacking, entertaining football, even if they lacked the killer instinct that was often necessary for victory, was the keystone of the legend.

For many years West Ham preached all the right ideals, but it had not done well at the one thing that would have proved that it understood the reason for keeping score. When the club returned to mediocrity after its initial success in the 1950s, it was at least still in the first division. It retained its commitment to the type of play that had brought it attention. Supporters could fall back on the 'West Ham way' to justify, if not explain, why the club was something different. Once West Ham had

This aerial view of the Boleyn Ground, taken in the late 1970s, shows the covered stands and terraces and the tower blocks that border the ground

succeeded, it was much easier to maintain that the club was devoted to a unique, and admirable, set of standards. In that light Greenwood might agree that success did more than attract 'the wrong kind of people' to the club: it also reinforced the right kinds of feelings and helped to consolidate in people's minds exactly the ideals that Greenwood wanted West Ham to represent.

There are many ways to dissect the experience of West Ham United. We could break it into its component parts – officials, management, players – but none could have existed alone: each has been changed by its complex set of relationships with the others. The supporters must be added to this brew. Professional football without an audience is almost a contradiction in terms, and the supporters changed the way players performed and influenced the conduct of both board and managers. Performances on the field gave birth to legends. The spectre of Sid Puddefoot loomed over the club and its supporters long after he was gone, and even after the club had gone on to successes unimagined during his career at West Ham. Other individuals stamped their characters on the club: the goals of Vic Watson, the attitude of Dick Walker, the cool detachment of the members of the 'Academy', the presence of Bobby Moore, and the tenacity of Billy Bonds. Each provided individual moments of glory, as did hundreds of other players, but only a few are remembered as symbols of the heart and soul of the club. That might explain why supporters could admire Malcolm Allison for what he did for their club, but not for the way in which he did it. Allison believed that he could be doing the same thing at almost any club, but supporters wanted to believe that their heroes were part of a long line of West Ham giants who would pass something on to succeeding generations. The club was an institution that would keep its traditions intact and continue to develop as each generation of players, management and supporters had an influence on it.

The mystique of West Ham has extended far beyond people who know anything about football. The ways in which the club has reacted to changing conditions say much about this particular part of London. It is clear for anyone to see that the game matters and West Ham United matters to untold numbers of people, many of whom would be hard pressed to explain how football has touched their lives. Even those who think the club is important find it difficult to explain exactly what it has meant to them. This confusion is the ultimate testament to how much a part of everyday life West Ham United has been. West Ham and its community have developed together, sharing the hard times, the triumphs and the drama of the past 90 years.

Epilogue
Into the Eighties

Winning is important, but you have to entertain as well.

John Lyall, West Ham manager, 1985.

This book was conceived as a history of West Ham United from 1895 to 1968. The final date was based on the changes that came in the wake of the 1966 World Cup, events that had a special place in the history of West Ham because of the trio of the club's players who were in the team. Many standards surrounding football changed and the game assumed a new place in English life. This epilogue makes no pretence at being inclusive; it deals with a few events and shows how they reinforced or modified the trends and traditions that had developed over the preceding generations.

At 7.30 p.m. on Wednesday 1 October 1980, the kick-off for the second leg of a first-round European Cup Winners' Cup match took place at West Ham. For almost two hours, the Boleyn Ground echoed to some of the strangest noises ever to accompany an important match. Individual voices could be heard throughout the ground, and a single cheer or casual comment achieved the same level as the lusty sound that usually came from the north and south banks. An unaccumstomed sound was the repeated thud of boot on ball as the match progressed. A reporter remarked that it was the first time in his career that he had heard that so consistently at a big match. This was no ordinary evening, even by the standards of international football. Few people will remember that West Ham overcame a two-goal deficit from the first leg. Even the goal scorers' names are lost to all but the most devoted of West Ham fans. The big story was the crowd: it was not there. The throng at the ground for the West Ham v. Castilla match was listed officially as 140 plus 122 reporters, commentators, ball boys and others considered necessary to stage the match. This was the famous 'ghost match' played behind the closed doors of West Ham as the UEFA punishment for the actions supposedly undertaken by the club partisans after defeat in Madrid a fortnight earlier.

It is interesting to look at the 'ghost match' and draw comparisons with other events in West Ham's past. How much might we be able to

The 'ghost match'. West Ham v. Castilla, 1 October 1980

conclude about both West Ham and English football by comparing the 'White Horse Final' of 1923 to the 'ghost match' of 1980? A huge, uncountable crowd in 1923, a crowd that could have been counted with absolute precision by one person in 1980. In 1923, the crowd moved back peacefully to wait for the match to begin; in 1980 violence had accompanied West Ham to Madrid. Even if UEFA did 'overreact' to what the West Ham chairman later called 'the disturbing and disorderly conduct of a very few who disgraced themselves', even if the events were 'grossly exaggerated' in post-match reports, the fact remains that European officials had cause to think that English fans were capable of doing what was linked to the West Ham supporters in Madrid.[1] West Ham might have been singled out for punishment as an example to other clubs and their supporters. If that was the case, the events of the next five years showed sadly that the lesson was not brought home with enough severity to dampen the excesses of crowds, either at home or abroad.

In May 1980 West Ham had beaten Arsenal to win the Cup Final at Wembley. As in 1923, West Ham was a second-division club matched against a top-quality first-division side. Familiar faces from 1923 were at the match: Jimmy Ruffell, the speedy winger, was in the stands waving

Scenes of jubilation in the borough on the day after West Ham's victory against Arsenal in the 1980 Cup Final

to his old friends and former fans; Reg Pratt, the recently retired West Ham chairman, was a few sections away from him. There were others who had attended both matches, including the historian S. T. Bindoff, who had come to Wembley in 1923 as a boy from Brighton.

For most West Ham supporters, the biggest change from 1923 was what happened on the field. A West Ham team that was given little chance by the book-makers and experts and none by Brian Clough scored a 1-0 victory. The only goal came from an unlikely source, the head of the 'thinking man's footballer', Trevor Brooking. The club was led by John Lyall, a no-nonsense figure, who was only the fifth manager in West Ham's history. The club was a composite of what most West Ham teams had been since 1923: the home-grown talent of Brooking, Pike and Allen; a bargain acquisition from Devonshire; purchases such as Stewart, Cross and Pearson and one very expensive buy in Parkes. Its second-division status also fitted into West Ham's past. How appropriate that the club should win the Cup while it was a second-division team against a club that had never been out of the first division since its arrival there. It was special that the victory was at the expense of Arsenal, the club for whom West Ham's leadership had shown such great respect.

The years between West Ham's reflected glory from the 1966 World

Cup trio and victory at Wembley in 1980 had contained ups and downs. One high point was the FA Cup win in 1975 against Fulham. The match was not one of the great or dramatic finals, but it had elements of drama tinged with a sense of melancholy. A positive way of describing the events was to note that the victorious club was managed by John Lyall and captained by Billy Bonds, men who came from the West Ham mould. However, the match was as noticeable for the men who were not there, at least in the way that West Ham followers had grown to expect. Ron Greenwood was at Wembley, but as an interested spectator. He was manager in name, but the team manager John Lyall in fact put the club on the field. Bobby Moore was there, but he was wearing a Fulham strip and trying to deny a second Cup victory to the Hammers. The 1975 Cup dramatically marked the end of what many had expected to be the golden age of West Ham football.

West Ham's triumphs and frustrations might be summed up in its two victorious Wembley appearances in 1964 and 1975. The first win seemed to open an almost unlimited horizon to the club. When the Cup Winners' Cup and the World Cup victories followed in quick succession, only the most sceptical supporter did not predict a glowing future for West Ham. Even the national press, which tended to treat the club and its supporters with a certain amount of condescension, became interested in what was happening at West Ham. Greenwood and his players were expected to restore a flair to English football and acquire trophies that would blot out the memory of years of frustration, but in fact during the eleven years between cup finals the club was unable to sustain a victorious pattern. Many journalists hoped that West Ham represented the way football would develop in the future. When success did not follow, they had to come up with something about West Ham that would redeem it: that West Ham did not have enough 'hard men'; that the club was more interested in playing good football than in winning; and that it lacked a hungry ambition to win. These ideas could have been applied to other football clubs, but they stuck to West Ham and became its public personality. The story was that West Ham did not win as much as it should, but at least it lost with dignity. It was supposed to be a club that would not stoop to unethical back-room procedures and would not allow its players to become thugs on the pitch just to win a match. Entertainment and ethics became codewords to describe West Ham United. This led journalists to look at West Ham's history to find out why it was different from other clubs. That meant looking at the club's unwillingness to sack managers, its attitude toward money, its antipathy to hangers-on, and its supposed dependence on local players. These characteristics were exactly what West Ham wanted to believe about itself.

Most of the threads of West Ham's history in the post-World Cup era were tied up on a mild spring evening at the ground in 1977. On 11 May, the Monday after the normal close of the season, West Ham faced Manchester United. The visitors were heading towards a Wembley victory later that week against Liverpool; the Hammers were trying to avoid relegation. West Ham did not make its task against United any easier when it conceded a goal to Gordon Hill less than 30 seconds into the match. That was only the beginning of West Ham's troubles. It misfired on the penalty shot that would have brought it equal. Then the match finally turned. The Hammers scored three unanswered goals, the first two by Lampard and Pike, products of the East End, the third by Pop Robson, a northerner who always seemed to fit in with the style and crowd at West Ham. Stuart Pearson brought United back to within a goal, but a second Robson goal in the seventy-fourth minute ensured another year of first-division football for West Ham.

At the conclusion of the match, the crowd stayed in their places and demanded that the club reappear for an encore. It was their way of showing appreciation for the evening's comeback and the fact that the players had salvaged a season that had been disastrous from the start. The post-match party in the board-room mirrored what had taken place in the stands and terraces shortly before. Celebration was mixed with a large dose of relief. That night, John Lyall's team had come back from adversity to win against the best. For that match the team truly deserved to be in the same league as Manchester United, even though it retained that position for only one more year.

Looking back at the 11 May survival match we know how ephemeral its result proved to be. The Hammers dropped back to the second division in 1978 shortly after Lyall took control, Ron Greenwood having departed to manage England. The board showed immediately that although appointing an ex-Hammer as manager was a tradition to be maintained, it did not plan to continue the club's other tradition of languishing in the second division. A record fee of £500,000 paid for Phil Parkes was only one sign that Lyall had the support he needed to rebuild the club. Purchases like David Cross and Ray Stewart, the development of the unknown Alan Devonshire, and the rapid maturing of Paul Allen and Alvin Martin provided the ingredients for the team that Billy Bonds led out at Wembley in 1980. A few weeks after Wembley, the board demonstrated that it did not intend to live off the Cup victory for long. Just before the new season, £1 million brought Paul Goddard to West Ham. The club already had players of star quality, it had the Cup, and it was competitive in the second divison. There could be only one reason for this huge investment - the manager was convinced that Goddard was the last piece of the jigsaw needed to bring promotion. He was in the tradition of Woosnam, Byrne and Parkes, but he had the most direct, recognizable effect of any of them. Goals *and* a championship came in his first season at West Ham.

One blemish on the victorious 1981-82 season resurrected another

John Lyall, who took over
as manager from Ron
Greenwood in 1977 and led
West Ham to two FA Cup
victories and a third place
finish (its highest ever) in
the first division in 1986

name from the 11 May 1977 survival match, that of referee Clive
Thomas. The Welshman's controversial decisions during the League Cup
Final against Liverpool on 14 March 1981 turned a semantic dispute
between him and John Lyall into a *cause célèbre*. There was no question
that the manager spoke to the referee as they left the pitch at the end of
the match. Had he called the referee a 'cheat' or had he said, 'We felt
cheated?' Thomas felt his integrity had been challenged, while Lyall
claimed that he was accused of something that he would never do nor
accept from anyone connected with West Ham. The FA disciplinary
committee refused to take any measures against Lyall, leaving his
reputation intact and allowing the dispute to be forgotten by all but the
most diehard West Ham supporters. Even defeat in the replay faded into
the background as Lyall's team went on to the best total for a
second-division side since 1920, scoring goals at a frantic pace. The team
also broke the mould of porous West Ham defences, allowing only 20
goals during the League season.

The Lyall-Thomas dispute, the League Cup run, the 'ghost match', the
virtuoso display by Dynamo Tiblisi at West Ham, and the Hammers'

courageous effort in the return leg were enough to make 1980-81 a memorable season. But everything was insignificant when weighed against the championship.

In May 1977 the club had barely survived in the first division. It had had to be torn apart and put back together again. By 1981 it was a vastly different organization, but much had remained the same. Wally St Pier had retired, but the new chief scout, Eddie Baily, was another East Londoner. The training staff was still made up of former West Ham players, ranging from the veteran Ernie Gregory to relative newcomers like Ronnie Boyce and Mick McGiven. There was a new chairman, Len Cearns, but he had been vice-chairman for years. The club had a president for the first time in many years, the former chairman Reg Pratt. West Ham created the position of chief executive, filled by Eddie Chapman who was entering his forty-third year with the club; his title recognised the role he had performed for so long. It was also a sign that the directors did not fear that their prestige might be usurped.

As West Ham entered the first division and its ninth decade, it might have been tempting to conclude that it exemplified the French proverb, *'Plus ça change, plus c'est la même chose'*. That would be too simple a judgment and distorts the essence of football. The sport provides a constantly changing set of personalities and events. Unpredictability is what makes it exciting and keeps the attention of millions. We must acknowledge the drama of the sport, and its ever-changing nature on the field and behind the scenes, before we can appreciate the stability that has existed at West Ham. Paradoxically, the club that prided itself on playing within the rules, on and off the field, has delighted in operating according to its own rules and standards. It has demanded that the men who represent the club accept these standards. If they do not understand them, there is no way to teach them. There has been a West Ham way of doing things. It might defy precise definition, but there is no question that people associated with the club, supporters and outside observers, recognized it when they saw it. In the last analysis, West Ham is as West Ham does, and its traditions have been strong enough to ensure the continuity of a shared set of ideas. The club has represented the hopes of its supporters, the beliefs of its officials and the standards of its community. West Ham has been more than a game, more than a club – it has been a way of life.

Notes

I was assisted in writing this book by grants from the American Philosophical Society; the Faculty Research Fellowship Fund, the Office of Research Administration and the Center for International Studies at the University of Missouri-St. Louis; and the American Council of Learned Societies.

Remarks in the text that are attributed to a specific individual were made in interviews or conversations with the author between May 1975 and May 1980. I have included references in the notes if the source of the remark might not otherwise be clear or if the statement was not made directly to me.

Chapter 1

1. 'Memorandum and Articles of Association of the West Ham United Football Club Ltd', registered 5 July 1900.
2. *Victoria County History: Essex*, V, p. 19.
3. E. G. Howarth and M. Wilson, *West Ham: A Study in Social and Industrial Problems* (London, 1907)
4. *The Victoria County History: Essex*, V, p. 19.
5. Howarth and Wilson, op. cit., p. 7.
6. Ibid., 23.
7. *Thames Ironworks Gazette*, 3 (June 1895), p. 65.
8. Ibid., 1 (January 1895), p. 1.
9. Ibid., 3 (June 1895), p. 66.
10. Ibid., 2 (March 1895), p. 34.
11. Ibid., 7 (June 1896), p. 83. The lead article in this issue, written by Hills, was entitled 'Our Clubs'.
12. Ibid., 5 (January 1896), p. 34.
13. Ibid., p. 35.
14. Gibson and Pickford, *Association Football and the Men who Made It* (London, 1905), III, p. 86.
15. *Thames Ironworks Gazette*, 10 (March 1897), p. 71.
16. Report of the secretary of the club in ibid., 12 (September 1897), p. 195.
17. Ibid., p. 196.
18. Ibid., 13 (December 1897), p. 47.
19. Roster of players in the report of the secretary of the club in ibid., 16 (September 1898), p. 211.
20. Ibid., 18 (March 1899), p. 284.
21. Ibid., 19 (June 1899), p. 338.

22. Ibid., p. 295.

23. Ibid.

24. Ibid., p. 338.

25. Gibson and Pickford, op. cit., p. 88.

26. *Thames Ironworks Gazette*, 19 (June 1899), p. 295. At the annual dinner of the Federated Clubs of the Thames Ironworks (5 February 1900) Hills proposed the toast. He wanted to 'throw out a few suggestions' about the future of the clubs: the foundation of the clubs must be young men coming from the Ironworks, even though some clubs should develop outside the structure of the Ironworks. If a club was to be connected with the Ironworks, it 'must always substantially as well as in name, be composed of Thames Ironworkers (hear, hear)' (ibid., 22 March 1900, p. 93).

27. *The Football Annual: 1896*, p. 13. The editorial was a defence of professionalism. The article pointed out the way in which 'amateurs' in cricket and other sports were 'paid more than any professional breathing'.

28. 'Memorandum and Articles of Association of the West Ham United Football Club Ltd', 5 July 1900.

29. Ibid. 30. Report of the AGM of the West Ham United Football Club (hereafter cited as Annual Report), 30 April 1902.

31. Annual Report, 30 April 1903. The figures are contained in the balance sheet for that year.

32. Annual Report, 20 June 1904.

33. Reported in minutes of special directors' meeting, 14 April 1904. The first mention of a possible move to the Boleyn Ground had been made at a meeting of the board on 21 March 1904.

34. Minutes of meeting of the board of directors of West Ham United (hereafter cited as Board Minutes), 25 April 1904. The resolution was passed unanimously.

35. Board Minutes, 18 April 1904.

36. Board Minutes, 25 April 1904.

37. Balance sheet, appended to Annual Report, 20 June 1904.

38. Report of the chairman in Annual Report, 20 June 1904.

39. Balance sheet appended to Annual Report, June 1905. Minutes of board meeting in 1905 discuss the loans as well as loans obtained from the Tottenham Football Club.

40. E. S. King, 'The Football History of West Ham United' in *The Book of Football*, ed. C. W. Alcock (London, 1906), pp. 187-8.

41. Gibson and Pickford, op. cit., III, 86.

42. Annual Report, June 1914.

43. Charles Edwardes, 'The New Football Mania' in *Nineteenth Century*, 32 (1892), p. 622.

44. Board Minutes, 11 April 1907.

45. Board Minutes, 26 March 1906.

46. Board Minutes, 3 May 1905.

47. Howarth and Wilson, op. cit.

48. Board Minutes, 5 April 1907.

49. Board Minutes, 18 June 1910.

50. Board Minutes, 6 January 1902 and 3 March 1902.

51. Board Minutes, 6 January 1902 and 13 January 1902.

52. Board Minutes, 30 December 1901, 23 March 1903, and May 1907.

Chapter 2

1. *The Los Angeles Dodgers 1958 Year Book – Souvenir of First Major League Season on Pacific Coast*, p. 5.
2. Roger Kahn, *The Boys of Summer* (New York, 1971).
3. 'Summary of Capital and Shares of the West Ham United Football Company Limited' (hereafter cited as 'Summary'), 21 November 1900 (filed in accordance with the Companies Acts, 1862 to 1898).
4. 'Summary', 5 June 1904.
5. 'Summary', 5 July 1910.
6. 'Summary', 1 July 1924.
7. 'Summary', 22 August 1939.
8. Ibid. and 'Summary', 1932 and 1933.
9. Board Minutes, 7 November 1927.
10. *Stratford Express*, 24 January 1950.
11. Report of the extraordinary general meeting, 21 March 1961.
12. Annual Report, 15 June 1914.
13. Annual Report, 20 June 1938.
14. Annual Report, 7 June 1943.
15. Annual Report, 3 July 1945. That meeting and the one held the previous year attracted the fewest number of shareholders, seven, at any AGM (except during war-time) in the history of the club.
16. Annual Report, 16 January 1962.

Chapter 3

1. They were William F. White, Lazzeleur Johnson, Henry Iggulden, G. F. Davis, and Harry Mattocks. Of the others, four had been elected to the board between 1906 and 1908 and one, J. W. Y. Cearns, lost his position on the board in 1904 and regained it in 1906.
2. *East Ham Echo*, 19 October 1934.
3. Annual Report, 12 June 1906.
4. Annual Report, 20 June 1904.
5. Ibid.
6. Carter was nominated in 1906, 1912 and 1914.
7. Annual Report, June 1910.
8. *East Ham Echo*, 3 August 1934.
9. Annual Report, 9 July 1936.
10. *Evening News* (London), 20 April 1936.
11. Board Minutes, 5 May 1936.
12. Ibid.
13. Annual Report, 9 July 1936.
14. Ibid.
15. Ibid.
16. Comment by Jimmy Ruffell in an interview with the author.
17. Comment by Reg Pratt in an interview with the author.
18. Ibid.
19. Ibid.
20. Ibid.

Chapter 4

1. 'Memorandum and Articles of Association of West Ham United Football Club Ltd', registered 5 July 1900.
2. Annual Report, June 1910.
3. Annual Report, June 1912.
4. Annual Report, June 1914.
5. Ibid.
6. Board Minutes, 17 May 1915.
7. Ibid.
8. Board Minutes, 25 April 1916.
9. Board Minutes, 14 April 1919.
10. Annual Report, 21 June 1920.
11. The co-operation of the bank was discussed in Board Minutes, 7 June 1920, and Cearns's willingness to set up terms for payment appears in Board Minutes, 1 June and 21 June 1920.
12. Puddefoot's transfer to Falkirk was noted in Board Minutes, 13 February 1922. Two weeks earlier the board had resolved to ask Chelsea and Tottenham to make their best offer, with the former having right of first refusal (Board Minutes, 30 January 1922).
13. *East Ham Echo*, 14 August 1925.
14. *East Ham Echo*, 4 September 1925.
15. *East Ham Echo*, 11 September 1925.
16. Board Minutes, 14 June 1926.
17. Board Minutes, 12 July 1926.
18. *East Ham Echo*, 30 March 1923.
19. *East Ham Echo*, 14 August 1925.
20. Annual Report, 10 June 1929. The club's financial situation was consolidated by Barclays Bank's decision to allow the club to be overdrawn by as much as £10,000 for the summer. The request is in Board Minutes, 11 March, notification of approval in Board Minutes, 27 May 1929.
21. Board Minutes, 5 January 1932.
22. Board Minutes, 15 November 1932.
23. Balance sheet of Annual Report, 18 July 1933.
24. Board Minutes, 6 June 1933.
25. Minutes of extraordinary meeting of shareholders, 25 July 1933. There were only seven shareholders present at the meeting besides directors. The AGM, held one week earlier, had attracted 26 shareholders.
26. Board Minutes, 1 August 1933.
27. Board Minutes, 16 January 1934. The bank's willingness to accept the arrangements was transmitted by the secretary to the board (Board Minutes, 11 December 1933).

Chapter 5

1. Reg Pratt in the second of a three-article series entitled, 'Behind the scenes in soccer' in *Stratford Express*, 11 August 1950. Pratt was describing his view of the history and traditions of the club. The articles appeared in the new features section, not on the sports pages.
2. Article entitled, 'Now for Wembley!' in *East Ham Echo*, 30 March 1923. The article celebrated West Ham's victory in the semi-final.
3. *East Ham Echo*, 23 January 1931.

4. *East Ham Echo*, 30 January 1931.

5. *East Ham Echo*, 23 January 1931.

6. *East Ham Echo*, 29 December 1933.

7. Balance sheet in Annual Report, 19 June 1922.

8. Annual Report, June 1913.

9. Board Minutes, 17 and 31 March 1919.

10. The board received three bids for the major work to be done. After obtaining minor revisions to the plans, it accepted the tender from Cearns Ltd for a total of £6,040 (Board Minutes, 27 April 1920).

11. Annual Report, 25 June 1923.

12. Annual Report, 16 June 1924.

13. *East Ham Echo*, 6 February 1925.

14. *East Ham Echo*, 4 September 1925.

15. Board Minutes, 21 May 1921 and 18 July 1921.

16. Board Minutes, 2 January 1922.

17. Board Minutes, 9 January 1922.

18. Board Minutes, 13 February 1922.

19. The chairman made a loan of £1,000 on 17 July and Mr Iggulden made a loan of £2,000 on 2 October (Board Minutes, 17 July and 2 October 1922).

20. *East Ham Echo*, 9 March 1923.

21. *East Ham Echo*, 23 November 1923.

22. *East Ham Echo*, 25 January 1924.

23. *East Ham Echo*, 18 April 1924.

24. Annual Report, 18 July 1933.

25. Annual Report, 23 July 1935.

26. Annual Report, 19 July 1937.

27. Annual Report, 9 July 1936.

28. Board Minutes, 30 October 1939.

29. Board Minutes, 12 September 1940.

30. Board Minutes, 1 October 1940.

31. West Ham's first problem with the Ministry of Works took place in 1944 when the club was refused a licence to make temporary repairs to the ground because of the damage caused by bombing (Board Minutes, 6 October 1944). The Ministry's refusal was contained in a letter forwarded to the club by a member of Parliament (Board Minutes, 30 November 1945). It was to him that the club made the reference about the local cinema (Board Minutes, 7 December 1945).

32. Board Minutes, 10 January 1946.

33. Board Minutes, 19 August 1947.

34. Board Minutes, 21 December 1948.

35. The figures submitted for enlarging the ground were based on 1 foot 6 inches per person. That would have allowed a capacity of 43,183. Once a safety margin was taken into account, the capacity would have been 38,947. The board decided to consider a capacity of 40,000 which would mean a safety margin of 7.5 per cent, a figure that Superintendent Higginbotham thought was acceptable (Board Minutes, 21 December 1948).

36. Reg Pratt, 'The Hammers' Future', in *Stratford Express*, 18 August 1950.

37. Board Minutes, 26 May 1959.

38. Board Minutes, 18 August 1959; Annual Report, 9 February 1960.

39. Board Minutes, 3 May 1960.

40. Board Minutes, 13 September 1960.

41. *Ilford Recorder*, 17 October 1957.

42. *Ilford Recorder*, 6 February 1958 and 17 April 1958.

43. *Ilford Recorder*, 1 May 1958 as part of a centre-page article entitled 'Division One Again – After Twenty-Six Years' and 'The Men Who Did It'.

44. Board Minutes, 3 May 1960.

45. *Ilford Recorder*, 13 November 1958.

46. *Ilford Recorder*, 22 September 1960.

47. Ibid.

48. *Ilford Recorder*, 17 November 1960. Pratt took the unusual step of issuing a long public statement to 'give the club's side of the much-criticized Woosnam-for-transfer controversy'. The statement was published in the match programme the following Saturday.

49. Ibid.

50. Ibid. During the 'controversy' there was no mention in the Board Minutes of any possible deal for Woosnam or the chairman's actions. That should certainly not be taken as proof that the issue had not arisen, but that more controversial items had appeared in the minutes.

51. Ibid.

52. *Ilford Recorder*, 24 November 1960. Cantwell left West Ham with a payment of £650 in accrued benefit and £300 additional payment. Both payments were sanctioned by the League (Board Minutes, 6 December 1960). Three weeks earlier, he had been fined £1 'for breach of discipline for failing to report back from Ireland at the appointed time' (Board Minutes, 15 November 1960).

53. *Ilford Recorder*, 24 November 1960.

54. The potential cost of the floodlighting was released to the press immediately. *Ilford Recorder*, 1 December 1960.

55. *Ilford Recorder*, 22 February 1962.

56. *Ilford Recorder*, 15 March 1962.

57. *Ilford Recorder*, 23 and 30 August 1962.

58. *Ilford Recorder*, 20 December 1962.

59. *Ilford Recorder*, 28 April 1966, 1 September 1966 and 20 April 1967. Some of the background of these transactions (or non-transactions) was supplied to the author by Reg Pratt and Ron Greenwood.

60. *Ilford Recorder*, 13 September 1962.

61. Ibid.

62. *Ilford Recorder*, 25 October 1962.

63. Trevor Smith in *Ilford Recorder*, 20 December 1963.

64. *Ilford Recorder*, 20 December 1963.

65. Ibid.

66. Ibid.

67. Ibid., quoting a statement made by Pratt in the *Daily Herald*.

68. *Ilford Recorder*, 21 May 1964.

69. Annual Report, 11 February 1964. In 1965 Pratt used the AGM following the victory in the FA Cup to remind the shareholders and the public of his previous statements, which at the time had been regarded as excuses for the club's lack of success. The meeting started with two quotes from reports that Pratt had made in 1959 ('We will hold our own with the best') and 1964 ('The value of the manager's sterling work is beginning to emerge'). Pratt may have been modest, but he certainly took advantage of the opportunity to remind his detractors that they might have underestimated the impact of his policies. Annual Report, 15 February 1965.

70. Annual Report, 11 February 1964.

71. Ibid.

72. Ibid.

73. Annual Report, 15 January 1963.

Chapter 6

1. *Ilford Recorder*, 16 March 1961.
2. West Ham has established a public personality for attributes like its style of football, its inability to sustain a winning record and its use of local players. It must be symptomatic of the expectations surrounding football that every journalist, historian, sociologist or observer of the sport that I spoke to about West Ham mentioned its few managers as one of the club's most significant features.
3. *East Ham Echo*, 27 April 1923.
4. Comment by Jimmy Ruffell in an interview with the author. Ruffell felt like that about King, even though Ruffell had not been much of a football fan before he played for West Ham.
5. *East Ham Echo*, 26 August 1904.
6. *East Ham Echo*, 10 May 1912.
7. *East Ham Echo*, 27 April 1923.
8. Comment by Dick Walker in an interview with the author.
9. Board Minutes, 11 May 1914.
10. Board Minutes, 3 May 1915.
11. Board Minutes, 25 April 1916.
12. Board Minutes, 21 May 1917.
13. Board Minutes, 28 April 1919.
14. Board Minutes, 19 May 1919.
15. Board Minutes, 13 April 1920.
16. Ibid.
17. *East Ham Echo*, 27 April 1923.
18. Board Minutes, 7 April 1931.
19. Board Minutes, 7 November 1932.
20. Minutes of emergency meeting of the directors, 8 November 1932.
21. Ibid.
22. Board Minutes, 15 November 1932.
23. Board Minutes, 22 November 1932.
24. Board Minutes, 2 July 1940. Two weeks earlier, Searles had received a bonus of £10.
25. Board Minutes, 3 January 1933.
26. *East Ham Echo*, 20 January 1933.
27. Board Minutes, 17 January 1933.
28. Board Minutes, 15 November 1932.
29. Ibid.
30. Board Minutes, 22 November 1932.
31. Ibid.
32. Ibid.
33. Ibid. During Paynter's first season as manager, there were many notations in the minutes of comments made by directors concerning specific players and their match performances. Paynter also gave explanations to the board for some of the decisions he made concerning the team, 'substituted of Puddefoot as the twelfth man because he was too late to perform duties'. This action was noted in the minutes as 'approved unanimously'.
34. Board Minutes, 20 December 1932.

Chapter 7

1. *Stratford Express*, 22 September 1950.
2. Ibid. For an informative and sensitively written tribute to Paynter, see Trevor Smith, 'Charlie – the greatest Hammer of them all', in *Newham Recorder*, 3 December 1970.
3. Board Minutes, 25 April 1933. The following week, the board revised the terms offered to Ruffell from £5 and £5 to £6 (season) and £5 plus an extra £1 for first team and Cup appearances. He accepted the terms (Board Minutes, 2 May 1933).
4. Board Minutes, 19 September 1933.
5. Board Minutes, 6 January 1936.
6. Board Minutes, 13 January 1936.
7. Board Minutes, 15 July 1938. Earlier that month, the board had decided to appoint a coach and asked Gibson to 'take on the position in addition to being chief scout'. It also decided to hire someone to help him with the coaching (Board Minutes, 1 July 1938).
8. Board Minutes, 15 July 1938.
9. Board Minutes, 2 July 1940.
10. Board Minutes, 5 November 1946.
11. Board Minutes, 24 June 1948.
12. Ibid.
13. The details were provided by Fenton in an interview with the author. He also discussed them in general terms in his book, *At Home with the Hammers* (London, 1960).
14. The same phrase ('West Ham run'), and description of it by Cartwright, was used by Frank O'Farrell, Noel Cantwell and Bernard Joy in separate interviews with the author.
15. Comments by Jack Turner in an interview with the author.
16. Comments by Peter Lorenzo in an interview with the author.

Chapter 8

1. The complete headline was 'Trevor Smith poses the question everyone is asking – WHAT IS GOING ON?', *Ilford Recorder*, 16 March 1961.
2. *Ilford Recorder*, 1 May 1958.
3. Ibid.
4. Ted Fenton, *At Home with the Hammers* (London, 1960).
5. Ibid., p. 118.
6. Comments by Jack Turner in an interview with the author.
7. Comments by Terry Venables in an interview with the author.
8. *Ilford Recorder*, 16 March 1961.
9. Board Minutes, 13 March 1961.
10. *Ilford Recorder*, 16 March 1961
11. Ibid.
12. There were no published rumours about Fenton's impending move, nor were there any comments in the Board Minutes about any discussion of the subject. The latter might have been a conscious attempt not to record it, but a more reasonable assumption, based on the actions taken by the club, is that the decision was reached very quickly and was made by the chairman.
13. *Ilford Recorder*, 21 January 1960.
14. *Ilford Recorder*, 17 November and 24 November 1960 and 19 January 1961.

15. *Ilford Recorder*, 23 March 1961.
16. Annual Report, 21 March 1961.
17. *Ilford Recorder*, 13 April 1961.
18. Greenwood discussed how he was hired in his book, *Yours Sincerely* (London, 1984), pp. 168-70. The title of the book reflects the man's personality, as does its straightforward prose style.
19. Ibid., pp. 169-70. There was no discussion in the local press about why Fenton left the club.
20. Comment by Colin Green (a supporter since 1944) to the author. The same sentiment was expressed in other interviews with long-time supporters.

Chapter 9

1. Board Minutes, 8 November 1932.
2. Board Minutes, 9 May 1939.
3. Annual Report, 3 July 1939.
4. Board Minutes, 17 August 1937.
5. Board Minutes, 25 September 1942.
6. Board Minutes, 5 November 1946.
7. Board Minutes, 17 October 1950.
8. Board Minutes, 31 July 1956.
9. Board Minutes, 15 September 1959. The text of the letter was published in the *Ilford Recorder*, 24 September 1959.
10. *Ilford Recorder*, 24 December 1959.
11. Comments by Bernard Joy in an interview with the author.
12. Jeff Powell, *Bobby Moore: The authorised biography* (London, 1976), p. 180.
13. Comments by Ken Brown and Jack Turner in interviews with the author.

Chapter 10

1. *East Ham Echo*, 3 March 1911. The match was the biggest thing that had happened to West Ham, there was a 'vast mass in and around the ground and above the playing field...even on telegraph poles'. At the end of the match 'scenes were incredible. Thousands dashed across the pitch to shake hands with the Hammers.'
2. Board Minutes, 24 February 1910.
3. Board Minutes, 27 April 1920.
4. The board responded by 'deferring consideration' (Board Minutes, 15 March 1920).
5. Ibid.
6. Board Minutes, 28 September 1920.
7. Board Minutes, 22 April 1924.
8. *East Ham Echo*, 8 January 1932.
9. Board Minutes, 18 April 1933.
10. Ibid.
11. Board Minutes, 18 September 1934.
12. *Stratford Express*, 16 March 1935.
13. Board Minutes, 2 July 1935.
14. *Evening News*, 20 April 1936 and above pp.34-7
15. Annual Report, 9 July 1936.
16. The purchase of Walker was noted in Board Minutes, 5 May 1936. Arrangements for Mangall's transfer were discussed then and made final in

Board Minutes, 4 June 1936.

17. West Ham's first offer was £2,000 (Board Minutes, 17 August 1936), its acceptable offer of £5,000 was made in Board Minutes, 31 August 1936. The club accepted, but Tweedie refused to move (Board Minutes, 15 September 1936).

18. Board Minutes, 26 July and 3 August 1937.

19. Board Minutes, 31 January 1938. The reply was one of the few times a phrase in the Board Minutes was in inverted commas and the only time it was capitalized for emphasis.

20. Board Minutes, 14 June 1937.

21. Comment by Dick Walker in an interview with the author.

22. West Ham v. Arsenal, 28 March 1942, West Ham v. Arsenal, 11 September 1943.

23. Board Minutes, 14 April 1942.

24. Board Minutes, 20 August 1940.

25. Board Minutes, 29 August 1940.

26. Board Minutes, 20 August 1940.

27. Board Minutes, 10 January 1946.

28. Board Minutes, 28 September 1945.

29. Board Minutes, 7 December 1945.

30. Board Minutes, 14 December 1945.

31. Board Minutes, 28 March 1946. The meeting took place six days after his request to be placed on the transfer list was denied.

32. Board Minutes, 14 November 1946.

33. Board Minutes, 19 November 1946.

34. Board Minutes, 10 August 1945.

35. Board Minutes, 28 February 1946.

36. Board Minutes, 25 April 1946.

37. Board Minutes, 22 March 1946 and 25 April 1946.

38. Comments by Dick Walker in an interview with the author.

39. Ron Greenwood, *Yours Sincerely*, p. 171.

40. Board Minutes, 15 May 1956, 28 August 1956 and 6 November 1956.

41. Comment by Ken Brown in an interview with the author.

42. The anecdote was mentioned again in a story after West Ham gained promotion, *Ilford Recorder*, 1 May 1958.

43. Ibid.

44. Board Minutes, 8 October 1957.

45. Board Minutes, 15 October 1957.

46. Malcolm Allison, *Colours of My Life* (London, 1975), pp. 36-7 and Powell, *Bobby Moore: The authorized biography* (London, 1976), pp. 7-10.

47. Board Minutes, 28 March 1960.

48. Powell, op. cit., p. 17.

49. Quoted in John Moynihan, *The West Ham Story* (London, 1984), p. 85.

50. Greenwood, op. cit., p. 176.

51. Ibid., p. 175.

52. Ibid., p. 178.

53. *Ilford Recorder*, 19 April 1962.

54. *Ilford Recorder*, 23 August 1962.

55. Greenwood, op. cit., p. 190.

56. Ibid., p. 194.

57. Ibid., p. 192.

58. Ibid., p. 188.

59. Powell, op. cit., pp. 59-60.

60. *Ilford Recorder*, 13 April 1967.
61. Ibid.
62. Two often mentioned examples of West Ham's unwillingness to change arrangements to purchase players were its failure to get Terry Venables and Alex Stepney. The stories were repeated in the wake of the purchase of Bobby Ferguson in place of Gordon Banks. *Ilford Recorder*, 20 April 1967.
63. Ibid. There was at least one similar instance in the late 1970s when West Ham lost a player it thought it had purchased when a higher fee was asked at the last moment.
64. *Ilford Recorder*, 18 May 1967.
65. *Ilford Recorder*, 11 May and 18 May 1967.
66. *Ilford Recorder*, 20 April 1967.

Chapter 11

1. Board Minutes, 19 January 1914.
2. Board Minutes, 2 March 1914.
3. Board Minutes, 13 April 1920.
4. Board Minutes, 2 May 1922.
5. Board Minutes, 27 September 1927.
6. Board Minutes, 20 September 1927.
7. Board Minutes, 18 April 1933.
8. Board Minutes, 25 April 1933.
9. Ibid.
10. Board Minutes, 18 April 1933.
11. Board Minutes, 5 August 1953.
12. Board Minutes, 24 June 1958.
13. James Walvin, *The People's Game* (London, 1975), p. 166.
14. Board Minutes, 25 May 1965.
15. Board Minutes, 20 April 1965.

Chapter 12

1. See above, p. 172, for the Lonsdale incident (Board Minutes, 19 January 1914).
2. Earlier, he had a knee problem that was serious enough for the club to enquire about surgery (Board Minutes, 6 June 1921). His suspension took effect on 5 October (Board Minutes, 4 October 1921). He rejoined the club and played in a match on 21 January 1922 (Board Minutes, 25 January 1922).
3. Board Minutes, 30 March 1914.
4. Board Minutes, 31 July 1928.
5. Board Minutes, 8 August 1946.
6. Board Minutes, 20 August 1946.
7. Board Minutes, 15 October 1946.
8. Compilation of properties from Board Minutes up to the board meeting of 24 August 1950.
9. Board Minutes, 11 August 1949.
10. Board Minutes, 3 November 1950.
11. Board Minutes, 28 March 1950.
12. Board Minutes, 7 November 1950.
13. Annual Report, 10 June 1929.
14. Board Minutes, 19 April 1915.
15. Board Minutes, 16 June 1930. Hufton had agreed to have his benefit (due in

1929) postponed for a year.

16. Board Minutes, 7 April 1930.
17. Board Minutes, 6 May 1930.
18. Annual Report, 13 June 1932.
19. Board Minutes, 23 April 1935. The amount was £400.
20. Annual Report, 9 July 1936.
21. Board Minutes, 2 May 1939.
22. Board Minutes, 9 May 1939.
23. Board Minutes, 27 June 1950. The management committee would allow West Ham to pay Hall a total of £650 based on 4½ years' service, if the club certified 'it would not re-sign the player'. The club made the statement and agreed to pay him on 1 August.
24. Board Minutes, 9 December 1952.
25. Comment by Frank O'Farrell in an interview with the author.
26. Board Minutes, 17 January 1933.
27. Board Minutes, 8 May 1933.
28. Board Minutes, 23 December 1933.
29. Letter dated 1 January 1935 entered in Board Minutes, 31 December 1934.
30. Board Minutes, 10 January 1956.
31. Ibid.
32. Board Minutes, 12 June 1956.
33. Board Minutes, 28 August 1956.
34. Board Minutes, 7 August 1956.
35. Board Minutes, 24 September 1956, 1 October 1956 and 15 October 1956.
36. Board Minutes, 23 October 1956.
37. Board Minutes, 30 October 1956.
38. Board Minutes, 18 December 1956.
39. Ibid.
40. Board Minutes, 8 January 1957.
41. Board Minutes, 15 January 1957.
42. Board Minutes, 22 January 1957.
43. Board Minutes, 12 February 1957.
44. Board Minutes, 12 March 1957.
45. Board Minutes, 9 April 1957.
46. Board Minutes, 30 April 1957.
47. Board Minutes, 15 May 1957.
48. Fenton was instructed again to 'discuss Walker's future with him. Meanwhile he is to be engaged on our staff at £10 per week' (Board Minutes, 23 July 1957). A month later the £4 per week offer was made to Walker (Board Minutes, 20 August 1957).
49. Board Minutes, 3 May 1960.
50. Board Minutes, 6 September 1960.
51. Board Minutes, 28 March 1961.
52. Board Minutes, 11 September 1962.
53. Board Minutes, 14 January 1964.
54. Board Minutes, 21 January 1964; *Ilford Recorder*, 23 January 1964.
55. Board Minutes, 24 March 1964.
56. Board Minutes, 28 April 1964.

Chapter 13

1. Comment by Arthur Clarke (a supporter for more than 50 years) in an interview with the author. These sentiments were repeated by various long-time supporters and officials.
2. Board Minutes, 10 November 1913.
3. Board Minutes, 2 September 1914.
4. Board Minutes, 30 November 1914.
5. Ibid. A month later, the board resolved that 'facilities on this ground shall not be given to representatives of those daily papers that do not publish our fixtures' (Board Minutes, 28 December 1914).
6. Annual summary in Board Minutes.
7. Board Minutes, 31 March 1924.
8. Board Minutes, 29 October and 5 November 1923.
9. Board Minutes, 11 February 1924.
10. *East Ham Echo*, 21 March 1924.
11. Board Minutes, 19 March 1935.
12. Board Minutes, 22 September 1938.
13. Board Minutes, 16 January 1939.
14. Board Minutes. Examples of collections are Dependants of Rawalpinde Victims (11 December 1940), Red Cross (8 February 1940), Comfort for Troops (6 May 1940), Essex War Welfare Committee (29 August 1940), Christmas for Troops (7 November 1940), and East Ham Wardens (19 September 1941).
15. The request was in Board Minutes, 30 December 1941 and the collection was set for 24 January 1942 (Board Minutes, 6 January 1942). The board's decision to add to the collection was noted (Board Minutes, 3 February 1942).
16. Board Minutes, 17 February 1942.
17. Board Minutes, 7 May 1943.
18. Board Minutes, 20 July 1945.
19. Board Minutes, 2 December 1947.
20. Board Minutes, 9 December 1947.
21. Board Minutes, 23 December 1947.
22. Board Minutes, 17 December 1947 and 24 June 1948.
23. Board Minutes, 20 January 1948.
24. Board Minutes, 13 January 1949.
25. *Stratford Express*, 26 August 1949.
26. Board Minutes, 13 November 1951.
27. Board Minutes, 25 November 1958.
28. Board Minutes, 25 April 1961.
29. *Ilford Recorder*, 8 February 1962.
30. *Ilford Recorder*, 21 May 1964.
31. Annual Report, 11 February 1964.
32. The damage occurred on 2 August 1944 and the club asked for assistance two days later (Board Minutes, 4 August 1944). The Ministry refused the permit two months later (Board Minutes, 6 October 1944). The chairman tried to bring the matter before a parliamentary committee with the assistance of Mr Will Thorne MP (Board Minutes, 3 November 1944). A permit to perform the minimum work necessary was received at the end of 1944 (Board Minutes, 8 December 1944).
33. Board Minutes, 23 March 1945, 3 July 1945, and 17 August 1945.
34. Board Minutes, 5 October 1945.
35. Comment by Reg Pratt in an interview with the author.

Chapter 14

1. For a brief history of the building, see the West Ham United *Information to Clubs and the Media*, 1948-1985.
2. West Ham's initial response was to 'call their [the Boleyn Club's] attention to the terms of their lease'. Board Minutes, 3 April 1941. Shortly afterwards, West Ham assisted in making the repairs. Notice about closure in Board Minutes, 2 December 1943.
3. Board Minutes, 27 April 1948.
4. Board Minutes, 8 May 1951.
5. Board Minutes, 5 April 1955.
6. Board Minutes, 9 December 1918.
7. Board Minutes, 25 February 1919.
8. Board Minutes, 17 March 1919.
9. Board Minutes, 25 March 1919.
10. John Osborn presents a very interesting analysis of how the attitude of the FA towards the League clubs showed the class distinctions that operated at the outbreak of the Great War in 'The British Sports Industry and the Opening of the First World War' (unpublished paper).
11. Board Minutes, 18 and 26 August 1919.

Epilogue

1. 'A Statement by Our Chairman, Mr Leonard C. Cearns' in *Hammer: The Official Programme of West Ham United FC*, 11 October 1980, pp. 4-5.

Directors and officials

Subscribers to the Articles of Incorporation, 5 July 1900

Cornelius Osborn (clerk)
J. W. Y. Cearns (clerk)
George Handley (contractor)
George C. Fundell (house agent)
Edwin Smith (timber converter)
Aitken Brown (brass founder)
Lazzeluer Johnson (clerk)

Chairmen

Lazzeluer Johnson (clerk)	1900-1903
Edwin Smith (timber converter)	1903-1904
Joseph Grisdale (coppersmith)	1904-1909
W. F. White (barge builder)	1909-1935
W. J. Cearns (contractor)	1935-1950
R. H. (Reg) Pratt (timber merchant)	1950-1979
L. C. (Len) Cearns (contractor)	1979-

Managers

E. S. (Syd) King	1901-1931
Charlie Paynter	1931-1950
Ted Fenton	1950-1961
Ron Greenwood	1961-1977
John Lyall (team manager, 1974-1977)	1977-

Secretaries

E. S. (Syd) King	1901-1931
Alan Searles	1931-1940
Charlie Paynter	1940-1946
Frank Cearns	1946-1956
Eddie Chapman (chief executive/ secretary, 1979-1986)	1956-1986

Directors

Lazzeluer Johnson (clerk/engineer)	1900-1932
J. W. Y. Cearns (clerk/accountant)	1900-1904; 1907-1934

243

Aitken Brown (brass founder)	1900-1902
Cornelius Osborn (clerk)	1900-1902
John Byford Jr (merchant)	1900-1903
Edwin Smith (timber converter)	1900-1903
George Handley (contractor)	1900-1903; 1907-1923
George J. Hone (patentee)	1900-1904
George C. Fundell (house agent)	1900-1908
Albert C. ('Bert') Davis (engineer)	1900-1906; 1923-1949
F. Hamlett (builder)	1902-1904
L. M. Bowen (clerk)	1902-1904
Joseph Grisdale (coppersmith)	1904-1909
Henry Mattocks (lighterman)	1905-1917
Joseph Moss (grocer)	1905-1909
Henry Iggulden (publican)	1905-1927
J. Reeves (photographer)	1905-1907; 1910
W. F. White (barge builder)	1905-1935
H. G. Sutton (tobacconist)	1906-1917
Thomas Taylorson (butcher)	1906-1925
G. F. Davis (engineer)	1909-1935
James Holden (contractor)	1910-1924
F. R. Pratt (timber merchant)	1924-1941
W. J. Cearns (contractor)	1924-1950
J. H. Rooff (builder)	1933-1945
F. A. Enders (film agent)	1933-1947
R. H. ('Reg') Pratt (timber merchant)	1941-1979
L. C. ('Len') Cearns	1948-
O. Thomas (doctor)	1948-1959
W. F. Cearns (solicitor)	1950-
H. Langman (squash courts)	1959-1960
R. G. Brandon (electrical business)	1960-1976
Brian R. Cearns (company secretary)	1962-
Jack Petchey (property developer)	1978-
Martin Cearns (banker)	1978-

Glossary

This glossary defines terms that may be unfamiliar to the non-British reader.

capped: to be selected to play for one's country in an international football match

cup tie: a match played in a cup competition

Cup Winners' Cup: a European-wide elimination tournament open to clubs that won their national club tournament the previous season

division one, division two, etc. (also known as first division, second division): the Football League is organized on a hierarchical basis with division one at the top. *See also* promotion

FA, *see* Football Association

FA Cup, *see* Football Association Challenge Cup

football = soccer = association football: the game as formulated by the Football Association

Football Association (formed 1863): the body that runs football in England. It establishes the rules, sets the standards of conduct for players and management, and controls the international aspects of the game

Football Association Challenge Cup: the trophy awarded to the winner of an elimination tournament that goes on throughout the season and is open to all professional and amateur clubs. The Final (played at Wembley Stadium in London since 1923) is the most important event of each season

Football League (founded 1888): the top level professional league in English football. The league championship is based on points awarded for wins and draws throughout the season played on a home and away schedule

ground: the football stadium – both the facility and the field of play

International: any player who plays for his country in an international match

League Cup: an elimination tournament patterned after the FA Cup. It was established in 1960 and is open to Football League clubs only

pitch: the field of play

245

promotion and relegation: at the end of each season, the bottom two (or three, depending on the rules in effect that year) teams in each division are sent down (relegated) to the division below and replaced by the top teams from that division

relegation, *see* promotion

reserve side: the second team players, many of whom can be called on to play with the first team during the season. The reserves play in an organized league

retain and transfer: the ability of a football club to keep a player until it decided to transfer him or release him from his contract. The equivalent of the baseball reserve clause

secretary: the chief paid administrative officer of a football club

side: the football team, also used to refer to the club rather than just the players for an individual match

Southern League: formed in 1894 as a parallel organization to the Football League – at the time most of the clubs in the Football League were in the industrial north of England. The Southern League lost its 'major league' status in 1920 when its first division clubs applied *en bloc* for entry to the Football League

stand: the part of the ground that contains seats and is usually under cover. Much of the area on the lower level is standing room

table: the Football League standings

terraces: uncovered standing room at the ends of the ground. Until recently, the vast majority of the crowd at most grounds stood either on the terraces or in the lower part of the stand

trainer: an assistant to the manager of a football club, responsible for dealing with the players and their skills as well as their physical fitness

transfer: the sale of a player by one club to another. Unlike baseball, almost every transfer in England is based on cash rather than trading players

UEFA (Union of European Football Associations): the association of the governing bodies of football from each European nation. It controls the Cup Winners' Cup

Wembley (the Empire Stadium, Wembley, London): a stadium opened in 1923 with the FA Cup Final between West Ham and Bolton Wanderers. The FA Cup Final is played there, as are most of the England national team's home games

Chronology

1895 June	Creation of the Thames Ironworks Football Club
1896 January	A committee of non-players is established to run the club
1897 September	First match at the Memorial Ground
1898 September	The Thames Ironworks Club joins the Southern League
1899 June	Arnold F. Hills (owner of the Thames Ironworks) condemns the football club for being professional
1900 July	Formation of the West Ham United Football Club Ltd.
1901 September	E. S. ('Syd') King is appointed as secretary of the club
1904 May	West Ham United moves to the Boleyn Ground, Green Street, Upton Park. The most contested election for directorships in the history of the club takes place
1905 June	West Ham United has an annual profit for the first time
1909 May	W. F. White is elected chairman and serves until 1935
1911 February	West Ham defeats Manchester United in an FA Cup tie at Upton Park before a club record crowd of 24,800
March	G. K. Webb of West Ham is capped for England – the first West Ham player to gain the honour
1912 June	West Ham pays off its remaining loans and debts
August	Charlie Paynter is appointed trainer and coach to the first team
1919 August	West Ham joins the Football League, second division
1922 February	Syd Puddefoot is transferred to Falkirk for £5,000, then a record fee for the transfer of an English player to a Scottish club
April	Debentures are issued and subscribed to by the directors
September	The club's offer of £20,000 for the freehold of the Boleyn Ground is refused by the landlord. A new 30-year lease is signed
1923 March	A benefit match for the Docklands Settlement is played with the Duke of York attending
April	West Ham defeated 2-0 by Bolton Wanderers in the first FA Cup Final to be played at Wembley – the so-called 'White Horse Cup Final'. West Ham is runner-up in the second division, and is promoted to the first division
May	West Ham becomes the first English club to visit Germany since the end of the First World War
August	West Ham plays its first match in the first division (v. Sunderland, a 0-0 draw) and its first home match in the first division (v. Arsenal; West Ham wins 1-0)

1924 June		W. J. Cearns and F. R. Pratt are elected to the board
1925 August		The west stand is opened
	October	King Faisal of Iraq is among the crowd of 28,000 at a match at Upton Park
1932 February		Syd Puddefoot rejoins West Ham
	April	West Ham is relegated to the second division
	7 November	Syd King is suspended as secretary
	15 Nov.	Alan Searles is appointed secretary
	22 Nov.	Charlie Paynter is appointed manager
1933 3 January		Syd King is dismissed
	12 January	Syd King commits suicide
	August	New debentures (£2,000) are issued and purchased by the directors
1935 March		Dr James Marshall is purchased from Arsenal for £2,000, then a record fee for West Ham
	May	W. J. Cearns is elected chairman
	July	An attempt is made to nominate a shareholder as a director, but fails for lack of a second. The attempt has never been made again
1936 April		A public outcry erupts after a statement by A. C. Davis (a West Ham director) that it might be better for West Ham to remain in the second division
	May	The board issues a statement 'clarifying' and disclaiming remarks attributed to Davis
	July	The Annual General Meeting takes formal notice of comments made by Davis and his retraction
1937 August		Eddie Chapman is engaged on the office staff and to train as a player
1940 June		West Ham wins the Football League War Cup (v. Blackburn Rovers, 1-0)
	July	Alan Searles, the secretary, is dismissed for 'defalcations', which are written off as a 'bad debt' by the shareholders
1941 January		Death of F. R. Pratt, succeeded on the board by his son, Reg
1944 August		The Boleyn Ground is struck by a flying bomb
1945 August		Len Goulden is transferred to Chelsea for £4,500. League soccer is resumed, with West Ham in the Football League (South)
1946 August		West Ham resumes play in the Football League, second division
1948 June		Ted Fenton is appointed assistant manager
1950 January		Reg Pratt is elected chairman after the death of W. J. Cearns
	July	Charlie Paynter retires; Teb Fenton succeeds him as manager
	September	Testimonial match for Charlie Paynter, with the elite of the Football Association and the Football League in attendance
1951 February		Malcolm Allison is transferred to West Ham from Charlton Athletic for £7,000
1952 September		The insurance scheme is set up, with contributions deducted from players' wages
1953 April		First floodlit match at Upton Park
1955 April		The Boleyn Castle is demolished
	October	Jack Turner is appointed property manager

1956 August		Eddie Chapman is named secretary
1957 September		Benefit match for Dick Walker
	October	Vïc Keeble is transferred from Newcastle for £10,000
	November	Malcolm Allison is diagnosed as having tuberculosis, and is out of the game for the rest of the season
1958 April		West Ham wins the second division championship and is promoted to the first division
	October	First League match for Bobby Moore
	November	An agreement is reached between West Ham United and the West Ham United Supporters' Club
1959 May		West Ham buys the Boleyn Ground for £30,000
1961 March		Ted Fenton resigns as manager
	April	Ron Greenwood is appointed manager
1962 March		Johnny Byrne is transferred from Crystal Palace for £65,000, then a record fee for a transfer between English clubs
1963 July		The High Court decision in favour of George Eastham in an action against Newcastle United establishes freedom of contract for players
1964 May		West Ham wins the FA Cup (v. Preston North End, 3-2)
	September	First West Ham match in a European competition (v. La Gantoise in the Cup Winners' Cup)
1965 May		West Ham wins the Cup Winners' Cup Final (v. TSV Munich, 2-0, match played at Wembley)
1966 July		England wins the World Cup, defeating West Germany 4-2 in the Final played at Wembley. Bobby Moore captains England and the goal scorers are Geoff Hurst (3) and Martin Peters (1). All three are West Ham players
1967 April		A formal arrangement is worked out between West Ham United and West Ham United Supporters' Club to set up a building fund
	May	Bobby Ferguson is transferred from Kilmarnock for £65,000, then a record fee for a goalkeeper
1968 May		The final remains of the 'chicken run' are demolished
1969 January		The east stand is opened
1974 March		John Lyall is appointed team manager
1975 May		West Ham wins the FA Cup (v. Fulham, 2-0)
1977 May		First 'all-ticket' match at Upton Park since before the Second World War. West Ham defeats Manchester United 4-2, ensuring West Ham's place in the first division for the following season
	December	John Lyall is appointed manager four days after the resignation of Ron Greenwood to become manager of the England team
1978 May		West Ham is relegated to the second division
1979 February		Phil Parkes is transferred from Queen's Park Rangers for £500,000, then a record fee for a goalkeeper
	July	Eddie Chapman is named chief executive/secretary
1980 May		West Ham wins the FA Cup Final (v. Arsenal, 1-0)
	August	Paul Goddard is transferred from Queen's Park Rangers for £800,000
	October	The second leg of the Cup Winners' Cup v. Castilla is played at

	Upton Park with no spectators allowed. This is the UEFA penalty for actions of West Ham supporters in Madrid after the first leg
1981 April	West Ham and Liverpool draw 1-1 in the League Cup Final. After the match, John Lyall is charged by referee Clive Thomas with questioning the integrity of the referee. Lyall is held blameless by a tribunal. West Ham loses the replay 2-1
May	West Ham wins the second division championship and is promoted to the first division
1986 May	West Ham finishes third in the first division, the highest in the history of the club

Special acknowledgement is due to Jack Helliar for his help.

Index